Evidence and Recovered Property

The Police Property Control Function

Second Edition

Robert A. Doran

Public Management Press
909 Euclid Avenue   P.O. Box 1464
Arlington Heights, IL 60006

This book is designed, in part, to provide the reader with information about the numerous legal issues associated with the collection, preservation, packaging, storage and disposal of physical evidence and recovered property.

The readers own situation may differ from those described in this book. State and federal laws are subject to change and varying interpretations from one jurisdiction to another. Case law related to property management is also subject to judicial review and change.

Police agencies are encouraged to refer all legal questions and issues to their legal counsel before taking final actions in the custody or disposal of property. Based upon the foregoing, this book is sold with the express understanding that neither the author nor the publisher is engaged in rendering specific legal services to any individual.

Library of Congress Cataloging in Publication Data

Doran, Robert A.
    Evidence and Recovered Property

        Bibliography p.
        Includes index
        1. Evidence I. Title

Printed in the United States of America
10 9 8 7 6 5 4 3 2 1

Library of Congress Catalog Number 93-83307

ISBN: 0-9636835-0-0

Contents

Preface

4 Preservation and Storage of Evidence

5 Managing Electronic Evidence

6 Handling and Disposal of Property

7 Record and Information Systems

8 Staffing The Property Control Function

9 Property Control Audits

Figures

Preface

The second edition of this book is again intended for the many sworn and civilian property control personnel in the small and medium size police agencies across the United States. Patrol officers, investigators and non-sworn personnel are too often assigned to this sensitive and critical position without training adequate to meet effectively legal, administrative and procedural standards. In recent years there has been a significant increase in the assignment of non-sworn personnel to the Property and Evidence Control function. This has resulted in significant cost savings to the police agency. In many instances, however, civilian property control personnel have little or no training in the investigation of crime, collection, preservation and storage of evidence, criminal and procedural law, and civil law as it pertains to the police property control function.

A primary objective is to familiarize both sworn and civilian property control personnel with the many legal issues, procedures and responsibilities that influence or direct the manner in which evidence and other property is handled, secured, stored and disposed of. The intent of this book is not to provide simple solutions to the property control problem but rather, intelligent choices to be considered in solving the problem.

Police administrators must provide a strong, steady influence on those responsible for the property control function to maintain an unbroken chain of evidence and ensure that the property control function attains its intended purposes. Administrators must understand and appreciate the reasons for property and evidence security and the associated processes in order to formulate the necessary policies and procedures for the inventorying, storage, disposition and audit of found property and evidence.

It is a hope that this book will also be of assistance to crime laboratory personnel and prosecutors in better understanding the police property and evidence control function. It may be too often presumed that the property control function deals strictly with evidence; overlooking the fact that the vast majority of items in the property control system include the many lost and abandoned items the police regularly must inventory and make reasonable attempts to locate and notify the owner.

No attempt is made to provide legal advice regarding the seizure, custody, continued possession or disposition of property. The treatment of property law in this book is intended only to inform the reader of the legal issues inherent in the property control function. Police agencies are encouraged to refer all legal questions to their legal counsel before taking final actions in the custody or disposition of property.

vii

Acknowledgments

A note of thanks is due several individuals who provided the benefits of their knowledge and experience in producing the first and second editions of this book. My brother, Captain Roger Doran (retired), Skokie, Illinois Fire Department, for assistance in gathering research materials on arson investigation and hazardous materials. Also, Sandi King, Property Control Officer, Clackamas County, Oregon, Sheriff's Department, for assistance as well as her friendship. Commander Tim McVicker and John Martins, Property Control Officer, Clark County, Washington, Sheriff's Department, for their time and assistance. Special Agent William Gleason, United States Customs Service, for providing insights into the federal property control system.

A special note of thanks is due my associate, Ann Kavanaugh, for the countless hours she spent reviewing the many draft manuscripts of this second edition as well as for her encouragement in this undertaking.

Finally, I must thank the numerous law enforcement officers and civilian property control managers throughout the United States who have attended our Management of Evidence and Recovered Property training seminars. Their initial suggestions that a book on this subject was needed, as well as reccomendations for this second edition, have been very helpful. I hope this book serves its intended purposes well.

Robert A. Doran

Training Available

A three day training seminar on many of the topics covered in this book is available. For further information regarding hosting, or attending this seminar contact:

R.A. Doran & Associates
Police Training Consultants
1519 North Patton Avenue   Arlington Heights, IL 60004
847-259-2792

Introduction

The desire to have a secure property control system must be supported with adequate management and quality controls. Modern law enforcement must have an effective quality control system which will monitor and detect deception, negligence, and human error. In addressing the problems of property and evidence management, the authors of one article state: "An all too prevalent practice within some law enforcement agencies is to recognize the seriousness of the problem and then to create, in varying degrees, a facade—a smoke screen—as a property control system. This practice is unintentionally created by neglecting to establish or to maintain a closed system." (Sullivan and O'Brien, 1979)

Present day property and evidence accountability lags far behind the modern police system that produces the evidence. Trained crime scene technicians, using sophisticated equipment and procedures, collect significant quantities of physical evidence that must be stored securely. With increasing volumes of evidence actually overflowing many property rooms, the mandatory use of an antiquated system should never be used as an excuse for a breach of system security and efficiency. A major weak link is evidence that has been processed through the court and the criminal case legally terminated. Since the primary objective, adjudication, has been attained, laxity sets in. Although the legal value of the evidence has diminished, the commercial value remains.

The development of a sound property control system starts with the identification of management and operational expectations of the property control system. These expectations are best stated in the form of objectives to be attained through the planning, administration and operation phases of the system.

Trends in Property Management

Planning for the processing, safe handling, storage and security of property taken into custody should incorporate a review of the events and trends--local, state, national and international--in crime, criminal activities and the types of potential evidence that may be collected. The property controller should be sensitive to these trends as they are reported in local newspapers and give some thought as to how they will impact upon the property control system. These events and trends should be viewed from the perspective of their actual, or potential impacts on the evidence and property control system. An example is the increase in seizures and storage of computers as evidence in prostitution, gambling, pornography, electronic mail fraud, sexual harassment and embezzlement investigations. This trend toward the increased use of computers in criminal enterprises, for example, should be seen as a need for additional, or dedicated space for the storage of computer related evidence. Another event that will influence property control is the recent United States Supreme Court Ruling that the property of an innocent owner may be forfeited if it is closely associated with a criminal act. This ruling may have the effect of causing changes in state laws pertaining to property forfeitures.

The trend toward police officers using lap top computers for field reporting; including property inventories, should also be considered. This trend may portend a reduction in the time required for the property officer to enter property descriptions into a computer system. Also, as property inventory computer programs become more "user-friendly" officers may be required to enter their own information into the property control computer system.

Current trends that should be considered include: increases in the volume of seized evidence, the costs of disposing of hazardous and toxic evidence, changes in the time associated with the criminal appeals process, the availability and level of funding for the property control function, crime rates, and the continuing trend toward computerization in police agencies.

Objectives of Evidence and Property Control

The law enforcement evidence and property control function has four major objectives. Each of these four objectives must be attained individually, and collectively, in order for the property control function to operate efficiently and be considered effective in maintaining the required chain of evidence and the safekeeping of property. The process of developing and adopting objectives itself encourages the development of measures and standards of performance by which to evaluate the property control function.

Meet Legal Requirements

The property control system must meet all legal requirements. These include federal, state, and local laws and ordinances. These statutes and ordinances very often dictate the methods and procedures for handling, storage and disposal of property. Seized property within the scope of federal statutes must be handled and disposed of according to federal statutes.

To be effective the property control system must establish and maintain a continuous chain of custody. The chain of custody must, by necessity, start with the initial location, seizure or custody of the property.

State laws pertaining to seizures, forfeiture of property, prisoner's property, retention of lost and found property and the sale of abandoned and unclaimed property must be considered fully in the establishment and operation of the property control function. In many cases, local ordinances have been established to expand upon or clarify state laws, or have created specific responsibilities for property custody and control. It is important that research be conducted to identify existing local ordinances so their provisions may be incorporated into property control policies and procedures.

Meet Administrative Requirements

Administrative requirements include proper reporting and the control and audit of property control operations. These requirements are most often included in agency policy and procedures manuals.

The property control system, through formally established policies and procedures, and the Property Control Officer, through practice, must ensure all property is fully and accurately described. To meet this objective administrative controls must require all property be inventoried, completely identified and must indicate the location of items while in custody.

A major deficiency observed in many law enforcement property control systems is inadequate property descriptions by investigating officers. Incomplete or inaccurate property descriptions may contribute to future problems, including allegations of theft, misplacement of property or incomplete audit trails. Complete descriptions are of significant importance also when property inventories are computerized. A computerized inventory may be used as a data base for correlating property reported lost or stolen with property taken into custody. It becomes apparent immediately that only complete and accurate property descriptions will contribute to the success of such a system.

The reporting function includes also the indexing of property in custody. Indexing is essential to rapidly and efficiently locate property in custody when complete property case information is not available immediately. Proper reporting includes also the documentation of the final disposition of property and the authority for disposal.

The development and adoption of reliable policies and procedures simplifies and supports internal inspections significantly. Uniform policies and procedures serve as guidelines for the day-to-day operations of the property control function and support the development of standardized procedures for conducting audits of the property control function.

The conduct of performance and compliance audits of property control management and operations is vital to fulfilling administrative responsibilities. The intent and scope of such audits is to act as a control device; to establish custodial responsibility and thereby minimize the risk of loss or unauthorized release of property.

An additional benefit of formal policies and procedures is in-service training of property control personnel will be improved. Based upon an analysis of the property custodian job description and the policies and procedures associated with the property control function, training needs can be identified.

Property control is a specialized job function. The individual assigned to the position of Property Control Officer should receive comprehensive training in all the skills, knowledge and ability areas associated with property inventory, control and disposition. Formal policies and procedures provide the basis necessary for understanding position requirements and identifying the skills necessary for acceptable performance. From this understanding, training requirements can be developed to improve and maintain the skills and knowledge of the Property Control Officer.

Property Handling and Storage

The safe and efficient handling and storage of evidence and recovered property is a critical component of any property control system. Considering the wide variety and nature of items entered into the property control system, planning should be conducted to identify contingent situations. These situations include the recovery of very large amounts of property, small amounts of very large or bulky property items, and the immediate need for secure temporary storage of evidence when the Property Control Officer is not available immediately.

Comprehensive guidelines contribute significantly to the prevention of injury, or health hazards to the Property Control Officer. These procedures are necessary also to protect the integrity of evidence from contamination, fire or other damage. Of particular concern is the handling and storage of firearms, ammunition, explosives, flammable, toxic and biohazard materials. Attention must be given also to the temporary and long-term storage of perishable items. Other related issues include the storage of bulk property and legally required retention periods for various classifications and types of property.

Protect Property Owner's Rights

While the owner or other person entitled to possession of evidence or recovered property may not enjoy immediate possession of the property, they none-the-less retain all their legal property rights. These property rights must be protected unless the property is contraband, or it has been ordered forfeited after a due process hearing.

The police agency's duties in protecting these property rights requires every reasonable effort to recover lost or stolen property, to identify owners or others rightfully entitled to possession and to assure the prompt return of all property. Crime

Victims' Rights Acts and professional police associations have established standards for the custody and return of property by police agencies. While property is in police custody adequate provisions must made to protect the property from damage, loss and unauthorized disposition. These provisions should include the identity of the individual to whom property is released, the reason for the release and documentary evidence that the release of property has been authorized by competent authority.

Aid In The Solution of Crimes

Maintaining the chain of custody, proper packaging and preservation, storage of evidence in a manner that prevents contamination, and the availability of the evidence to the investigating officer in a timely manner can contribute significantly to the investigative effort. These procedures may also assist in the identification of the offender and ensure the admissibility of the evidence at trial. The property control system should be viewed from this perspective by police administrators, investigators and the Property Control Officer.

Chapter Notes

Sullivan, R.C. and O'Brien, K.P., *Law and Order*, May 1979:34.

Chapter 1

Legal Issues In Property Management

In order to efficiently operate the property control function, develop policies and procedures and gain a comprehensive understanding of property control systems, it is necessary to have uniform definitions for the development of new policies or the assessment of existing policies and procedures. The definitions and legal principles provided here serve as the basic foundation for the property control storage systems presented in later chapters.

Property and Ownership

In a legal context property is defined as "... an aggregate of rights which are guaranteed and protected by the government." Also, a "Collection of rights to use and enjoy property, including the right to transmit it to others." (Black, 1968) There are several rights associated with property. These rights involve the power of freedom of action to possess, use and enjoy the property, to sell or lease it, to destroy it (unless prevented by some agreement or covenant which restrains that right), to give it away as a gift or devisement (a disposition of land or realty), to lend the property, or abandon all rights to the property. Collectively, these rights are referred to as the "Bundle of Rights." These rights must be considered in relationship to one another in order to fully understand the legal implications of police custody of found, abandoned and seized property.

Possession of Property

Physical possession of property concerns itself with the detention and control of property either as the owner or as one who has a qualified (less than absolute) right to the property. The true owner of property having possession of the property (one of his property rights) may exercise power over the property at his pleasure and to the exclusion of all others. A qualified owner for example, one who finds lost or mislaid property, may exercise rights to possession over everyone except the true owner.

Derivative possession of property is lawful possession by a person, not under a claim of title or ownership, but under a right derived from another, such as a bailee, licensee or tenant. Thus, a sheriff in possession of property under a levy, a bailee in possession of property bailed (temporary custody of property belonging to another) and the finder of lost goods, have derivative possession of property (a qualified, temporary or limited nature possession).

Under most circumstances title to special property does not pass to the person merely by fact of possession, since possession does not give a perfect title. Perfect title confers to a person the absolute right of both possession and property. A possessor of lost property has only presumptive title; title of the lowest order, arising out of simple possession without any right to hold and continue possession against the true owner.

Property In Police Custody

Police custody of property implies a responsibility, on the part of the police agency to care, preserve and secure the property while it is under its control. Possession of property gives the police agency only qualified, or temporary rights to the property. Unless there is an abandonment or forfeiture of property rights, the true owner of the property retains all rights to possess it in the future, to sell it, lease it, or to give it away as a gift.

Once property is delivered into the custody of a police agency, a bailment is created and the agency becomes a bailee. A bailment is broadly defined as "a rightful possession of goods by one who is not the true owner." (Black, 1968) A bailee is liable for conversion (the equivalent of criminal law theft), regardless of negligence, if he or she wrongfully refuses to deliver, or if he or she delivers the property to the wrong person.

Bailment and Custody

A bailment occurs "... when the owner of goods places them in the physical control of another but does not intend to relinquish the right of dominion over them. In this situation there is no bailment or possession but only custody." (Survey, 1985) A bailment may take the form of a gratuitous or involuntary bailment depending upon individual state laws.

Gratuitous bailment. A gratuitous bailment is a delivery of property creating a bailment from which the bailee (law enforcement agency) receives no profit or benefit through the use of the property. A gratuitous bailee is not accountable for the loss of property unless the loss is the result of gross negligence on the bailee's part. When police handle lost property as a gratuitous bailee for the benefit of the true owner, the police are liable for acts of gross negligence or bad faith. (State V. Ching) "A bailee cannot delegate his duty to others and he is liable for the negligent acts of persons to whom he entrusts the bailed property." (1 Am. Jur. 2d.)

The Missing Motorcycle

Issue: What is the degree of care a police department owes for the safekeeping of property after it is seized and taken into police custody.

Facts: A motorcyclist was stopped by a police officer of the City of North Platte, Nebraska. The officer learned the motorcyclist did not have a valid driver's license on his person and did not posses a registration for the motorcycle. Upon checking with the National Crime Information Center (NCIC) the officer learned the motorcycle engine had been reported stolen. The officer impounded the motorcycle and placed it in a locked, fenced police impoundment area.

The owner of the motorcycle proved later, to the satisfaction of the North Platte Police Department, the motor was purchased from a dealer in North Platte. The parties to this law suit conceded the plaintiff was an innocent purchaser of the motorcycle engine. The motorcycle remained in the custody of the North Platte Police Department at its impoundment area for three months. At that time the impoundment area was broken into and the motorcycle was stolen. The owner/

plaintiff eventually filed action against the City of North Platte for the value of the motorcycle.

The city alleged any claim against it was barred by way of a tort claims act and further, it had exercised due care in the impounding and protection of the plaintiff's motorcycle. After a finding for the city the plaintiff appealed.

The Supreme Court of Nebraska, after hearing the case, ruled: "... in an action for the bailee's failure to exercise required care whereby bailed property has become lost, destroyed or injured, the plaintiff has the burden of proving the negligence of the bailee which proximately caused the loss or injury. However, loss or injury of bailed property while in the hands of a bailee ordinarily raises a presumption of negligence (with citations)...." The finding of the District Court was reversed and the case was remanded for a new hearing.

After hearing the case on remand, the County Court found for the City Of North Platte and, upon appeal again, the District Court affirmed the County Court ruling. The plaintiff again appealed to the State Supreme Court and the case was reheard.

The Court found the liability of the city was governed by a section in the State Statutes that provided "...property seized and held as evidence 'shall be safely kept' by the officer seizing it unless otherwise directed by the court."

The court defined "safely kept" as: "*The care required ... which men of average prudence would exercise in the conduct of their own affairs and be commensurate with the dangers involved, having regard for the nature and situation of the property. The officer is responsible for reasonably foreseeable contingencies which could have been prevented by the exercise of reasonable care*" [emphasis added]. Evidence was provided that showed the "...city had stored the motorcycle within a fenced area which had a gate secured by a chain and padlock. The motorcycle itself was not chained or otherwise secured, and could be seen by anyone looking into the pound area ... and could have been easily removed from the pound once entry had been gained into the fenced area."

The decision of the lower court was reversed and the plaintiff was awarded damages in the amount of $2,400 with interest and costs. (Nash v. City of North Platte)

Involuntary bailment . An involuntary bailment involves a delivery of property arising out of the accidental leaving of personal property with another without negligence on the part of the owner. In a California case the court held: "The contention of the police that an inventory search is necessary to protect the police and the storage bailee from tort claims is not convincing. An involuntary bailee has the obligation to use 'slight care' for the thing deposited. "(Mozzeti v. Sup. Ct.)

Property coming into the custody of a law enforcement agency as the result of the seizure of property through a warrant or warrantless search may create a bailment of a higher order. This is an implied-in-law bailment. Some authorities have held this type of bailment places a more stringent liability on the law enforcement agency regarding the care of the property while it is in police custody.

The Damaged Boat

Issue: Can a police agency be held liable for damages associated with a legally authorized search that was unreasonably conducted.

Facts: On July 3, 1975 the New York State Police questioned Mr. Terranova (plaintiff) while conducting a homicide investigation. During this questioning Mr. Terranova signed a consent for the search of his boat, a 35-foot pleasure craft. The next day the State Police conducted an initial search of the boat. They requested the boat be taken to Governor's Island (in New York City) for further search and testing. On July 5th, Terranova, in the company of State Police Officers, drove the boat to Governor's Island and left the boat there along with the keys.

The plaintiff made several requests for the return of his boat, but to no avail. The plaintiff later served a summons and complaint on the State Attorney General, dated September 22, 1975, seeking return of the boat or damages.

On November 14, 1975, the State returned plaintiff's boat to him. The boat was damaged and items previously on the boat were either missing, stolen, destroyed or damaged. The engine was inoperable and the boat had to be towed back to its original mooring location. The plaintiff brought a lawsuit against the State of New York.

The Court found that while the state was statutorily authorized to search and seize the plaintiff's boat under a warrant, that "power must be exercised reasonably and with a scrupulous regard for constitutionally guaranteed rights ... the concept of reasonableness comprehended that the state exercise reasonable care to safeguard the property in its custody and inflict or allow only such damage as was reasonable for the purposes of the search and seizure. This also included retaining claimants property only as long as it was reasonable for said purposes." The court concluded: "...upon concluding such searching and testing and finding no proper evidence, the state has no further right to retain claimant's property."

The court found the proper factual support for the state's liability in that the damage arose from "... the neglect of the state to properly secure and protect the boat from weather and other foreseeable detrimental agents ...." Since the seizure of the boat was for the sole benefit of the state, "...the standard applicable to that type of bailment is extraordinary care, with slight negligence being the basis for liability." Based upon the facts the plaintiff was awarded, and the state was ordered to pay, $9,250 with interest for actual damages to the boat. (Terranova v. State of New York)

Based upon this court decision, extraordinary care must be taken to secure and protect property seized for investigative purposes.

Type of Property	Degree of Care
Seized	Extraordinary Care
Lost / Safekeeping	Ordinary Care
Abandoned	Slight Care

Figure 1.1
Standards of Care For Property In Custody

Department Property

Department property includes any property within the control of the police agency by purchase, administrative action, or statutory provision. This includes evidence, contraband, lost and recovered property, as well as abandoned property that is retained permanently by a police agency for agency use or benefit. Statutory provisions for such administrative action must be adhered to or an action for conversion (civil law theft) may be brought by the owner of the property.

Police Investigations and Property Custody

For the purposes of the police property control function, the definition of property is expanded to include those physical items taken into police custody in conjunction with one of four events:

- The investigation of a crime; evidence
- Recovery of lost or stolen items
- Safekeeping and return to the owner
- Abandonment by owner

These four property classifications will be used later to differentiate the methods used to handle, store, and dispose of property.

Evidence

Evidence is property that has significance as a means of determining the truth of an alleged matter of fact being investigated. While legal requirements for the handling, storage and return of property apply to all classes of property, the most exacting requirements apply to evidence.

One purpose of physical evidence collection is the reconstruction of the crime; what the evidence can tell us about such factors as the method, motive, and time associated with a criminal act.

Evidence that should be identified for collection and preservation includes that can:

- Establish the elements of the crime;
- Link a suspect to the crime scene(s);
- Link the suspect to the victim, the victim to the offender;
- Link the suspect to physical evidence left at the scene, or in the suspect's possession.

Forensic evidence. Forensic, or scientific evidence consists of clues associated with a crime that can play a role in establishing or reconstructing a crime, or link a suspect to the victim or crime scene. This includes blood and semen stains, hairs and fibers, drugs and alcohol, firearms, toolmarks and fingerprints. In a criminal prosecution, this evidence is characterized by the availability of the results of a laboratory analysis and a forensic expert prepared to testify regarding the analysis and the interpretation of the results.

A 1987 research study conducted by the National Institute of Justice found that scientific evidence has a significant effect on the case clearance rates for burglary, robbery, and aggravated assault. The study design controlled for the variables of availability of suspects, eyewitnesses, and elapsed time between crime discovery and reporting to the police. Clearance rates for crimes with evidence scientifically analyzed were approximately three times greater than for cases where such evidence was not used. (Peterson, 1987)

Inspection and Production of Physical Evidence

Property controllers often raise several questions regarding access to physical evidence by criminal defense attorneys for their inspection and possibly independent testing. Many police property controllers have stated that they have received unannounced visits by defense attorneys requesting to inspect evidence in custody. While there is little uniformity among the state laws and court decisions that address this issue, the defense generally has the right to inspect, or compel the production of, physical evidence that may be introduced as evidence at trial. Police agencies should, however, adopt written policy on the inspection of evidence by the defense prior to trial. This policy must be drafted in accordance with applicable state laws and court decisions.

Policy and procedure. It is recommended that all defense requests directly to the police agency for inspection of evidence prior to trial be in writing and specify the items of evidence that are to be inspected. Standard procedure should include notification of both the prosecutor and the criminal investigator assigned to the case. Physical inspection of the evidence should take place in the presence of the prosecutor, the investigator and the property custodian to ensure that the interests of each official is maintained. A chain of custody entry should be recorded that reflects the fact that the evidence was retrieved for inspection by the defense, the identities of those examining or handling the evidence, and the fact that package seals were broken. Evidence should be repackaged and sealed in the presence of those conducting the inspection. The handwritten initials of those present should also be written across the new seal to document their presence at the time of resealing.

Case law. Several state courts in Illinois, Arizona, Iowa, Nebraska and Colorado have directed the production of physical objects involved in the commission of an offense which the prosecution intends to introduce at trial.[1] At least one court has indicated, however, that the inherent power to permit the inspection of physical exhibits in the custody of the prosecution or police should be exercised with great caution,[2] or that a defendant must establish a valid reason for the inspection.[3]

Other court decisions have addressed specific types of physical evidence that are sought by the defense for independent examination or testing.

One state's discovery laws do not require that the prosecution produce physical evidence it intends to use at trial, except such items as a taped confession or confiscated narcotics. Georgia courts have denied production since no statute or rule provides for it.[4] In one case a skull was not discoverable where the state did not intend to offer it in evidence and the defendant failed to establish that an examination of the skull would be material and favorable to the defense.[5]

Production may be ordered of weapons and shells for ballistics testing,[6] tissue samples taken by a surgeon conducting an autopsy,[7] clothing, blankets, and materials found at a murder scene,[8] and a rape victim's clothing.[9]

Breathalyzer test apparatus and ampoules,[10] and stolen merchandise[11] have also been the subjects of production for independent examination.

In a Florida case is was ruled that the defendant was entitled to independent verification of a stolen vehicle's secondary identification number. Since the location of the number is to remain secret, the inspection was performed by the official court reporter who was prohibited by the judge from disclosing the location to anyone other than the trial judge.[12]

Federal and state courts have ordered the production of controlled substances for independent testing.[13] A defendant requesting delivery of marijuana for testing must identify his expert and outline the circumstances and conditions of the proposed test.[14]

In several states it was held that a trial court should order the production of all photographic arrays from which witnesses identified the defendant.[15] Composite drawings based on witnesses' descriptions of a suspect have also been ordered produced.[16] One court held, however, that a failure to produce such a drawing is not prejudicial if the victim or witness is

adequately cross-examined concerning the physical characteristics on which the identification was based.[17]

A defendant may also obtain photographs of a crime
scene,[18] although a failure to disclose such photographs is not
prejudicial if the defendant had access to the site[19], and inspection of a crime scene site may be permitted under the *Federal
Rules* of *Evidence.*[20]

Contraband

Contraband is property which, by federal or state law, or
local ordinance is inherently illegal and prohibited from private
ownership, use, or possession. Property seized as contraband
is that which the mere possession of would subject the possessor to criminal penalties. "Contraband property properly
admitted at trial or suppressed because it has been unlawfully
seized will not be returned to the person from whom it was taken.
To return such would frustrate public policy against the possession of such objects. In this instance the government, through
legislative declaration, has asserted a superior interest in the
property and the property is subject to forfeiture." (Haywood v.
U.S.)

Also included within this definition is derivative contraband:
property not inherently illegal but put to some illegal use which
subjects the property to seizure. Examples of derivative, or
noninherent contraband include vehicles, boats, aircraft and
U.S. Currency. Generally, derivative contraband must be specified by statute as being subject to seizure and forfeiture. Such
specification is generally found in a state's narcotics and dangerous drugs statute. Derivative contraband will ordinarily be
returned to the person from whom it was taken if they are the
lawful owner or otherwise entitled to possession. This return of
property occurs if it has been seized illegally, if the owner had no
knowledge of the illegal use of the property, or if the criminal
offense alleged is not proven in court.

Seizure of Property

A seizure occurs when police take custody of property
through a search, either with a warrant or warrantless, or as the
result of an arrest. A seizure is the involuntary dispossession of
property from the person in possession. Because a seizure is an

involuntary dispossession; the owner is required to give up possession under the laws of seizure, a police agency may be held to a more strict standard for the care and custody of the property.

Generally, property that is lawful to possess but has been illegally seized by the police will be ordered by the court to be returned to the owner. Property may also be seized for the purpose of recapturing the property from a person so that the true owner will not be deprived of it. The return of such property is generally qualified by the provision that the property will be retained by the police agency until it is no longer needed as evidence.

Forfeiture

Forfeiture is the legal authority for a police agency or a court to retain permanent possession or order the destruction of seized property. The practical effect of a forfeiture is to extinguish legally all of the rights an owner may have in their property. An order of forfeiture will generally direct the police agency in the final disposition of the forfeited property.

The provisions for property forfeiture proceedings include: criminal, civil, administrative and summary forfeitures. The law of forfeiture is basically statutory in nature; that is, a state or federal statute must authorize a forfeiture under circumstances related to the criminal offense before a forfeiture is permitted. A forfeiture generally may be ordered only by a court of competent jurisdiction after a forfeiture hearing.

Innocent third party property owners are protected against forfeitures. It is generally accepted that a forfeiture will not be ordered if any one of three conditions exist with respect to the property in question. These three conditions are generally referred to as the *exceptions to forfeiture*:

> 1. The owner was not privy to or consenting to the illegal act.

"Privy to" means the owner knew or should have known of the future illegal use of the property. "Consenting to" means the owner knew of the pending illegal act and either affirmed the act, or took no action to prevent the property from being used for the illegal activity.

2. The property was in the possession of a person who acquired possession in violation of state or federal laws.

The owner of stolen property is considered to be neither privy to nor consenting to the use of their property and is thereby protected from forfeiture.

3. Lien holders are generally protected to the extent of their lien.

An innocent lien holder will not loose their equity in the property if the debtor's actions place the property in jeopardy of seizure and forfeiture.

Subsequent to the seizure, property may be forfeited to the state. The issue often arises as to whether a conviction of the criminal offender is a condition precedent to an order of forfeiture of property used in or related to a criminal offense. The answer to that question depends upon the type of forfeiture proceeding that may be pursued.

A criminal forfeiture is an *In Personam* action; an action against an individual. A criminal forfeiture is totally dependent on convicting the defendant of the substantive criminal offense. If there is no criminal conviction there can be no criminal forfeiture. The burden of proof required in a criminal forfeiture is guilt beyond a reasonable doubt.

A civil forfeiture is a proceeding against the property or an asset; an *In Rem* action. A civil forfeiture action is independent of any criminal action against a person. The burden of proof is a preponderance of the evidence, a lower standard than guilt beyond a reasonable doubt. The outcome of the civil proceeding determines if the state will take ownership of the property.

A criminal or civil forfeiture action is generally required for *derivative contraband.* Derivative contraband is property that is not inherently illegal but is put to some illegal use that subjects it to seizure and forfeiture. An example of derivative contraband is a firearm in the possession of a convicted felon. It should be noted that some states do not recognize the concept of derivative contraband under common law. In those states, derivative contraband must be identified in a criminal statute. The practical effect of this is that property that has not been defined statutorily as contraband may have to be returned to the owner after it is no longer needed as evidence.

Summary or administrative forfeitures may be used for *per se contraband*. This is property that is inherently illegal and prohibited from possession, ownership or use. *Per se contraband* may be seized and forfeited without notice and hearing. While some state and federal statutes do expressly require a conviction prior to forfeiture, other statutes, in some cases in the same state, do not require a conviction. To resolve this issue, in a specific case in a particular state jurisdiction, requires a careful reading of the precise terms of the controlling statute.

The Auctioned Armaments

Issue: Can police dispose of "derivative contraband" without a judicial forfeiture proceeding and without due process.

Facts: The Greenwood, Mississippi and the Leflone County Sheriff's Department police executed a search warrant of an animal hospital owned by Cooper's son-in-law and seized 201 firearms. Cooper was indicted and convicted for possession of the firearms as a convicted felon in violation of the *National Firearms Act*. The City of Greenwood later sold the firearms at public auction and received $30,000. No court authorization to dispose of the firearms was sought or obtained.

Cooper claimed ownership of the firearms and brought a legal action against the City and the county alleging violations of his 4th and 14th Amendment constitutional rights and sought $30,000 in damages.

The general rule is that seized property, other than contraband, should be returned to its rightful owner once criminal proceedings have terminated.

Contraband is of two types: contraband per se and derivative contraband. Contraband per se consists of objects which are intrinsically illegal in character; the possession of which constitutes a crime.

Derivative contraband, however, includes items which are not inherently unlawful but which may become unlawful because of the use to which they are put - an automobile used to commit a crime, for example. Because a property interest in derivative contraband is not extinguished automatically when put to an unlawful use, the forfeiture of such an item is permitted only as authorized by statute. Cooper's claim against the City was upheld and the City was ordered to pay the monetary damages sought. (Cooper v. City of Greenwood, Miss.)

The Contraband Money

Issue: Can an administrative forfeiture against property be obtained if criminal charges are dismissed.

Facts: In a case involving the New York City Police Department, a narcotics officer conducted a surveillance of a suspect. During this time the suspect engaged in a number of transactions believed to be narcotics sales, including an undercover buy. The drug charges against the suspect were later dismissed as a result of the prosecution's failure to produce a laboratory report. The police property clerk brought a proceeding pursuant to the Administrative Code of the City of New York seeking forfeiture of $1,206.00 seized from the suspect at the time of his arrest. The trial court directed the return of the money to the suspect on the grounds of dismissal of the charge against him. The property clerk appealed this decision. On rehearing, the Appellate Court held the fact that charges against the suspect being dismissed was not determinative of his right to the return of the money. A separate forfeiture hearing was required. This hearing was to determine whether the suspect was able to overcome the property clerk's prima fascia showing that the money was proceeds of illegal narcotics activity. (Property Clerk v. Hurlston)

The time when forfeiture of property rights takes place is an important consideration. Criminal offenders have attempted to subvert forfeiture laws by disposing of property before a forfeiture is perfected. This may be by actual or bogus sale or gift of the property to another person. When a forfeiture is declared by various state statutes; either upon commission of the offense, seizure of the property, or condemnation, determines when the forfeiture of rights takes effect. This in turn effects the sale or gift of the property by the owner/offender.

If, for example, a statute declares property forfeited upon the commission of the criminal act, then the forfeiture relates back to the time of the commission of the offense. This voids all sales or gifts of the property by the property owner after the commission of the crime. If, however, the statute declares the property forfeited upon seizure, then the forfeiture relates back to the time of seizure and voids only sales or gifts of the property after the seizure. Figure 1.2 depicts these circumstances.

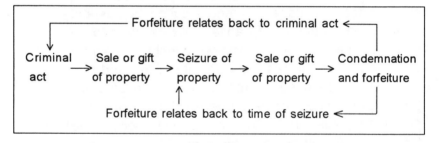

Figure 1.2

Time of Forfeiture

A Fatal Delay in Filing

Issue: Is there a time limitation for the filing of a forfeiture action.

Facts: On December 1, 1986, the DEA seized a vehicle from the defendant. The owner filed a claim and bond for the vehicle on January 12, 1987. In February, 1987, the case was referred to the U.S. Attorney for institution of a civil forfeiture proceeding.

After continued efforts by the owner's attorney to obtain the release and return of the vehicle, the U.S.

Attorney filed the forfeiture action in June, 1988, 18 months after the seizure.

The Court applied the test for delay established by the U.S. Supreme Court in *U.S. v. $8,850*, 103 S. Ct. 2005 (1983), and concluded the delay of 18 months in this case where "... the government can offer no credible reason for substantial delay" is a violation of due process. (U.S. v. One 1984 Nissan 300 ZX)

As a general rule, the title to forfeited property vests immediately in the government. However, such title is not perfected (the property cannot be disposed of by the law enforcement agency) until a forfeiture hearing and condemnation of the property has taken place (U.S. v. Stowell, and Motlow v. MO)

There Must Be a Remedy

Issue: Must notice be given to the owner of the seized property before it can be forfeited and offered for sale.

Facts: A gun dealer sold a 16-gauge shotgun to a customer on a conditional sales contract. The plaintiff gun dealer was to retain title to the shotgun until the full purchase price was paid.

A year later the purchaser was arrested by a game warden for using lights for shooting deer at night. The warden seized the shotgun as contraband and turned it over to the defendant, Sheriff of Clay County, Mississippi with instructions to the sheriff to advertise and sell the shotgun as provided for by Mississippi law. The sheriff proceeded to advertise the sale of the shotgun. The gun dealer sought and was issued a writ of replevin.

At trial, the Justice of the Peace entered a judgement for the defendant sheriff. The case was appealed to the Circuit Court of Clay County and the decision of the Justice of the Peace was affirmed.

Upon appeal to the Supreme Court of Mississippi, the legal issue considered was the constitutionality of the state statute as applied to the facts in this case. That particular state statute declared certain property contraband if it were used for hunting deer at night with any lighting device. Further, the statute declared the property is to be confiscated, delivered to the sheriff of the county in which the offense took place and forfeited to the State of Mississippi.

The game warden followed strictly the provisions of the statutes in seizing the shotgun, declaring it contraband and thus forfeited, and in advertising it for sale at public auction.

The issue before the court was whether the statute was constitutional. The statute did not provide for notice to be given to the owner who was out of possession of the seized property before it was declared forfeited and offered for sale. This, it was contended, was a violation of the Fourteenth Amendment "Due Process of Law" clause of the United States Constitution.

Citing a 1904 Nebraska case (*McConnell v. McKillipp*, 71 Neb. 712, 99 N.W. 505, 65 L.R.A. 610), the court's opinion stated: "There is a clear and marked distinction between that species of property which can only be used for an illegal purpose, and which therefore may be declared a nuisance and summarily abated, and that which is innocent in its ordinary and proper use, and which only becomes illegal when used for an unlawful purpose ... if property is of such a nature that, though innocent in itself and susceptible of a beneficial use, it has been perverted to an unlawful use, and is subject to forfeiture to the state as a penalty, no person has a right to deprive the owner of the property summarily without affording the opportunity for a hearing and without due process of law."

The court ruled portions of the state statute unconstitutional on the grounds:

- It provided no remedy for the owner of derivative contraband property seized and confiscated
- It required no notice to the owner of the property nor to any other interested persons
- It authorized no proceeding against the property
- It made no provision for a forfeiture hearing for the owner

Based upon these findings the Court reversed the judgement of the lower court and the shotgun was ordered returned to the plaintiff gun dealer. (Kellogg v. Strickland)

Abandoned Property

Abandonment of property relates to the act of intentionally relinquishing absolutely; and without reference to a particular person, or for any particular reason, all right, title, claim and possession of the property with the intent of terminating ownership. Abandonment of property involves both voluntary and intentional acts by the owner in placing the property where it is eventually found by another. (Columbus-America Discovery Group, Inc. v Unidentified, Wrecked & Abandoned Sailing Vessel, *et al*) One who abandons property severs his or her relationship with that property. The result is that he or she may not thereafter claim their Fourth Amendment protection has been violated. (Parman v. U.S.)

Tests of Abandonment

Abandonment is generally restricted, by state statute or case law, to personal property. Several tests may be applied to determine if property is abandoned, rather than lost or mislaid.

1. The property is of such a character as to make it clear that it had been voluntarily abandoned by the owner (1 Am. Jur.).

Money, for example, will not generally be considered abandoned if it is discovered under circumstances indicating it was lost or mislaid. The mere relinquishment of possession is not, in itself, legally sufficient to demonstrate an abandonment.

2. Relinquishment of possession (the act) must be accompanied by an intent (state of mind) to permanently part with the property.

3. An owner's intention to abandon must be shown; "reasonable cause" is insufficient to believe abandonment of property was intended.

The burden is upon the party alleging abandonment to prove such by clear, unequivocal and decisive evidence. An owner's intention to abandon may be inferred from the owner's words, acts and other objective facts. (U.S. v. Cella)

Denial of Ownership as Abandonment

An individual who denies ownership in property to a law enforcement officer relinquishes his right of privacy in that property. The individual cannot later challenge a search or seizure of that property.

The Abandoned Briefcases

Issue: Does a person give up their expectation of privacy after abandoning property.

Facts: As two defendants were approached by police officers they placed two briefcases on the sidewalk. When questioned about the briefcases the two defendants denied any knowledge or ownership of the briefcases. The officers stopped them again as they walked away from the officers and the briefcases. Upon opening the briefcases, the officers found a sawed-off shotgun in each of the two briefcases.

The U. S. Court of Appeals, in confirming the defendants' convictions for possession of unregistered sawed-off shotguns, stated: "The issue is not abandonment in the strict property right sense, but whether the person prejudiced by the search had

voluntarily discarded, left behind, or otherwise relinquished his interest in the property in question so that
he could no longer retain a reasonable expectation of
privacy with regard to it at the time of the search ... the
government may argue, without self-contradiction, that
a defendant had possession at one time for purposes
of conviction, but at a later time lacked sufficient
possession to confer standing to object to search and
seizure of the property." (U.S. v. Colbert)

Finder's Rights in Abandoned Property

Abandoned property is considered to revert to a state of
nature; that is, it has no owner. It becomes subject to appropriation by the first finder that takes possession. This person
acquires an absolute right to title to the property against the
former owner.

Law Enforcement Custody of Abandoned Property

Police agencies, under their state derived law enforcement
powers, have the right to take charge of apparently abandoned
property. The state may take over the care of the property by
escheat (reversion of property to the state for lack of an owner)
if there is provision for notice to claimants. It is recommended
that police agencies adopt the necessary procedures to notify
the known owner, in writing, of police custody and provide the
owner with a reasonable time limit within which the owner must
claim their property. The *Property Owner Notification Letter* in
Chapter 5 should be adapted to meet the needs and requirements of the police agency. If the property is not retrieved by the
owner within a reasonable length of time the property should be
declared abandoned and processed for final disposal.

Abandoned Automobiles

The Cost-Benefit Test

Issue: Are there civil and constitutional rights
violations for the destruction of property (an automobile) without a post-seizure notice or hearing.

Facts: A 19 year old auto was parked on a public
street for two months. An officer placed a bright

orange sticker on the windshield warning that if the auto was not moved it would be towed and destroyed. Ten days later the officer placed a bright yellow sticker again warning that if car was not moved it would be destroyed. The stickers provided the telephone number and hours of operation of the abandoned vehicle office.

• Evidence was offered that owner could obtain an extension of time by telephoning the police officer in charge.

• Evidence was offered also that officers make "considerable and extensive efforts to locate owners." "such as ... identification through department computer, ... telephoning the owner at home, and ... a neighborhood canvass to identify the owner"

The court applied a "cost-benefit test" as established in *Matthews v. Eldridge* (424 U.S. 319, 96 S.Ct. 893, 1976) for determining whether due process requires a particular type of notice and hearing before property can be disposed of.

This cost-benefit test balances the:

1.) Value of the property interest at stake

2.) The extent to which the proposed proce dures would decrease the probability of an erroneous determination.

3.) The cost of the procedure.

Failure to provide a formal notice (letter) and a hearing (to determine if the vehicle was junk or illegally parked) in these unusual circumstances would accomplish little, the court reasoned, and due process does not mandate these procedures. (Propert v. District of Columbia)

Treasure Trove

According to the common law, treasure trove consists of any form of gold or silver found concealed in the earth, in a structure, or other private place, the owner of which is unknown. While, strictly speaking, treasure trove is gold or silver, it has been held to include the paper representatives thereof; paper currency and gold certificates, especially where found hidden with those precious metals. It is not essential that treasure trove was hidden in the ground; some cases have held that it is sufficient if found concealed in other articles, such as bureaus, safes, or machinery.

Treasure trove carries with it the implication of antiquity. Treasure trove must have been hidden or concealed long enough as to indicate the owner is probably dead. Proof of the age of found property has included dates stamped or printed on coins or paper money. Evidence of the length of time that it had been hidden has included: its possession has been illegal since a certain date, its container had rusted to disintegration, its place of concealment was constructed on a certain date, and it was buried in ground that did not indicate recent digging.

Treasure trove must be found under circumstances indicating it had originally been concealed for safekeeping. A finder of treasure trove acquires the same rights as a finder of lost property. Some states, however, (Florida and Texas) have never recognized the doctrine of treasure trove.

Property Embedded In The Earth

"Property embedded in the earth" includes anything other than gold or silver which is so buried, and is distinguished, in this respect, from treasure trove. An aerolite, an ancient Indian canoe found embedded in a river bank, valuable earthenware, and gold-bearing quartz found embedded in the soil have been classified as such. The property must be found under circumstances indicating that some person had placed it where it was found. Property need not be totally buried to satisfy the imbeddedness requirement. (Chance v Certain Artifacts, Ga, 1986)

Lost and Mislaid Property

Lost property. Lost property is defined as property which the owner has involuntarily parted with through neglect, carelessness, or inadvertence. The essential test for lost property is whether the owner parted possession with the property *involuntarily* and has no knowledge of its whereabouts. Stolen property may be considered "lost property" for certain purposes since theft is an unintentional parting with one's property.

Mislaid property. Mislaid property is property which the owner *voluntarily and intentionally* laid down and then forgets where it was laid.

The place where property, including money, is found is an important element in determining if the property is lost or mislaid. If property is laid-down in a public place, or if it is hidden, and later cannot be located, it is mislaid property and considered to be in the constructive, as distinguished from the physical, possession of the owner.

Lost or Mislaid Property ?

Issue: Can an action be brought against a police agency by a finder to recover lost property.

Facts: A young boy, while playing in front of his home, found unregistered bearer bonds with a value of $75,000. Accompanied by his father, the boy delivered the bonds to a police station and received receipts for the bonds.

The bonds were not claimed by the owner within the time prescribed by law and the boy claimed ownership three years later, demanding the property clerk of the New York City Police Department (defendant) return the bonds to him. The property clerk refused to do so and the boy filed suit to recover the bonds.

The court held that the boy was the true owner and awarded him $75,000 together with interest from the date of ownership claim to the date of the court decision. (Fuentes v. Wendt)

Inventory of Lost and Found Property

The extent to which the police may search lost property has been the subject of several cases. The standard laid down in these cases has been presented as: The ..."State's burden (is) to show that lost property contained valuables or dangerous objects and that *search was necessary to safeguard valuables, protect the police from false claims, or negate the danger presented* [emphasis added]. If the facts do not sustain this burden the police must handle lost property by less intrusive means of enclosing it in a sealed envelope." (State v. Ching)

The Supreme Court of Hawaii ruled a police inventory of lost and found property is a "search" within the meaning of the Fourth Amendment of the United States Constitution.

The Cocaine Caper

Issue: Does the true owner of lost property give up all expectation of privacy in their property.

Facts: An eleven year old boy found an unzipped leather pouch next to a car in a public lot. The pouch was later turned over to the Honolulu Police and an officer inventoried the pouch's contents pursuant to routine department procedure for lost and found property.

The officer found the pouch contained the owner's drivers license, charge card, key ring and keys and an opaque brass cylinder two inches long and one half inch in diameter. The officer opened the cylinder by unscrewing its brass top and found inside a white powder alleged to be cocaine. The property owner was subsequently arrested. At trial the court suppressed the contents of the cylinder as evidence. The Court stated "...the argument that an owner gives up all expectations of privacy in lost property is too extreme. Property is lost through inadvertence, not intent. Although owners of lost property must expect some intrusion by finders, common sense dictates that they do not forfeit all expectation of privacy in their property as though they have intentionally abandoned it."

The court went on to establish a standard by which Hawaiian police officers could search lost property: "Unlike a post-arrest inventory, identification of the owner far outweighs the state's other search purposes in searching lost property. When lost property is turned over to the police, their paramount goal must be to ascertain its ownership and return it to the owner in substantially like condition as it was received. We therefore hold that police may validly search lost property to the extent necessary for identification purposes." (State v. Ching)

Escheat

Escheat is the power of the state to possess property within its jurisdiction for which there appears to be no owner. This may be the result of an abandonment, or the inability to identify and locate the owner of the property. Through the power of escheat, property is brought into a legal ownership where it will serve the state. This applies to unclaimed money or property in the possession of a public officer.

Civil Action For Return of Property

If a property owner seeks the return of his property from the police and the property has been seized under a civil (as distinguished from a criminal) statute the proper remedy is an action for replevin.

Replevin is an action brought by an individual to regain the possession of the specific property taken or detained. An action for replevin is against the person in possession of the property sought. (Kuchar v. Bernstrauch) If the plaintiff seeks only damages, an action in trespass or unlawful distress is the proper remedy.

The Liquor and the Law

Issue: Can possession of seized property be gained through replevin.

Facts: The Chief of Police of Scappose, Oregon seized various items of personal property, with an alleged value of $250, at the time he arrested the plaintiff and others for violation of a city ordinance involving minors in possession of alcoholic beverages.

The plaintiff filed an action for replevin for the return of the property seized or the value of the property, for $1.00 actual damages and for $10,000 in punitive damages. The plaintiff's action was nonsuited in circuit court.

On appeal the Supreme Court of Oregon heard the case. The court held that where the action for replevin was filed 13 days after the arrest, it is reasonable to assume that all of the cases had not been finally disposed of at the time of the filing of the action. Further, it was held: "It is a general rule of law that property seized in enforcing the criminal laws is in the custody of the law (*custodia legis*) and cannot be replevied and property held as evidence in a criminal prosecution cannot be replevied." (Denny v. Alder)

When property has been seized under a criminal statute and the person claiming ownership files suit for the recovery of the property, the proper remedy is an action under the applicable criminal statute allowing the seizure. (People v. Herman)

Owner's Civil Remedies

The improper handling or disposition of property by police can be the basis for an action for trespass, conversion or damages to property.

Trespass. Trespass is an action brought by an individual for injuries to personal property as a result of the seizure of the property.

Conversion. Conversion is an unauthorized assumption and exercise of the right of ownership over personal property belonging to another. The "... essence of conversion is not the acquisition of the property by the wrongdoer, but a wrongful deprivation of the owner thereof." (Caicos v. Hansaker) The intent required for a conversion is simply to use or dispose of the goods of another without a lawful exercise of police power. (Spear v. City of Dodge City) Conversion may occur when property is wrongfully acquired or wrongfully retained. (Scheduling Corp. of America v. Massello) There can be no action for conversion of money, (Johnson v. Studholme) and one who deprives another of possession of his or her property can be held liable for damages. (Causey v. Blanton)

An action for conversion will lie against a public official who, by unauthorized act, wrongfully deprives an owner of his property. Such deprivation need not result in the official's acquiring the property, but any exercise of right of ownership to the exclusion of the owner's rights would be actionable. (Wilkins v. Whitaker)

The elements necessary to prove the civil offense of conversion are:

- Unauthorized and wrongful assumption of control or ownership by one person over property of another.
- The other person has rights in the property including the right to immediate possession of the property
- A demand for possession (A.T. Kearney v. INCA Intern, Inc.)

There has been a significant amount of litigation over the loss of prisoner's property in custody. A California court held a prisoner could sustain a cause of action for conversion of a silver belt buckle taken from him while in custody. The court held that while he had no right to possession of the buckle while in prison, he did have a right to it immediately upon his release. (Fearon v. State of California)

The Missing Mail

Issue: Can a deprivation of property be the basis for a civil rights law suit.

Facts: The plaintiff, a prison inmate, complained that prison officials deprived him of his property without due process of law when prison procedures for the handling of mail resulted in the loss of hobby materials he had ordered.

In this case, the Court held that the deprivation of property interests could be the basis for a civil rights law suit based on the theory of negligence, as well as intentional deprivation.

The essential elements of a federal civil rights due process law suit are that the conduct the complainant alleges was committed by a person acting under "color of state law" and deprived the complainant of rights, privileges, or immunities secured by the U.S. Constitution or federal statutes.

By "color of law" means the individual engaging in the act asserts official authority to undertake their actions. "Under color" means something more than having actual authority to do the wrongful act complained of. If an officer asserts the authority to engage in some act under any statute, ordinance, regulation, custom, or usage, (regardless if the officer actually has such authority) the officer may be found to be acting under color of law. (Federal Civil Rights Act, Sec. 1983; Parratt v. Taylor) The Sixth Federal Circuit held that state remedies were available to prisoners for the loss of personal property while in custody. (Brooks v. Dutton)

The Converted Motorcycle

Issue: Can an investigative seizure be the basis for a civil law suit.

Facts: In a 1984 Louisiana case a plaintiff was awarded $2,000.00 in actual damages and $20,000.00 in punitive damages for an improper police seizure of plaintiff's motorcycle.

The officer, while investigating motorcycle thefts, seized the plaintiff's motorcycle and maintained it in custody for over two years. The basis for the officer's decision was a claim the serial number was altered and a warrant was issued.

It was found later that the serial number was correct and the motorcycle was not stolen. In addition, it was held that the serial numbers could have been quickly verified as valid, therefore, there was no basis for the seizure and lengthy custody of the motorcycle. (Hunt v. Chapman)

Damage to property legally possessed by a law enforcement agency is an issue that has been frequently litigated. A municipality may be liable for damages even though municipal officials acted in good faith. This liability may attach if there is an unconstitutional policy, procedure or custom adopted or used by the municipality regardless of the fact the policy or decision-making government officials acted in good faith. (Owens v. City of Independance)

Where's The Beef?

Issue: What can constitute "damage" to property.

Facts: After the plaintiff's truck, carrying perishable meat, crashed through a guardrail and caught on fire, the driver was killed. After extinguishing the fire the officer in charge of the accident scene ordered the cargo to be disposed of in a nearby landfill.

The officer's decision was based on the fact the meat was not salvageable because of the fire, a diesel fuel spill and water contamination from the firefighting effort.

The plaintiff, later upon inspecting the meat, found much of it was still in good condition and, while it was not fit for human consumption, could be still legally salvaged as pet food. Because the meat had been dumped on top of some dead animals however, none of it was now usable.

After subsequent appeals, the Utah Supreme Court upheld the verdict of the original trial court. The Court assessed the sheriff $19,377.00 in damages for the destruction of the truckload of meat. (Hagen Trucklines v. Sheriff of Weber County)

Inventory Searches

The Fourth Amendment to the United States Constitution protects against governmental intrusion in the form of unreasonable searches and seizures. There is a presumption that warrantless searches are unconstitutional and the burden rests upon the prosecution to show that a warrantless search was proper. The basic rule was set forth in *Katz v. United States* wherein the Supreme Court stated that warrantless searches are "per se unreasonable" under the Fourth Amendment -- subject to only a few established and well delineated exceptions. In the case of *Illinois v. Lafayette* the Unted States Supreme Court held that the 4th Amendment does not support any prohibition of inventory searches.

The established exceptions to the search warrant rule are:

- Search Incident To Arrest
- Open Fields
- Seizure Of Items In Plain View
- Abandoned Property
- Automobile Searches
- Inventory Searches
- Consent Searches

The following cases illustrate the application of this warrantless search exception to the Fourth Amendment.

Inventory Search or Investigation?

Issue: When a driver is intoxicated, arrested and placed in a cell the law enforcement agency becomes the temporary custodian of the individual's property. Does this property become subject to an inventory search.

Facts: The U.S. Supreme Court gave broad approval to automobile inventory searches in S.D. v. Opperman. When a vehicle is lawfully impounded, routine inventorying, including locked components, is permissible. (Also *U.S. v. Prescott*, 599 F.2d, 103, 105, 5th cir 1979).

Since the Opperman decision many lower courts have restricted inventory searches.

Inventory searches are intended to serve the police "caretaking purposes" and may not be used simply as a pretext for an investigation, or to uncover evidence.

The valid purposes of an inventory search are:

1. Protect property
2. Prevent danger to law enforcement personnel
3. Discourage false claims against the police for lost or damaged property.

Some states, South Dakota and Montana, for example, use state grounds to limit inventory searches by the police.

Standard Procedures and Good Faith

Issue: Does the inventory of a vehicle before a police tow to an impound lot include the opening and inventory of closed containers within the vehicle.

Facts: An officer opened a backpack found in a car and found cocaine and a large amount of money. Police department procedures mandated the opening of closed containers and the inventorying of contents.

The Court's opinion stated that opening backpack was legitimate in view of three reasons:

1. Preserving property
2. Guarding against claims of theft, vandalism and police negligence
3. Averting danger to police and others

Since the police were following standard procedures and there was no showing that they acted in bad faith, or for the sole purpose of an investigation, the search was upheld. (Col v. Bertine)

It should be noted that the police department had regulations and procedures for the inventory of property. These department standards required the opening of closed containers and the listing of contents once the police impounded a vehicle. The standards spelled out officers' discretion in inventory-ing closed containers; all closed containers were to be inventoried.

Inventory Policies Were The Key

Issue: When does an inventory search end and an investigative search begin.

Facts: Federal Customs and DEA agents were maintaining a prolonged surveillance on the plaintiff, Andrews, who was suspected of involvement in the importation of narcotics into the United States aboard a seagoing tugboat.

After several days of surveillance the agents observed Andrews driving erratically after visiting several bars and reported this to the Moss Point Police Department. A police officer arrived and stopped Andrews shortly thereafter. Andrews failed several field sobriety tests. At the scene of the arrest the officer conducted a routine inventory search of Andrew's vehicle. This produced, in part, a spiral notebook containing diagrams and several names, and an electronic radio frequency detector.

The officer opened the spiral notebook and observed a diagram he believed might be of evidentury value to the DEA. Based upon this information a search was later conducted of the fuel tanks of the tugboat. The search revealed a hidden compartment containing four thousand pounds of marijuana with a street value estimated at 3.6 million dollars.

The defendant, Andrews, was convicted in federal district court of importing and possession of marijuana with intent to distribute and sentenced to 136 months imprisonment. He later appealed the conviction, in part, on the grounds that the search of his vehicle was an unreasonable search in violation of the Fourth Amendment.

Upon reviewing the record of the trial court the appeals court found that the Moss Point, Mississippi

Police Department (MPPD) had a policy on inventory searches. This policy required officer to:

- Conduct an inventory search;

- Complete an inventory form;

- The purpose of which was to protect the City from claims of lost property.

The court found that: "An officer who engages in 'a general rummaging in order to discover incriminating evidence' exceeds his authority under MPPD inventory search policy" It went on to state that: "... *inventory policies must be adopted which sufficiently limit the discretion of law enforcement officers to prevent inventory searches from becoming evidentury searches*". [emphasis added]

The "inventory exception" to the search warrant requirement is no longer available once the purposes of the inventory search have been fulfilled. The MPPD officer was aware of the evidentury value of the notebook before a second look was taken by federal agents. An inventory search may extend to a page by page review of a notebook found in an impounded auto. Based upon this the court upheld the search and the conviction. (U.S. v. Andrews)

Three points about inventory searches should be keep in mind:

1. Once the notebook was seized pursuant to a valid inventory search the defendant lost any reasonable expectation of privacy to its contents;

2. The purpose of the notebook inventory search was to locate items ("cash, credit cards, negotiable instruments and other items ... hidden between the pages which might ... give rise to a claim against the city if lost");

3. Diagrams in the notebook appeared to depict a marijuana importation and distribution network.

Protection Or Liability

Issue: Towing of defendant's vehicle

Facts: The impounding officer testified that the police department tows vehicles following arrests for the vehicle owner's protection and the department's liability. The defendant's girlfriend, who had driven the car and had possession of the keys, was prepared to remove the car from the street. The defendant's brother was also present at the arrest and could have moved the vehicle.

The court held that the impoundment of the defendant's vehicle following his arrest was not justified in the exercise of the impounding officer's "caretaking" function". The city did not have a duty to remove the car from the high-crime area where it was parked and, moreover, the city's liability was increased by impounding the car. (U.S. v. Duguay)

Some state courts have held that when an alternative is available; such as a family member, or friend to take custody of the property, the police must allow this. (FL, IL, MN, WA)

Inventory Searches of Prisoner's Property

The United States Supreme Court stated it is reasonable for police to undertake routine administrative procedures which incorporate searches of individuals under lawful arrest.

The Supreme Court approved intensive searches of prisoners and pre-trial detainees, even where no suspicion focused on a prisoner. (Bell v. Wolfish) and, an inmate has no reasonable expectation of privacy entitling him to 4th Amendment protection. (Hudson v. Palmer) This is a permissible warrantless search incident to the booking and jailing of the individual.

The basis for such inventory searches is to:

- Protect the officers' safety and that of other prisoners
- Prevent contraband from being smuggled into detention facilities
- Protect officers and their departments from

unjust accusations of theft

• Protect the property of the arrestee

Considering the frequency of these inventory searches, the Court pointed out: *"It is important that police departments adopt uniform policies and procedures to govern these searches. In addition, it is important that record-keeping practices require thorough inventory of the property found, as well as, policies and procedures for the storage and custody of the property.* [emphasis added]." (IL v. Lafayette; S.D. v. Opperman; Florida v. Wells).

The Illinois Supreme Court has ruled once an arrestee's belongings have been subjected to an initial, valid inventory police may reexamine the items they had already seen incident to the first inventory. The reasoning was a legal arrest substantially diminishes the defendant's legitimate expectation of privacy in his person and his clothing.

"Second Look" at Prisoner's Property

Issue: May a prisoner's inventoried property, once seen by the police, be viewed again in connection with the same, or a different crime without first obtaining a search warrant.

Facts: During a burglary investigation a Peoria Heights, IL, investigator learned a suspect had been incarcerated in a nearby jail. The police at the jail searched and inventoried the prisoner's personal effects pursuant to standard procedure. This property was secured in a manila envelope and stored outside the presence of the defendant.

The investigator telephoned the jail and learned that an unusual necklace, fitting the description of one taken in the burglary, was among the prisoner's personal effects. The investigator accompanied the victim to the jail, the necklace was removed from the closed envelope, and the victim identified it as being taken from her house during the burglary.

The investigator interviewed the defendant, advised him of his Miranda rights and showed him the necklace. The defendant initially denied knowledge of the necklace until told it was found in his property envelope. The defendant later made a written statement confessing to the burglary.

The trial court held the second look was a search within the meaning of the Fourth Amendment, and since no warrant had been obtained, the results of the search were suppressed. The Illinois Appellate Court upheld the suppression of evidence and the State appealed to the Illinois Supreme Court.

The State argued the defendant lost all reasonable expectation of privacy when the necklace was viewed during the initial jail inventory. The defendant argued that while his expectation of privacy was diminished as a result of the jail inventory, this expectation was renewed when the envelope was sealed for safekeeping.

The Illinois Supreme Court found the defendant had not sought to preserve his expectation of privacy in the necklace by concealing it in a container, but rather, carried it openly on his person. The court concluded, "The second look was not conducted to search for and discover evidence previously concealed in some way from the inventorying officers. We agree ... that no reasonable expectations of privacy are invaded and no search occurs when police officers simply look again at what they had already lawfully seen. (People v. Richards)

Towing and Impoundment of Vehicles

All seizures and searches of vehicles by government officials must comply with the requirements of the Fourth Amendment. Seizures and searches without a warrant are unreasonable unless they fall within one of the "exceptions" which the courts have adopted by case law. Non-evidentury seizures of vehicles must conform to the Due Process rights of the Fourteenth Amendment. Although procedural due process is not normally required prior to towing, it is clear that the vehicle owner has a due process right to adequate notice and a meaningful, impartial hearing as soon as possible after the "deprivation" of property rights in the vehicle occurs.

Retention of Vehicle as Security

Governmental or private retention of vehicles as "security" for payment of fine, towing and storage charges is in a state of uncertainty. Some courts require that when the owner appears for the vehicle it must be returned and another form of security be obtained. Other courts have not decided this issue, or else permit the continued retention of the vehicle. The propriety of the governmental action, however, will be determined by the swiftness with which the legality of the seizure and towing is adjudicated.

A violation of a vehicle owner's Fourth and Fourteenth Amendments constitutional rights may subject the public official and the employing municipality to a federal civil rights suit under *Section 1983 of the Civil Rights Act*, or to a state civil suit for conversion or illegal deprivation of property.

There is no distinction in "public towing" situations whether the towing and storage is accomplished by the government, or by a private concern at the request of government officials pursuant to government policy, procedure or regulation. Municipal statutes, policies, procedures or custom may subject a governmental jurisdiction to a civil rights liability if that custom or policy is unconstitutional and the responsible officials should have recognized the unconstitutional aspects of the law or statute. (Northwestern University Traffic Institute, 1981)

Chain of Custody

One of the most important functions of the property control system is to maintain the chain of custody over evidence placed into the system. The chain of custody, as a process, consists primarily of the signing in and out of all movements of evidence between persons or locations outside of the property control room. The chain of custody relates to the total accounting for evidence and the continuity of possession. The chain is made up of all individuals who have had custody of the evidence since its acquisition by the police agency. Each individual in the chain of custody is responsible for the particular piece of evidence to include its safekeeping and preservation while it is under his or her control. The chain of custody of electronic evidence -- computers, audio and video recordings, and surveillance recordings -- because of their technical nature, is addressed in the chapter on Electronic Evidence.

Necessity for Chain of Custody

The chain of custody is necessary in order to establish the legal sufficiency of evidence once it has come into the custody of the police agency. The basis for this legal sufficiency is that the evidence has not been lost, that no tampering of the evidence has occurred, and the evidence has not been contaminated; by other evidence stored nearby, or by the container in which the evidence is stored.

In a practical sense, the maintenance of the chain of custody allows the investigating officer to testify with confidence in court that the evidence is, at the time of introduction at trial, in the same form as it was at the time it was taken into police custody. "Any disruption in the chain of custody may cause evidence to be inadmissible. Even if admitted, a disruption [in the chain of custody] can weaken or destroy its probative value. Accordingly, the rule is to have the least possible number of persons handle the evidence." (Osterburg and Ward, 1992)

Maintaining the Chain

The chain of custody is established and maintained by adhering to the following standards:

- The number of persons handling evidence from the time it is secured should be limited.

When the evidence leaves the possession of an officer, he must record in his notes to whom the evidence was given, the date and time, and the reason it was turned over.

- Individuals who handle the evidence should affix their names, badge numbers and assignment to the package containing the evidence.
- A signed receipt should be obtained from the person accepting the evidence.

• A receipt should be signed by the investigator when the item is returned to him or her.

• The investigator, after an item has been returned to him, should determine if the item is in the same condition as when it was discovered.

Any change in the physical appearance or characteristics of the evidence must be called to the attention of the court. (U. S. Dept. of Justice, undated)

Photographic film developing. The use of commercial film developers may raise chain of custody questions. When the film is delivered to a commercial developer the police agency is not in possession and has no control over the developing process or the negatives. Many police agencies, and some commercial film developers, require that a chain of custody entry be recorded when the film is delivered for processing. The film is handled, processed and stored by the commercial firm under controlled conditions. Conditions that will support future testimony pertaining to the chain of custody while the film is in the possession of the firm.

A Question of Good Faith

Issue: Can a defendant's due process rights be violated by police mishandling of evidence.

Facts: The defendant, Larry Youngblood, abducted a ten year-old boy from a carnival, took him to a house and sexually assaulted him. After the assault, the boy was taken to a hospital where tests were performed using a sexual assault kit. After receipt of the boy's underwear and teeshirt, which contained semen stains, the police failed to refrigerate these items.

It was not until two years later that the underwear and tee/shirt were examined. Neither the clothing nor the test results from the sexual assault kit conclusively connected Youngblood with the crime. Nevertheless, Youngblood was convicted on the basis of other evidence, including the eyewitness identification by the boy.

On appeal, Youngblood argued that if the boy's clothing had been properly preserved by the police, it may have exculpated him. Upon hearing the case the United States Supreme Court, in a 5-4 decision, upheld Youngblood's conviction.

In addressing the issue, whether the defendant's due process rights had been violated by police mishandling of the evidence, the Court disagreed strongly among itself and issued three separate opinions. The simple majority focused on the good faith efforts of the police officers in preserving the evidence. Chief Justice Rehnquist stated it is unfair to "impose on the police an undifferentiated absolute duty to retain and to preserve all material that might be of conceivable evidentury significance.

A good faith standard limits the police officer's duty to preserve evidence and protect the defendant in cases where the police themselves, by their conduct, indicate the evidence could form a basis for exonerating the defendant." (Arizona v. Youngblood)

Under the good faith standard, if police actions indicate they realize the probative value of evidence that may potentially be used to determine the defendant's innocence, and they maliciously destroy the evidence, there is a presumption the evidence would have exonerated the defendant. If the police officer is merely negligent in failing to preserve evidence, there is no due process violation if he or she is acting in good faith.

The difficulty with the Youngblood decision is that while the Supreme Court established a standard for the handling of criminal evidence, it did not go beyond this and establish effective guidelines by which to apply the standard. This leaves several questions unanswered such as; what constitutes "bad faith" other than malice. Does gross negligence or recklessness constitute bad faith.

The dissenting justices rejected the good faith standard. They argued it is not in accordance with normal police practices to negligently handle evidence. On that basis the dissenters argued, Youngblood's decision should be reversed.

Relying on *California v. Trombetta*, Justice Blackmun wrote, the first determination must be whether the destruction of the evidence was "in good faith and in accordance with normal police practice."

Justice Stevens, in a separate dissenting opinion, referred to a "fundamentally unfair" standard. Justice Stevens, in upholding the conviction, stated he was doing so because the trial was not "fundamentally unfair."

The promise of Justice Stevens' approach is it shifts the burden from the police officer's action to the fairness of the trial itself. In essence, it eliminates uncertainty from the police point of view and it places a proper due process emphasis on whether the defendant receives a fair trial.

In this case, *Arizona v. Youngblood*, there are three standards articulated by various members of the United States Supreme Court relating to police handling of evidence: *the good faith standard, the fundamentally fair standard* and *the good faith in accordance with normal police practice standard.*

A possible development in future cases before the United States Supreme Court on this issue may be one in which the police acted in good faith but destroyed evidence so crucial as to deny the defendant a fair trial. The "fairness standard" articulated by Justice Stevens, may well be the standard applied in future cases.

The "Single Action" Revolver

Issue: What effects can a material alteration of evidence have on evidence admissibility.

Facts: In an unusual case, the defense objected to the introduction of a pistol used in a robbery on the grounds that its condition had changed while in police custody. It was alleged that at the time of seizure the pistol could only be fired by thumbing the hammer.

While the investigating officer was occupied with the completion of his report, a second officer picked up the pistol and, finding a loose screw, tightened the screw causing the pistol to be capable of firing double-action.

The court ruled the weapon was admissible since its ability to fire at the time of the crime was not at issue, nor was it contended the defendant ever fired the weapon. The attempt to introduce the pistol was solely to show that the victim relinquished his money because he feared he would be shot. In this case, the court ruled, the alteration to the weapon did not affect its evidential value. (State v. Griffith)

In this case the alteration of evidence did not have a negative effect on the outcome of the trial. Consider, however, the outcome if the contention was that the defendant fired the weapon.

Chain of Custody and Property Audits

Another purpose of the chain of custody is to support the property audit function. In order to audit the movement, custody, location and disposition of property and evidence, it is necessary that exact records be maintained. Chain of custody entries on the Property Inventory Report form provide a significant portion of the information required to trace property movements and final disposition.

Chain of Custody Relating to Expert Analysis

The chain of custody relating to a specimen or object analyzed requires that the specimen or object was in fact derived or taken from the particular person or place alleged: "The chain of custody is an essential quantum of proof in any case involving bullets, cartridge cases and weapons, fingerprints, hair, stained clothing, drugs and urine, blood or breath specimens." (Moenssens et al, 1973) A New York trial court ruled that DNA evidence to be offered at trial must be accompanied by chain of custody documents to adhere to pre-trial procedures. (People v. Castro)

In these instances the chronicle of custody includes:

• The initial possession of the specimen or object

by an officer
- The journey to the laboratory
- The method of storage at the laboratory prior to analysis
- The possession of the unused portion of the specimen or the object after analysis and up to the time of trial

Disposal of Personal Property

To address fully the issue of the disposition of property several related issues must be addressed. Disposal may include custody as ordered by a court, disposal at public sale, destruction or return to owner. Disposition of property may also include continued custody, possession and use of the property by the police agency through administrative action. This administrative action must be through a court-ordered possession or statutory provision allowing continued possession of the property.

Where there are conflicting claims as to the ownership of property, between the person from whom the property was taken by the police and the person from whom it was allegedly stolen, the matter must be resolved in a civil action. Applicable state and federal property statutes should be reviewed to determine the exact requirements and procedures for disposing of various classifications of property.

Only if the government has a superior right in the property does a law enforcement agency have the right to withhold the property from its rightful owner. Illinois Criminal Statutes, for example, require the return of property to one from whom it was seized if the person is not charged with an offense. This does not apply to contraband, or other property known or suspected to be stolen.

In the many cases addressing the disposition of seized property at issue is the extent to which the government's property interest is superior to that of the property owner or person in possession. It has been recognized that the Fourth Amendment protection of privacy allows property to be seized as "mere evidence" in which the government claims no superior property interest. Thus, the lawful seizure of property by the police implies no denial of ownership nor does it restrict the owner's right to regain possession once the property has served its evidentury function. (Warden, Maryland Penitentiary v. Hayden)

The Forgotten Stolen Auto

Issue: Can the neglect to notify a property owner of recovery be the basis for a constitutional deprivation.

Facts: A car reported stolen was recovered by the police the same day and towed to a private tow operator's lot. Thirty five days later the victim was notified of the recovery of the car. The towing and storage charges of $150 would have to be satisfied before the release of the car. The victim paid $85 in charges, but the car was never returned nor was the money paid returned.

The United States Court of Appeals reversed a District Court ruling and allowed the victim to proceed with a civil suit against the police officer that ordered the tow and the private tow operator. The basis for this decision was the violation of the victims civil rights in that the victim was deprived of property without due process of law. (Bunkley v. Watkins)

The improper sale of property held by law enforcement agencies without adequate notice to the property owners has been held to violate the due process clause of the Fourteenth Amendment. In one case the court held the sale of the defendant's vehicle, while he was in custody, on the pretext it was abandoned was a Fourteenth Amendment violation. The court stated the officers could have easily notified the plaintiff, his lawyer or parents regarding the status of the automobile. (McKee v. Aggy)

Notification Before Disposal

Issue: Does a failure to properly notify the true owner of property before it is disposed of constitute an unlawful conversion of the property.

Facts: The chief of police of the Village of Chatham, New York received a teletype from police in Fairfield, CA that a Camaro 228 reported as stolen was in the possession of the plaintiff in the Chatham area. The information was said to have come from the owner of the car, Norris, who had filed a complaint with the Fairfield, CA. Police Department. The owner alleged the plaintiff in this law suit had stolen the car and intended to forge her name on the ownership papers. Several hours later the car and driver were located. The driver, plaintiff, was arrested for possession of stolen property and the car was impounded. The Chatham Police requested a tow by Taconic Automotive.

The alleged owner of the automobile, Norris, later dropped the charges of auto theft against the plaintiff and the chief of police released the hold on the car. The tow operator sent a registered letter to the plaintiff regarding the release of the auto. The plaintiff had moved, however, and the letter was returned. Plaintiff later went to the tow operator to retrieve the car and a dispute ensued over the storage fees.

The chief of police later informed the tow operator that the cars owner was the person who originally reported it stolen. Norris, however, took no action to recover the vehicle. Plaintiff filed an action for conversion of the car against the police department and the tow operator, Taconic Automotive. One year later the tow operator foreclosed on its liens for storage of the vehicle. The owner of the tow firm purchased the vehicle at auction.

After a jury trial the plaintiff was awarded $13,000 in compensatory damages against the police department and the tow operator and $5,000 punitive damages against the tow operator. The defendants appealed the judgement.

On appeal, the court found that the police department and tow operator had unlawfully converted the car (civil law theft); each had interfered with plaintiff's use and enjoyment of the car.

Although required by the criminal court to release the car to its owner -- and only the plaintiff produced ownership documents -- the police told the tow operator to release the car to Norris. The tow operator, fully aware of plaintiff's ownership claim, instituted foreclosure proceedings against Norris only and did not inform plaintiff of the impending sale of the car. The judgement of the trial court was upheld. (Warner v. Village of Chatham)

Reported Stolen Auto

Issue: Is the negligence of an officer impounding a vehicle, which was later released to the prior owner who had reported it stolen, actionable under *Section 1983 of the Civil Rights Act*. This issue arose in a 1997 case that was tried in federal court.

Facts: Plaintiff Williams purchased a truck from the City of Kansas City at an abandoned vehicle auction. Months later, Richard Fowler notified police he had located his stolen truck on a Kansas City street. Detective Soligo investigated and found the truck parked near Williams' salvage business. Soligo observed the VIN was for another truck and the truck's license plate was for a Chevrolet registered to Williams. Williams produced a bill of sale for the truck from the city vehicle auction and bearing the illegitimate VIN.

Detective Soligo impounded the truck pending further investigation and had it towed to a city lot where he placed a "hold" on it. Soligo checked the tow lot sales records which confirmed Williams' bill of sale. Detective Soligo concluded the truck was the one reported stolen by Fowler and turned the license plate and illegitimate VIN plate over to the police property room. He then released his "hold" on the truck without further instructions.

Shortly thereafter, Fowler filed a claim with the Police Auto Release Desk producing a certificate of title for the truck. The claim was processed and the truck was released to Fowler.

Williams brought a *Section 1983* negligent deprivation suit against Officer Soligo under the 14th Amendment. Williams alleged Soligo should have informed him of the hold release so he, Williams, could have filed a claim for the truck.

The court held that Officer Soligo took no action depriving Williams of his property. The officer impounded the truck, later released his investigative "hold", and simply turned the matter over to city officials who were authorized to release a towed vehicle to the proper claimant. (Williams v Soligo)

Conclusion

Key words and phrases appeared in the legal principles and case law that were presented in this chapter. These words, and the associated legal principles, should serve as a basis for the development or revision of property control policies and procedures. Phrases such as chain of evidence, good faith, preservation, retention, materiality, contraband, seizure, custody, possession and abandonment should be incorporated into property management procedures. Equally important is an understanding of the practical meaning and intent of these legal principles as well as their application in the operation and administration of the property control function. A plea of ignorance to these basic principles of property management after a property owner has been deprived of their rights will not serve as an effective defense before a criminal or civil court.

A due process determination following a good faith, but failed effort by the police, to preserve evidence will often be decided by these significant factors:

- The materiality of the available evidence;
- The possible prejudice to the defendant that results from the loss or destruction;

- The procedural formalities associated with the loss or destruction.

The intentional, reckless, or negligent destruction of physical evidence is always illegal and often unconstitutional. The trend of judicial decisions addressing these situations is the recommendation, or requirement for formal procedures for the collection, preservation, testing and disposal of evidence. As a practical matter it is a sound practice to apply these same standards to nonevidential property.

A finder's rights to the several classifications of property are summarized as follows:

- A finder of lost property acquires title to the property against all others except the true owner.

- A finder of misplaced (mislaid) property does not obtain title or right to possession. Instead, the owner of the property on which the misplaced property is found is deemed to be the bailee of the mislaid property for the true owner.

- A finder of abandoned property is entitled not only to possession, but also to ownership as against all others.

- Treasure trove is treated as lost property and belongs to the finder. (Survey of Law of Property)

Chapter Notes

Book References

Black, Henry C., *Black's Law Dictionary*, 4th ed. (St.Paul: West Pub. Co., 1968).

Survey On The Laws Of Property, p. 689.

1 Am. Jur. 2 *Abandoned, Lost Property.*

25 Proof of Facts 671, p. 697.

Boyer, Ralph, *Survey on the Law of Property*, 3rd Ed. (St. Paul: West Publishers, 1981).

Northwestern University Traffic Institute, *Impounding, Towing, Search and Inventory of Vehicles*, 1st. Edition, (1981).

U.S. Department of Justice, *Drug Enforcement Administration Handbook,* undated.

Moenssens, Andre; Moses, Ray and Inbau, Fred; *Scientific Evidence In Criminal Cases,* (Mineola, N.Y.: The Foundation Press, 1973).

Osterburg, James W.; and Ward, Richard H.; *Criminal Investigation: A Method For Reconstructing The Past,* (Cincinnati: Anderson Pub. Co., 1992), p. 180.

Peterson, Joseph, "Use of Forensic Evidence by the Police and Courts", (National Institute of Justice, 1987).

Section 1983, *Federal Civil Rights Act of 1873.*

Court Cases

Arizona v. Youngblood, 109 S. Ct. 333 (1988).

A.T. Kearney, Inc. v. INCA Intern., Inc. 87 III. Dec. 798, 477 N. E. 2d 1326, III. App. 3d 655, appeal dismissed (III. App. 1 Dist. 1985).

Bell v. Wolfish, 441 U.S. 520, 99 S.Ct. 1861(1979).

Brooks v. Dutton, 751 F. 2d 197 (1985).

Bunkley v. Watkins, 567 F. 2d 304 (C.A. 5th Fla. 1978).

Caicos Petroleum Service Corp. v. Hunsaker, 551 F. Supp. 152 (D.C. III. 1982).

California v. Trombetta, 467 U.S. 479 (1984).

Causey v. Blanton, 314 S.E. 2d 346, 281 S.C. 163 (S.C. App. 1984).

Chance v Certain Artifacts Found & Salvaged from The Nashville, 606 F Supp 801, AMC 609, affd without op (CA11 Ga) 775 F2d 302, 1986 AMC 1216, ((SD Ga, **1985).**

Col v. Bertine, 479 U.S. 367, 107 S. Ct. 738 (1987).

Columbus-America Discovery Group, Inc. v. Unidentified, Wrecked & Abandoned Sailing Vessel, 974 F2d 450, 1992 AMC 2705, 24 FR Serv 3d 14, cert den (US) 123 L Ed 2d 183, 113 S Ct 1625 (CA 4 Va). Also, Campbell v Cochran, 416 A2d 211 (Del Super); Foster v. Fidelity Safe Deposit Co., 264 Mo 89, 174 SW 376; Foulke v. New York C. R. Co., 228 NY 269, 127 NE 237, 9 ALR 1384; Ferguson v. Ray, 44 OR 557, 77 P 600.

Commonwealth of Pennsylvania v. Wetmore, 447 A.2d 1012 (Pa. Super., 1982).

Cooper v. City of Greenwood, Miss., 904 F.2d 302 (5th Cir. 1990).

Denny v. Alder, 482 P.2d 723 (OR 1971). See also, Kellogg v. Strickland 191 So. 2d 536, (Miss. 1966) and Price v. Green 186 So. 2d 460 (Miss. 1966).

Fearon v. State of California, 209 Cal. Rptr. 309 (Cal. App. 1984).

Fuentes v. Wendt, 436 N.Y.S.2d 801 (1981).

Hagen Trucklines v. Sheriff of Weber County, 669 P. 2d 871 (Utah 1981).

Haywood v. United States (CA.7 Ill.) 268 F. 795, cert. den. 256 U.S. 789, 65 L. Ed. 1172,41 S. Ct. 449; and United States v. Rabinowitz, 339 U.S. 56, 94 L. Ed. 653, 70 S. Ct. 430.

Hudson v. Palmer, 104 S. Ct. 3194 (1984).

Hunt v. Chapman, 458 So. 2d. 206 (La. App. 1984).

Illinois v. Lafayette, 103. S.Ct. 2605 (1983).

Johnson v. Studholme, 619 F. 2d 908 (D.C. Colo. 1985).

Katz v. United States, 389 U.S. 347 (1967).

Kuchar v. Bernstrauch, 219 N.W. 2d 764 (NE. 1974).

McKee v. Aggy, 703 F.2d 479 (10th Circuit 1983).

Mozzeti v. Sup. Ct., 4 Cal. 3d 699, 94 Cal. Rptr. 412, 484 P.2d 84 (1971). See also State v. Opperman 228 N.W. 2d 152 (S.D. 1975).

Nash v. City of North Platte, 288 N.W. 2d 51 (Neb. 1980).

Owen v. City of Independence, 445 U.S. 622, 100 S.Ct. 1398 (1980).

Parman v. United States, 399 F.2d 559, (D.C. Cir. 1968), cert. denied 393 U.S. 858 (1968).

Parratt v. Taylor, 451 U.S. 527 (1981).

People v. Herman, 103 Ill Dec. 525, 501 N.E. 2d 842, (Il. App. 2 Dist. 1986). Also, Denny v. Alder 258 Or. 295, 482 P.2d 723, 726 (OR. 1971).

People v. Richards, 69 Ill. Dec. 839, 445 N.E. 2d 319, 94 Ill. 2d 92 (1983). See also, U.S. v. Guevera 589 Fed. Supp. 760 (D.C.N.Y. 1984).

People v. Castro, 545 N.Y.S. 2d 985, 45 Cr. L. 2375, (N.Y. Sup. Ct., 1989).

Propert v. District of Columbia, 741 F. Supp. 961 (D.D.C., 1990).

Scheduling Corp. of America v. Massello, 74 Ill. Dec. 796, 456 N.E. 2d 298, 119 Ill. App. 3d 355, appeal after remand 104 Ill. Dec. (Ill. App. 1 Dist. 1983).

Speer v. City of Dodge City, Kan. App. 636 P.2d 178.

State v. Ching 678 P.2d 1088 (Hawaii 1984) citing State v. McDougal 228 N.W. 2d at 678; State v. Keller 265 Ore. 622, 626, 510 P.2d 568, 570 (1973).

State v. Gwinn, 301 A.2d 291, 293-94 (Del. Supr. 1972).

State v. Griffith, 94 Idaho 76, 481 P.2d 34 (1971).

Terranova v. State of New York, 445 N.Y.S. 2d 965.

Warden, Maryland Penitentiary v. Hayden, 387 U.S. 294, 18 L. Ed. 2d 782, 87 S. Ct. 1642.

Wilkins v. Whitaker, 714 F.2d 4, certiorari denied 104 S. Ct. 3586, 468 U.S. 1217, 82 L. ED. 2d 884 (C.A.N.C. 1983).

U.S. v. Andrews, 22 F.3d 1328 5th (Cir. 1994).

U.S. v. Cella, 568 F.2d 1283 (9th Cir. 1977).

U.S. v. Colbert, 474 F.2d. 174, (C.A. 5th 1973).

U.S. v. Duguay, (C.A.7-Ill, 1996).

Warner v. Village of Chatham, 598 N.Y. 2d 863 (1993)

Williams v. Soligo, 104 F3d 1060, 8th Cir., (1997)

End Notes

[1] *State v Fowler*, 101 **Ariz** 561, 422 P2d 125; *State v Winsett*, 57 **Del** 344, 200 A2d 237; *People v Endress*, 106 **Ill** App 2d 217, 245 NE2d 26 (superseded by statute on another point as stated in *People v Williams*, 87 **Ill** 2d 161, 57 Ill Dec 589, 429 NE2d 487); *State v Eads* (**Iowa**) 166 NW2d 766; *State v Superior Court*, 106 **NH** 228, 208 A2d 832, 7 ALR3d 1; *People v Brown*, 104 Misc 2d 157, 427 **NYS**2d 722; *Commonwealth v Brown*, 29 **Pa** D & C2d 626, 47 Del Co 120.

[2] *Walker v People*, 126 **Col** 135, 248 P2d 287.

[3] *State v McCreary*, 179 **Neb** 589, 139 NW2d 362, cert den **384 US** 979, 16 L Ed 2d 689, 86 S Ct 1877.

[4] *State v Brumfield* (**La**) 329 So 2d 181. *Bryan v State*, 224 **Ga** 389, 162 SE2d 349,

[5] *State v Oliverez*, 34 **Or** App 417, 578 P2d 502.

[6] *Barnard v Henderson* (CA5 **La**) 514 F2d 744, later app (CA5 **La**) 531 F2d 1332; State ex rel. *Mahoney v Superior Court of Maricopa County*, 78 **Ariz** 74, 275 P2d 887; *People v Tribbett*, 90 **Ill** App 2d 296, 232 NE2d 523, affd 41 Ill 2d 267, 242 NE2d 249 and (superseded by statute on another point as stated in *People v Williams*, 87 **Ill** 2d 161, 57 Ill Dec 589, 429 NE2d 487); *Application of Hughes*, 181 Misc 668, 41 **NYS**2d 843; *Doakes v District Court of Oklahoma County* (**Okla** Crim) 447 P2d 461.

[7] *Schindler v Superior Court of Madera County* (3d Dist) 161 **Cal** App 2d 513, 327 P2d 68 (disapproved on other grounds People v Garner, 57 Cal 2d 135, 18 Cal Rptr 40, 367 P2d 680, cert den 370 US 929, 8 L Ed 2d 508, 82 S Ct 1571).

[8] *State v Wright*, 87 **Wash** 2d 783, 557 P2d 1.

[9] *People v Loftis*, 55 **Ill** App 3d 456, 13 Ill Dec 133, 370 NE2d 1160; *State v Gray* (**La**) 351 So 2d 448.

[10] *Lauderdale v State* (**Alaska**) 548 P2d 376; *Rogers v Municipal Court of Rogers*, 259 **Ark** 43, 531 SW2d 257; *State v Michener*, 25 **Or** App 523, 550 P2d 449; *State v Raduege* (App) 100 **Wis** 2d 27, 301 NW2d 259.

[11] *State v Davis* (**Mo**) 556 SW2d 45.

[12] *State v Moore* (**Fla** App D1) 356 So 2d 838.

[13] *United States v Sullivan* (CA5 **Fla**) 578 F2d 121; *Patterson v State*, 238 **Ga** 204, 232 SE2d 233, cert den 431 US 970, 53 L Ed 2d 1067, 97 S Ct 2932, reh den 434 US 882, 54 L Ed 2d 167, 98 S Ct 248; *People v Taylor*, 54 **Ill** App 3d 454, 12 Ill Dec 76, 369 NE2d 573; *State v Hopkins* (**La**) 351 So 2d 474; *People v Bell*, 74 **Mich** App 270, 253 NW2d 726; *Latham v State* (**Tenn** Crim) 560 SW2d 410.

[14] *State v Faraone* (**RI**) 425 A2d 523.

[15] *Washington v United States* (**Dist Col** App) 377 A2d 1348; *Rowe v State*, 262 **Ind** 250, 314 NE2d 745; *Commonwealth v Clark*, 3

Mass App 481, 334 NE2d 68 (all noting that the prosecution need not preserve arrays from which no identification was made).

[16] *People v McCabe*, 75 **III** App 3d 162, 30 III Dec 852, 393 NE2d 1199; *State v Brown*, 220 **Kan** 684, 556 P2d 443.

[17] *State v Brown*, 220 **Kan** 684, 556 P2d 443, *People v Rosa*, 49 **III** App 3d 608, 7 III Dec 228, 364 NE2d 389, 13 ALR4th 1350.

[18] *People v Coleates*, 86 Misc 2d 614, 376 **NYS**2d 374.

[19] *State v Le Clair* (**Me**) 382 A2d 30.

[20] *United States v Ahmad* (DC **Pa**) 53 FRD 186.

Chapter 2

Property Control Policies and Procedures

Comprehensive, well-written and up-to-date policies and procedures are an essential component of any property control system. Property and evidence processing is one functional area in which the discretion of department personnel should be restricted. Due to the sensitive and often valuable nature of property taken into custody, this is not an area in which flexibility of discretion is desirable. Therefore, the agency must formulate clear, specific guidelines for personnel and ensure that these guidelines are followed.

Policy

Policy consists of general statements of philosophy concerning the objectives, principles and values which guide the performance of department activities as established by the Chief of Police.

The distinguishing features of policy are:

- Policy is formulated by analyzing objectives and determining, through research, those principles that will best guide the department in achieving its objectives.

- Policy is based upon ethics, experience, the desires of the community and the mandate of the law.

- Policy is objective, rather than situation oriented, and is broad enough in scope to encompass most situations. Policy, therefore, must be stated in general terms.

- Property control policy is articulated to inform the

public and department employees of the principles that will be adhered to in the performance
of the property management function.

Policy can be characterized as a method for forming attitudes about the manner in which a job and related tasks and activities will be accomplished. Policy is intended to influence the way one thinks about the job.

Procedures

Procedures are more specific than policy and direct behaviors in the accomplishment of a task associated with the job. The characteristics of procedures are:

- A method of performing an operation or a manner of proceeding on a course of action
- A series of steps to be followed in definite order
- A checklist of things that must be done before a task is completed
- A particular way of accomplishing a task

Rules

Rules are specific statements of prohibition or requirement to prevent deviations from policy and procedure. A rule applies each time the situation or activity which is the subject of the rule occurs. The characteristics of rules are:

- Behind each rule there is a policy; written or implied
- Rules tell you exactly what or what not to do
- Rules are rigid and leave no room for discretion since they direct conduct, action or usage

Legal Requirements

In many instances the courts have decided cases pertaining to chain of custody and civil liability issues on the basis of the existence of such policies. The failure to have any policy regarding the disposition of seized property may be the basis for agency liability.

Several recent court decisions have held that the failure to have a policy gives unbridled discretion to police officers and may lead to a denial of a individual's property rights without due process of law. The failure to have a property disposition policy has been also the basis for judicial decisions in reviewing the policies, or lack of policies, and procedures employed in safeguarding property in police custody. These decisions have included issues of loss of property while in police custody, damage to property, disposition of property, and chain of custody issues.

Ohio statutes, for example, require each law enforcement agency that has custody of any property subject to the Code to adopt a written internal control policy that addresses the procedures the agency will follow in disposing of the property. (Ohio) The Wisconsin courts have held there is a necessity for police policy regarding the inventory search of closed containers. (*State of Wisconsin v. Weide*, 1990)

Inventory Searches

Issue: What policies and procedures are required for inventory searches.

Facts: A locked suitcase was found in a automobile trunk after a D.U.I. arrest. The officer opened the suitcase and found a "considerable amount of marijuana."

The defendant won the case in the United States Supreme Court since the "Florida Highway Patrol had no policy whatever with respect to the opening of closed containers encountered during an inventory search." The Supreme Court stated ... "absent such a policy, the search was not sufficiently regulated to satisfy Fourth Amendment requirements.

The policy and procedures specified by the Court are:

- Standardized criteria or established routine must regulate opening of containers and produce an inventory.
- The policy or practice governing inventory searches should be designed to produce an inventory.

The U.S. Supreme Court has held: "It would be ... permissable ... to allow the opening of closed containers whose contents officers determine they are unable to ascertain from examining the container's exteriors". (*Florida v. Wells,* 1990). One Federal Court decision held that there is no Fourth Amendment violation where the: "Police Department had an established, but unwritten inventory policy". (*United States v. Walker,* 1991).

Policy and Procedures On Property Returns

Issue: Does the disposition of property seized during a criminal investigation require notice to property owners under the Fourteenth Amendment, Due Process clause?

Facts: Police officers lawfully seized property belonging to plaintiffs including: stereo equipment, video recorder, movie projector, three cameras, binoculars, two briefcases, silverware, gold coins, hunting knives and rifles.

The property was tagged and turned-over to Houston Police Property Division. The Property Division stored the property, but the seizing detectives controlled the property's disposition through completion of a "Disposition Authorization Form."

After holding the property 90 days, the Property Division sent a Disposition Authorization Form to the detectives.

The Disposition Authorization form listed seven options for handling the property:

1) Hold for court case.

2) Hold for investigation,

3) Hold for possible surety bond indemnity agreement,

4) Photograph and release to owner,

5) Release to owner (or authorized person)

6) Dispose of as authorized by city ordinance

7) Not wanted by this division, seek authorization from _____.

A city ordinance requires officers to "make good faith effort to identify, locate and give notice to the owner of any unclaimed property." It does not specify, however, how officers were to determine owner identity. Three months later the seizing officers directed the Property Division to dispose of one batch of the property. The Disposition Authorization Form was not properly signed and dated as required.

After an internal investigation by the Police Department it was concluded that human error caused the unauthorized disposition of the property.

Plaintiffs repeatedly asked for the return of their property. A judge gave them a court order instructing the city to return the property. When plaintiffs presented the court order they found the city had sold most of the property and converted the rest to city use. Plaintiffs did recover some of the converted property.

Plaintiffs now sue the city under the *Civil Rights Act* (42 USC 1983) challenging the disposition of property and alleging it violated due process for a failure to provide notice and opportunity to be heard prior to disposition of the property. Plaintiffs were awarded $55,374 compensatory damages, $25,241 prejudgment interest and $67,164 attorney fees and costs; a total of $147,779.

The court, after reviewing the Houston City Ordinance for the disposal of property, identified three major deficiencies:

1.) The ordinance instructs police officers to notify only "lawful" owners of property in police custody. It does not instruct officers to notify other persons with claims to the property; for example, the persons from whom the officers seize the property unless the officers believe they are the lawful owners.

2.) The ordinance creates a high risk of erroneous deprivation because it does not require notification but only requires officers to make a "good faith effort" to identify, locate and notify "lawful owners." The system does not require some other type of notice such as newspaper advertisements when officers cannot notify directly persons with interests in the property.

3.) It neither establishes nor incorporates any guidelines for satisfying its "good faith" requirement or for identifying and locating "lawful owners." The ordinance allows each officer to decide when she has satisfied the good faith requirement. Nothing in the system checks the officer's determination that she cannot notify the owner or need not notify persons with a claim to the property.

The court identified procedural safeguards for the notification and return of property.

1.) Requiring officers to notify all persons with claims to the property including these from whom the officers seize the property.

2.) Detailed directions on how to identify and locate persons with claims and guidelines outlining the steps necessary to satisfy the ordinances "good faith" requirement. This would curb the officers almost complete discretion.

3.) Formally reviewing officers decisions and actions before disposing of property to safeguard individuals' property interests.

4.) If the city cannot notify persons with claims to the property because it does not know where to reach them and has tried to do so, the city can attempt to safeguard interests by publishing a notice in newspapers most likely to be read by people having claims to the property.

(*Mathias v. Bingley*, 1990)

Policy On Personal Privacy

Issue: Is police disclosure of a citizen's HIV status a violation of the right to privacy and actionable under the Civil Rights Act, Section 1983.

Facts: Plaintiff filed a civil rights complaint against Officer Tibbetts for an alleged violation of plaintiffs right to privacy and against the employing town for its alleged failure to adequately train and supervise Officer Tibbetts in the protection of the privacy of individuals with AIDS.

Officer Tibbetts came into possession of a mislaid container of prescription medication identified as belonging to plaintiff and which is used to treat AIDS patients. Officer Tibbetts later contacted plaintiff to confirm that the medication belonged to her. When plaintiff refused to explicitly identify the medication, Tibbetts told plaintiff he knew what the medication was. Tibbetts then asked the plaintiff if she was "HIV positive." Plaintiff, believing she would not get her medication without answering Tibbetts questions, said she was HIV positive.

It was alleged that Officer Tibbetts later told a neighbor plaintiff was a "sad case," had an illness, and that children should be kept away from plaintiff's home. Sometime after the incident the plaintiff moved from her apartment due to the stress resulting from people knowing she had AIDs.

Officer Tibbetts testified he had received some training in HIV disease and its transmission. He was not, however, aware of the privacy rights of those with HIV infection.

The court found that the plaintiff has a constitutional right to privacy which includes nondisclosure of her HIV status. (*Doe v Town of Plymouth*)

Issue: What degree of personal privacy does an individual with access to prisoner's property have in that setting.

Facts: An California appeals court found that a person who accepts employment in a prison or jail setting may have diminished expectations of privacy in that setting. The court found that deputy sheriffs lacked an objectively reasonable expectation of privacy against being videotaped in a county jail's release office, in which inmates' property was stored. The court ruled that a warrantless video surveillance of the office, as part of a theft investigation, was not an unlawful search and seizure in violation of the deputies' civil rights. (Sacramento County Deputy Sheriff's Association v. Sacramento County)

Property Control Directives and Training

The Property Control Manual, and the written directives contained within it, are not intended to serve as the primary, or sole training of property control officers, patrol officers or investigators. Its intended purpose should be to support and emphasize the formal training officers have already received in the collection, handling, packaging and disposition of evidence and other property classifications. A balance can be struck between property control directives and training when the detailed, training-oriented information is related to highly sensitive issues or situations of a hazardous nature. Examples are the weighing, packaging, handling and storage of narcotics and dangerous drugs, chemicals and biohazard materials.

There is significant potential for the contamination of other evidence by improperly packaged or handled narcotics. There is also the possibility of officers inadvertently ingesting narcotics substances through uncovered skin, mucous membranes or the eyes. Detailed instructions, the inclusion of available training information, and warnings pertaining to personal health should be included in the Property Control Manual. Recent OSHA guidelines require health and safety warnings be communicated to all personnel. The requirements addressed by these guidelines are presented in Chapter 5.

Written Directives and Discipline

Written directives and internal agency discipline are counterparts. Written directives are, in part, the basis for a sound system of discipline. In this context, discipline is defined as the agency work conditions that exist when an officer is fully aware of and knowledgeable of his duties and responsibilities, and the methods and procedures by which these duties and responsibilities are to be fulfilled. This implies the officer knows how to carry out his job activities and is willing and able to function in the prescribed manner.

If policies and procedures have been adequately researched, are well written and effectively communicated to agency personnel there should be an infrequent need to invoke "disciplinary action" related to the handling of property and evidence. It is only when job behavior is not in accordance with written directives that "disciplinary action" should be necessary or referred to. Thus, the written directives in the property control manual are intended to establish a sound foundation for the property control system and guide its operation.

Property control directives contribute directly to a major purpose of the property control function: to make every reasonable effort to recover lost or stolen property, to identify owners or others rightfully entitled to possession and to assure its prompt return.

Assessing The Need For Policy

The need for policy is dependent upon several factors, most of which have been presented. In addition to the legal, training and disciplinary aspects of policy development, the size of the law enforcement agency, the complexity of the property control function and the past experiences of the agency are factors that should be given consideration.

Several symptoms of the need for improved or additional property control policy are:

- A feeling that organizational goals controlling the property control function are not well understood
- Too much time is expended "putting out fires" because of the improper or negligent handling,

storage or disposition of property or evidence
- Plans are made to accomplish objectives and things still do not get done
- A feeling, or the reality, people are not being held accountable for their actions or achieving results
- People feel a lack of information critical to the effective processing of property
- Management feels the property control function is not truly under control

Steps In The Development of Policy

Step 1: Determine the objectives of the property control function.

The objectives of the property control function were presented in the Introduction. These objectives are: meet all legal requirements, meet administrative requirements of proper reporting, control and audit, the safe and efficient handling and storage of property, protect property owners' rights while property is in police custody and aid in the solution of crimes.

Step 2: Outline problems which will require patrol officers, investigators, supervisors and property control personnel to make decisions in reaching these objectives.

Each of the objectives is analyzed, one at a time, to determine the general types of situations and associated problems that may occur. This analysis should address the principles, values and legal requirements personnel should consider in making decisions about how to proceed in work-related situations.

Step 3: Write general, flexible guidelines in a positive context and in a clear manner.

Sound policy statements are those that will promote initiative, improve the acceptance of job responsibilities, and serve as a useful instructional device for future situations.

Step 4: Consider the practical aspects and requirements policy must meet.

- Does it meet requirements of the law or basic authority it seeks to support?

- Is it reasonably attainable?
- Is it too radical or likely to develop unintended controversy?
- Can it be reduced to writing succinctly?
- Does it provide for flexibility of action so that a great mass of rules will not be needed in its application and interpretation?
- Have all affected agencies had a part in its formulation?
- Have senior staff and command personnel had a part in its formulation in its

final developed form?

Property Control Policies and Procedures

Based upon the previous assessment of the need for policy, agency policy and procedure statements should, at a minimum, address the following issues:

- Policy statements addressing the property and evidence control function in general
- Specific property and evidence control functions
- Maintenance and filing of property management reports
- Confidentiality of information related to investigations

    Property Control Officers should be in formed of the confidential nature of information they are privy to and restrictions on dissemination to anyone other than the investigating officer(s).

- Procedures for taking found property and evidence into custody
- Written policy statement on inventory searches of property

    This policy should require officers to:

    1. Conduct an inventory search;

    2. Complete a Property Inventory Report form;

3. Thoroughly describing the property in custody.

The purpose of which is to protect the police agency from claims of lost, damaged or contaminated property.

Inventory policies must be adopted which sufficiently limit the discretion of law enforcement officers as a means to prevent inventory searches from becoming evidentury searches.

- Procedures mandating the opening of closed containers and the inventorying of contents.

- Procedures for dealing with hazardous, oversized or otherwise unique property or evidence

- Procedures for logging property or evidence that has been taken into custody

- Procedures for packaging, labeling and admitting property into secure storage and the property room

- Procedures for the Property Control Officer upon refusal of any property that has been improperly inventoried, packaged or secured

- Special procedures for perishable evidence, i.e.; blood samples and other types of evidence that may deteriorate over time

- Procedures and regulations applicable to the processing of firearms, narcotics and dangerous drugs, money and other property

- Procedures and regulations for removing property from the property control room for laboratory analysis, court testimony, investigator review or witness identification

- Procedures and regulations for the final disposal of property; return to owner, destruction, transfer for permanent agency use and forfeiture procedures

- Procedures for property disposal should deter- mine whether due process requires a particular type of notice and hearing before disposal and should incorporate the cost-benefit test found in the U.S. Supreme Court case, *Matthews v. Eldridge*.

1.) The value of the property interest at stake;

2.) The extent to which the proposed procedures would decrease the probability of an erroneous determination of property ownership;

3.) The cost of the procedure.

The necessity for formal notice via letter, and a hearing prior to property disposal, should consider the due process requirements of the Fourteenth Amendment.

- Property management personnel training
- Procedures relating to the maintenance of property records

    Information management practices and policies must comply with legal require ments for public records and sound records management principles.

- Property Control Room audit and control procedures
- Procedures for the handling and custody of prisoners' property

    Prisoner's personal effects are searched and inventoried pursuant to standard proce dure

- Asset forfeitures and the custody and storage of property during and after forfeiture proceedings
- Provisions for the physical safety of evidence and recovered property from fire, theft and alteration as well as access by employees and contractors
- Evidence management disaster contingency plan

Examples of Property Control Policy Statements

The following are illustrative examples of the characteristics of property control policy statements:

- The Property Control Officer, under the direction of the Chief of Police, shall act as custodian of all property seized, or otherwise coming into the custody of the department. The Property Control Officer shall not be required to take possession of, or to make a disposition of, any seized, lost or stolen property, the disposition or possession of which is otherwise provided for in this policy.

• The department will make every reasonable effort to recover lost or stolen property, to identify its owner or person otherwise entitled to possession and to insure its prompt return.

• The handling, storage and disposition of such property is to conducted within the constraints of statutory and case law and out of necessity for proper performance of the property control function.

• Personal property taken as evidence remains the property of the person legally entitled to its possession prior to its seizure as evidence unless the property is contraband under a state or federal law.

• Property kept as evidence must be returned to the person entitled to possession at the earliest possible time that it is no longer needed as evidence.

• Unclaimed or forfeited property held as evidence may be disposed of only after a court of competent jurisdiction has determined the unclaimed or forfeited property is no longer needed as evidence.

Property Control Procedures

Procedures represent a method of performing a particular activity or task or a way of proceeding under specific circumstances. Policy is stated as broad principles for job behavior or performance; procedures are more specific. Policies define the outer limits of acceptable job behavior; it is attitude forming— procedures direct behavior within those limits. In summary, procedures inform personnel what is expected of them in commonly occurring situations.

The following statements illustrate the characteristics of property control procedures:

• Officers will mark evidence as soon as possible after discovery in order to assure its identity at a later date. The evidence marks should be small and legible, while at the same time be distinctive and not easily duplicated.

- Identification marks should be placed on an item so as to prevent the marks from being altered. These identification marks should also be affixed in a manner and in a location which does not alter or destroy the value of the evidence or the property value itself.

- The original of the Property Inventory Report will be forwarded by the Property Control Officer to central records after the final disposition of all items in the inventory.

Rules and Regulations

Rules and regulations set specific requirements or specific limits on behavior. They are the most narrowly drawn written directives and allow the least discretion and interpretation by agency personnel. Rules and regulations may be thought of as representing precise commands which personnel are expected to follow to the letter unless a condition of an exceptional nature arises.

Examples of Rules and Regulations

The following examples illustrate the characteristics of rules and regulations as they relate to the property control function.

- Upon taking possession of evidence or found property from a citizen, officers will note the citizen's name, address and telephone number, and will take the citizen's statement regarding how, where and when the property was found.

- It is the duty of all officers to care for, control and promptly process all evidence or property that may come into their possession. Every officer shall follow the proper chain of custody at all times to ensure no contamination of evidence while it is in the officer's custody. At no time will a member of the police agency remove, use, loan, give or otherwise dispose of any property of another for personal gain.

- Officers shall not, under any circumstances, convert to their own use, any item of property coming into their possession. No officer shall destroy any item of property or evidence in their possession unless directed to do so through a Property Disposal Order issued by the chief of police.

- Whenever an officer conducts an investigation and takes possession of any physical evidence or property, the officer will retain possession of the evidence and will turn the evidence into the Property Control Room as soon as possible, but no later than the end of their work shift.

- If an officer is in doubt whether an item should be inventoried as evidence or found property, the property shall be inventoried as evidence.

- Evidence and found property coming into an officer's possession will be promptly tagged and a Property Inventory Report form completed prior to the property being placed in a temporary secure locker. Small items of property and evidence will be placed into paper bags provided with completed property inventory tags attached to the bags.

- Property marked and tagged items of found property and evidence will be placed into the property control temporary secure lockers. Officers placing property into the lockers will ensure the locker door is secure prior to leaving the immediate area.

- Under no circumstances will an officer remove property from the Property Control Room without the approval and supervision of the Property Control Officer, and then only after entering the required information on the chain of custody form.

- Officers will not check out any property from the Property Control Room except when necessary for laboratory analysis, court testimony, investigative case review or witness identification.

- When checking-out property for these purposes, officers will do so only with the permission of those officers assigned to the property control function.

- Officers will, at the time of checkout, complete a property sign-out on the Property Inventory Report. Upon returning the property or evidence, officers will complete the appropriate chain of custody entry on the Property Inventory Report.

Property Control Manual

Policies and procedures should be compiled into a Property Control Manual. The policies and procedures contained in such a manual are the agencies goals and objectives expressed in operational terms. As a communications device, the manual informs agency personnel of their responsibilities and the methods by which these responsibilities may be met. In addition, the manual outlines methods of accomplishing tasks and establishes general performance standards for the efficient operation of the property control function.

A Property Control Manual provides distinct advantages in maintaining control and instilling uniformity within the property control system.

Meet Legal Requirements

Many courts have taken judicial notice of Property Control Manuals as expressions of agency policy. A comprehensive Property Control Manual may demonstrate the agency has shown due regard in directing the actions of its personnel in the proper handling, storage and disposal of evidence and other property classifications.

Information Repository

The property control manual serves as a single document that contains all policies, procedures, legal requirements, forms, and processing steps related to the property control function. This promotes both management consistency and operating efficiency.

Useful Management Tool

A Property Control Manual provides a means by which lines of authority and accountability for the property control function, as well as the handling and packaging of evidence, are clearly established. A clear statement of authority and accountability communicates to all agency personnel the property control function is considered an important element of investigative case management as well as overall department effectiveness. If policies or procedures are in need of modification, the manual provides an overview of the entire function, making it easier to assess any potential modifications and their effects on the entire Property Control System.

Encourages Analysis of Issues

The planning, research and development of a Property Control Manual and the policies it contains encourages management personnel to address issues that might not otherwise be addressed. A well developed Property Control Manual reduces the tendency to react to emergencies or crisis situations with policies and procedures that may be less than useful in the long-term. A common reaction to emergency situations is to address the effects, rather than the causes, of problems encountered. The effective executive knows that well-written and developed policies and procedures places the organization one step closer to rational, goal-oriented management, and away from management-by-crisis.

A Communication Device

The Property Control Manual serves also as an important communications device to agency personnel and outside agencies concerned with the proper handling and disposition of property and evidence. The courts, prosecutors office, defense attorneys and crime laboratories are equally concerned with the manner in which evidence is routinely handled and stored by the police agency introducing the evidence. Comprehensive policies and procedures provide a degree of assurance that evidence has been handled and stored in a legally acceptable manner.

A Basis For Property Control Audits

The property control audit function cannot be planned successfully nor conducted effectively without formal policies and procedures to serve as standards. These standards establish operating guidelines and controls and provide a measure against which property control operations can be evaluated. The development of a representative sample--number-- of property items to be included in an audit is dependent, in part, upon the presence and adherence to comprehensive policies and procedures. To the extent such policies and procedures are informal or do not exist, the audit sample must be considerably larger in order to draw any reliable conclusions about the reliability of the audit findings. A larger audit sample translates into more time, and therefore more cost, to conduct the audit.

Developing A Property Control Manual

The Property Control Manual should be viewed as a means of systematically providing written directives to all members of the agency regarding the objectives and functions of the property control system. The manner in which the policies, procedures, rules and regulations are formatted and presented to agency personnel is of relatively little importance. The important issue is that property control policies address general guiding principles and procedures for the handling of particular situations, activities or property. This is accomplished by clear, specific orders addressing the responsibilities and duties of each division and unit as they relate to, and must coordinate with, the property control function.

Patrol officers and investigators, as well as others that are regular contributors to the property control system, must be considered during the development of the manual. This consideration suggests policies relating to the handling of evidence at a crime scene and the seizure of contraband must be included. Policies addressing the process by which lost and found or abandoned property is taken into custody should also be included.

A sample Table of Contents for a Property Control Manual, shown as Figure 2.1, may be helpful in planning and researching the development of policies and procedures.

Property Control Manual

Sample Table of Contents

VI.   Disposition of Motor Vehicles
            Abandoned, Lost and Stolen Vehicles
            Unclaimed Vehicles
            Altered, Destroyed VIN Numbers
            License Plates
            Vehicle Registration and Titles

Figure 2.1
Sample Table of Contents

OSHA Regulations

The Occupational Safety and Health Administration (OSHA) has issued regulations to protect workers from infection from AIDS, Hepatitis B and other bloodborne diseases. The standard covers all employees who could be "reasonably anticipated," as the result of performing their job duties, to come into contact with blood and other potentially infectious materials. OSHA's "universal precautions" are based on the premise that all human blood and bodily fluids are potentially infectious for HIV, HBV and other bloodborne pathogens.

The standard became effective March 6, 1992, and was to be fully implemented by employers by July 6, 1992. The standard covers occupations were exposures occur and includes emergency responders, law enforcement, and correctional facilities. These regulations require interactive training, which goes beyond a videotape presentation during roll call. A trained individual must be present to answer questions raised during the training sessions.

Despite the requirement that employers develop such a plan and make personal protective equipment (PPE) available to their personnel, many police agencies have not taken the necessary steps to implement a plan or make equipment readily available to personnel at their work stations or on their person.

Developing The OSHA Compliance Plan

• Employers are required to identify, in writing, those that could reasonably be exposed to infectious substances.

• A written exposure control program that details how the OSHA requirements will be implemented as well as the procedures that will be used to evaluate the circumstances surrounding exposure incidents.

• Testing of those who have been exposed to pathogenic materials to show whether there has been transmission of infection, follow-up treatment to prevent illness, and counseling to modify the individual's behavior to prevent the infection of others. All diagnoses related information must remain confidential.

Medical records for employees with occupational exposure must be kept in a confidential status for the duration of employment, plus 30 years.

The agency must maintain training records for three years; including the dates, contents of the training program, the trainer's name or qualification, and the names and job titles of those attending the training.

The OSHA standard requires employers to:

• Establish and maintain a written exposure control plan

The plan must be available to employees and must be made available to OSHA. The plan must include engineering and work practice controls (such as puncture resistant containers for used needles and accessible hand-washing facilities) to eliminate or minimize occupational exposure to contaminated items or surface areas. Also, the development of housekeeping standards to ensure the work-site is maintained in a clean and sanitary condition. Specific components of this plan are addressed in Chapter 5, Handling and Storage of Hazardous Materials.

• Identify workers with occupational exposure to blood and other potentially infectious material

• Offer, at their expense, voluntary Hepatitis B vaccinations to all employees with occupational exposure

• Prescribe appropriate medical follow-up and counseling after an exposure incident

• Provide personal protective equipment

OSHA requirements are that each officer be supplied with latex gloves; sharps containers for hypodermic needles, razors or other sharp objects; masks; and eye protection to protect the mucous membranes from blood- and airborne pathogens.

The Occupational Safety and Health Administration (OSHA) and the environmental Protection Agency (EPA) have identified four levels of personal protection based upon an assessment of risk associated with exposure to hazardous materials. These risk levels and associated equipments are presented in reverse order; most frequent to least frequent encounters in the context of the police property control function.

- Level D. Affords minimal protection against "nuisance contamination". Personal Protective Equipment (PPE) includes safety glasses, chemical splash goggles, gloves, coveralls and boots.
- Level C. Respirator, chemical resistant clothing, gloves and footwear.
- Levels A and B. Requires Self-Contained Breathing Apparatus (SCBA).

Comply with mandated training requirements

Employee training must include making accessible a copy of the regulatory text of the OSHA standard and explanations of its contents. There must be an opportunity for questions and answers, and the trainer must be knowledgeable in the subject of bloodborne diseases. This training must be provided at no cost to the employee , during working hours and, ..." At the time of initial assignment to tasks where occupational exposure may take place ... and at least annually thereafter." (OSHA, Final Rule)

Records of training provided to employees must be maintained by the employer for a minimum of three years. Medical records of employees with an occupational exposure must be kept for the duration of their employment plus an additional 30 years.

Blood- and Airborne Pathogens

Acquired Immune Deficiency Syndrome (AIDS) has a variety of manifestations that range from no symptoms to severe life-threatening primary and secondary infections. These infections include a severe form of pneumonia and cancer. The Center for Disease Control in Atlanta, Georgia has noted a significant increase in tuberculosis associated with AIDS.

The AIDS virus itself has been isolated from blood, bone marrow, saliva, lymph nodes, brain tissue, semen, cell-free plasma, vaginal secretions, cervical secretions, tears and human milk. (Bigbee, 1987) The Property Control Officer should be particularly cautious when handling evidence associated with offenses for which bodily fluids or secretions are associated: DUI, rape, aggravated battery and homicide cases.

Another potential health hazard is dried and liquid blood samples. Research has determined the AIDS virus can survive at least 15 days in dried and liquid blood samples maintained at room temperature. This potential threat suggests strongly that property control personnel be particularly careful when handling liquid blood samples or handling clothing with dried blood on it.

The AIDS virus generates the deepest fear since there is no cure, and death is the inevitable outcome. The chances that the AIDS virus will be contracted on the job, however, are less than one percent. A far greater danger is with tuberculosis (TB), hepatitis and meningitis.

Hepatitis B. Hepatitis B (serum hepatitis), known also as HBV, is a viral infection that causes jaundice, cirrhosis, and sometimes, cancer of the liver. The Hepatitis B virus is often found in human blood, urine, semen, vaginal secretion and saliva. The hepatitis virus may enter the human body through exposure of mucous membranes and contact with broken skin, in addition to accidental injections by hypodermic needles. HBV can result in liver cancer, cirrhosis and acute and chronic active hepatitis.

This bloodborne pathogen that can live outside the body longer than the HIV virus. One study found that the HIV virus in a deceased person dies after 21 hours. HBV not only lives longer, but is found in greater concentrations in the blood. A safe and effective vaccine to prevent HBV is available and can provide at least 90 percent protection for up to seven years.

Tuberculosis. Tuberculosis is transmitted through the air by coughing, hacking and wheezing. The tuberculosis bacteria is transmitted also through saliva, urine, blood and in some cases, other bodily fluids by persons infected with it. It enters the body through droplets that are inhaled and primarily causes lung infections. The Tuberculosis bacteria form spores, similar to seeds in plants, that are highly resistant to drying and other physical means that would easily kill other bacteria. The modern strain of TB is drug-resistant, and even those who test positive for it may not show symptoms because TB generally affects people whose immune systems are already weak.

Because of increased incidents of tuberculosis among persons with AIDS, property control personnel should be cautious and concerned with this bacterial disease. Property control personnel should be concerned with dried blood, urine and other bodily fluids on evidence as well as liquid forms of these bodily fluids.

Meningitis. Also spread by airborne transmission, this disease causes inflammation of the membranes that surround the brain. Although it is not fatal, its three forms; viral meningitis, tuberculosis meningitis, and bacterial meningitis, can result in headaches, fever, vomiting, stiff neck and sensitivity to light.

Crime Laboratory Personnel

There is special concern for the forensic analysts who routinely unpackage, handle and analyze crime scene evidence. In a survey of crime laboratories throughout the country. Researchers found that mechanical systems did not work, safety functions were substandard, space was severely limited, and air handling units and fume hoods did not properly function. (Pilant, 1995)

One of the principals of the study stated: There are a lot of lab planners who do pharmaceutical labs, animal testing labs, and research labs at universities. None of these labs take(s) firearms apart or do(es) an acid wash looking for serial numbers. None has the chain of evidence requirement imposed on them, or the necessary level of security because of the drugs and valuables in the lab. The planners may have lab experience, but none of them have the experience to deal with forensic specialties. (Pilant, 1995)

The need for universal precautions and the use of personal protective equipment is vital in the crime laboratory. Much of the evidence received by crime labs is seized from drug users and other high-risk individuals. The HBV can remain active a week on unprotected surfaces when it has dried at room temperature. Particles of dried blood can become airborne and be inhaled by workers, or recirculated throughout the rest of the building via the HVAC system, if the proper filters are not present on the airhandling system.

Chapter Notes

Bigbee, Paul, D.; "Collecting and Handling Evidence Infected With Human Disease-Causing Organisms", *FBI Law Enforcement Bulletin*, (July, 1987), p.2.

Commission on Accreditation of Law Enforcement Agencies, Inc., *Standards for Law Enforcement Agencies: The Standards Manual of the Law Enforcement Agency Accreditation Program,* (Fairfax, VA. **1989).**

Doe v. Town of Plymouth, 825 F, Supp. 1102, D. Mass (1993).

Florida v. Wells, 495 U.S. 1, 110 S.Ct. 1632, (1990).

Ohio, RC 2933.41 (A) (1).

OSHA Final Rule 29 CRF 1910.1020 and 1030 (d)(3)(i) to (g)(B)(2)(iii) and NPFA Standard, 471, 472, *Training and Competency Standards*, 1993.

Mathias v. Bingley, 906 F.2d 1047, 5th Cir. (1990).

Matthews v. Eldridge, 424 U.S. 319, 96 S.Ct. 893 (1976).

National Advisory Commission on Criminal Justice Standards and Goals; Task Force on the Police, U.S. Government Printing Office, (Washington D.C., 1973).

Pilant, Lois, "Infection Control", *Police Chief Magazine*, Nov. 1995.

Sacramento County Deputy Sheriff's Association v. Sacramento County, 59 Cal. Rptr. 2d 832, Cal. App.3 Dist., (1996).

State v. Weide, 155 Wisc. 2nd. 537 (1990).

United States v. Walker, 931 F.2d 1066, 1068-69, 5th Cir. (1991).

Chapter 3

Inventory and Packaging

The classification of property taken into custody is an initial decision to be made by the inventorying officer. This classification procedure is necessary to make packaging decisions and expedite the routing and storage of the property by the Property Control Officer.

Classification and packaging of property in the manner depicted below will assist the Property Control Officer in routing or storing property without having to open a package sealed by the inventorying officer

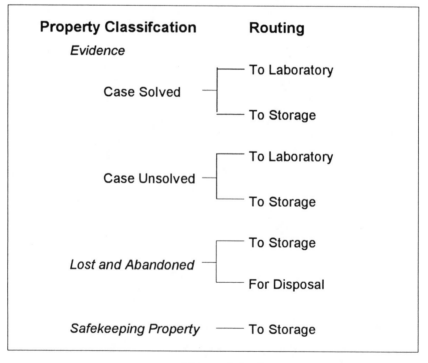

Figure 3.1
Packaging and Routing Property

Property Descriptions

A major problem observed repeatedly during property control studies and audits is the incomplete, and thereby inadequate, descriptions of property taken into custody. Complete and accurate property descriptions are essential for several reasons.

- Complete property descriptions are essential as a means of identifying property in custody that was previously reported stolen or lost.

When serial numbers or unique identifying marks are not present, property can be identified positively only through matching available property descriptions.

- Comprehensive and reliable audits of the property control system rely to a great extent upon matching the recorded property description with that of the physical item in custody.

Therefore, all items of property listed on the Property Inventory Report should include the brand or maker's name, serial and model numbers, and size and color. Owner-applied initials, marks or other identification features should be recorded also. The following is a list of many common items of property that come into the control of the police agency. Recommendations for identifying and describing these items is provided.

Currency and Valuables

All currency and other valuables seized as evidence or taken into custody as found property should be afforded maximum security. When practical, the Property Control Officer should be assigned the initial processing of evidence and found property with significant monetary value.

The Two-Count Rule

All currency and other valuables should be counted by the Case Officer in the presence of a second officer who acts as a witness to the counting of the currency, or verifies the description of the valuables.

Currency should be sorted by denomination, portrait-side-up with the portraits facing in the same direction. The currency count should be the number of bills of each denomination, not the total face value of the bills. As this count proceeds, the number of bills of each denomination are recorded on paper. At the end of the count the number of bills for each denomination is multiplied by the face value. The totals for each denomination is then foot-totaled to arrive at the final count.

An example of such a counting process is:

$$
\begin{array}{lll}
50 \ldots & \$100 \text{ bills} = & \$5,000 \\
26 \ldots & 50 \text{ bills} = & 1,300 \\
10 \ldots & 20 \text{ bills} = & \underline{\quad 200} \\
& \text{TOTAL} & \$6,500
\end{array}
$$

The same sorting, processing and description should be done also for coins.

This inventory and count process provides three essential elements of information that are useful for evidence control and audit purposes: the total number of bills or coins, the denominations and the total value of the inventoried money.

There should be independent counts of all inventoried currency by the Case Officer and the officer who witnesses the count and inventory. Any discrepancies between the two counts must be reconciled before the inventory is finalized. The final count and the number of bills and denominations should be entered on the Property Inventory Report. The witness should also sign the Property Inventory Report.

Property in General

Clothing should always be described fully. In addition to identifying the item as a dress, coat or hat the following information should be recorded on the Property Inventory Report:

Style: for example; single breasted sport coat, fingertip fur stole, and

Color: brown and white tweed, dark green satin, flowered print, red on green, and

Size: maker's label and laundry or cleaner's marks, and

Identifiable defects: tears, stains, and location

Men suits: The description should include: whether

single- or double-breasted, two- or three-piece
suit and plain or pleated trousers

Men's coats: Overcoat, hip- or waist-length, rain-
coat, single- or double-breasted, type of
trimming, lining and other specific identifiers

Other men's clothing: Includes sweaters, socks,
ties and shoes. Descriptions should include
color, size and style

Women's dresses: Describe as a house dress,
evening dress, or suit. Describe trimming, if any,
such as fur, lace, metallic and one- or two piece-
style

Women's coats: Describe as full-length, waist- or
three-quarter length, evening, sport or dress type
coat. Provide full description of trim, buttons, etc.
Complete descriptions should be recorded for fur
coats to include length, color of fur, color of lining
and labels

Jewelry must always be described in detail. The following
descriptors should be reported as they apply to the article being
described: color and type of material, number, color, cut and
size of stones.

Mounting: The type of mounting of stones on
jewelry should be described as filigree, plain,
engraved, etc.

Inscriptions: Dates, engravings, initials, serial
numbers and jeweler's markings should also be
recorded when present

Caution is advised in recording the description of precious
metals—gold, silver and platinum—unless a qualified jeweler or
metallurgist has inspected the item and identified the metal. As
a general policy, jewelry should be described as a "gold-colored
metal ring with red stone," not "gold ring with a ruby." This will
eliminate erroneous conclusions about the metal content or gem
stone and the item's value.

Silverware descriptions should include maker's label, type
of metal (when the metal is listed on the item itself), owner's

initials or other inscriptions, type of decorative pattern and number of pieces.

Radios, stereos, televisions and other sound equipment descriptions should include brand name, serial number, portable or full-size item, description of wood or metal components, color and type of trim.

Firearms descriptions should include the manufacturer's name, caliber or gauge, color of metal, serial number and type and color of grips or stock. Any marks, inscriptions or initials should also be recorded. Also, state whether the weapon is a revolver, pistol, rifle or shotgun, the number of barrels and the shell capacity.

Tire descriptions should state the size, manufacturer's name, color, tread design and serial number. Also state if the tire is mounted on a rim, and if so, describe the rim's size, color, material and design.

Office equipment includes cash registers and terminals, calculators, typewriters, computer terminals, printers and check protectors. State manufacturer's name, size, model and serial numbers and color. Include also any marks, labels or inscriptions.

Cameras and photographic equipment descriptions should include manufacturer's name, model and serial number, lens brand and number and speed. Describe the camera body and camera equipment case material.

Knives must be described as hunting, pocket, butcher, throwing, etc. Describe the color of the knife, color and material of the handle, and any numbers, inscriptions and carrying case.

Sporting goods description include manufacturer's name, serial or model numbers, color, type of material, and initials or other inscriptions.

Tool descriptions should state the type of tool, size, serial number, manufacturer or brand name and owner's initials or other identifying marks.

Bicycle descriptions include the brand name, men's or women's model, frame size, the size of wheels, color and serial number. Also, the type of seat, number of speeds, tires, baskets and other accessories, bicycle registration number, owner's initials and other identifying marks.

During the inventory process a search for a bicycle registration decal should be conducted. These decals are issued by many local jurisdictions for bicycle licensing purposes. The National Bike Registry in Sacramento, California registers bicycles for a fee and issues registration decals. Registrants are instructed to affix the decal above the front derailleur or under the seat of the bicycle. If a Bike Registry decal is located the Registry can be contacted at 1-800-848-2453 and owner information obtained.

Narcotics and Dangerous Drugs

Because of the sensitive nature of narcotics and dangerous drug evidence taken into custody, inventory policy should require that all such evidence be weighed as soon as possible after it is seized. Evidence in the nature of pills and capsules should, in addition to the initial weighing, be counted by the seizing officer immediately after the seizure.

The inventory of seized narcotics by investigators of the New York City Police Department was a central issue in a later internal investigation into an allegation of corruption within the department.

The French Connection Case

In 1962 the New York City Police Department seized a considerable amount of heroin in the infamous "French Connection Case." In late 1972 it was discovered that approximately 169 pounds of heroin and 131 pounds of cocaine were missing from the Property Control Room.

In response to the discovery of the missing narcotics the Police Department reported that a substantial portion of the discrepancy was the inaccurate reporting by the department's Narcotics Bureau of the quantity of heroin seized.

At the time of the seizure it was reported that 112 pounds of heroin had been seized. A later weighing by the police laboratory resulted in a weight of 97 pounds;

a discrepancy of 15 pounds. During the course of the internal investigation, narcotics investigators asserted the 97 pound weight was the amount of heroin stored as evidence in the Property Control Room.

An investigative commission impaneled to investigate corruption in the New York City Police Department directed that eight 1970 narcotics seizure cases be analyzed. This analysis uncovered a 68 pound difference between the amount of narcotics originally reported as seized by investigators and the resulting weight after the narcotics were weighed by the police laboratory. In the Commission's July, 1971 report it was stated that: "... the size and regularity of discrepancies in reported seizures and the amounts later officially impounded 'were disturbing'." Among the numerous observations made by the Commission in its 270 page report was: "Supervisors in the Department had taken no notice of the fantastic discrepancies and should look into the situation immediately."

In December, 1972 the Police Department disclosed that 81 of the 97 pounds of the French Connection heroin stored in the Property Control Room had disappeared between the time of its seizure in 1962 and 1969.

The former Deputy Chief Inspector that headed the Narcotics Bureau at the time of the 1962 seizure said he reported a 115 pound amount to the Police Commissioner as a "rounded figure;" it had been to commend the investigators on their record seizure. (New York Times, 1972)

Many questions pertaining to this investigation remain unanswered today. Were there originally 112 pounds of heroin, and were 15 pounds "lost" during its journey to the crime laboratory? How did 81 (or 97) pounds of heroin come to disappear from the property control room? One result of the totally inadequate inventorying and custody procedures that were in effect, accurate answers and a final resolution of this problem may never be realized.

Weighing and Counting

If drugs or narcotics are in a container or other packaging material when seized, the gross weight of the items should be recorded on the Property Inventory Report. Recording weight and count information in this manner will assist in a later audit should there be some question as to the weight or count of the evidence when it was initially taken into custody.

Weights should be determined prior to packaging the evidence for storage or shipment to the laboratory. Immediately upon receipt, the Property Control Officer should also conduct a weight and count of the evidence if the packaging does not prevent such a count. In every case, the evidence should be weighed by the Property Control Officer. This policy necessitates two sets of balance scales. One set maintained in an area always accessible to patrol officers and investigators and the second set of scales maintained in the Property Control Room.

Sample Weights and Counts

The weight and count of the evidence should be noted on the Property Inventory Report form. If the amount of pills or capsules are so numerous to make a count nonfeasible, or preclude an efficient count, a sample of one hundred pills or capsules should be weighed. The sample weight is recorded and the entire quantity of pills or capsules is then weighed together. The weight recorded for the sample of one hundred pills or capsules is then divided into the total weight of all the pills or capsules seized. The result is the approximate number of pills or capsules seized. In all instances when approximate counts or weights are used, the quantity should be recorded as an approximate weight or count on the Property Inventory Report, e.g.; "approximately 934 capsules by weight."

Prior to destruction a similar weight and count should be conducted. The initial weight or count when seized, minus the amount of substance expended in laboratory analysis, should equal the weight or count of the evidence at the time it is destroyed. Any discrepancies between the initial weight and the weight at the time of destruction, other than very slight discrepancies that are accounted for by packaging material (paper, tape, string) should be considered cause for investigation. This investigation should include an analysis of the weights recorded during the processing of the evidence; from seizure to destruction, persons handling the evidence, and any plausible explanations for the weight discrepancy.

Weighing Powder-Type Evidence

In those instances when the net weight of a large amount of powder-type evidence is to be determined, the entire amount of powder substance is weighed to obtain the gross weight. If possible, at least three empty containers of a similar size and nature to the ones used to package the powder substance should be weighed separately and the average weight calculated.

The average container weight is multiplied by the number of containers of the substance. The total weight of the empty containers is subtracted from the total gross weight of the containerized powdered substance, resulting in the net weight. The resultant net weight represents the actual weight of the powder substance and does not include the weight of the containers.

Capsule-Type Evidence

In those instances in which seized drugs are in capsules, the gross weight should be reported as well as the number of capsules. This is particularly important when the evidence is illicit drugs since the capsules may not contain an equal amount of the powdered substance. If a large number of capsules is present in the seized evidence the relatively small difference in weight between each capsule may become a significant weight discrepancy when multiplied by the number of capsules seized.

Liquid-Type Evidence

Liquid-type evidence measures should be estimated by volume in metric units; liters or milliliters. If only a sample of the liquid-type drug evidence is to be retained it should be placed in a clean, glass-stoppered bottle and sealed with adhesive evidence tape.

Bulk-Type Drug Evidence

The weight of bulk-type drug evidence, such as marijuana in packaged form, should be determined by gross weight. If the evidence is contained in several packages the weight of each individual package should be determined as well as the gross weight of the entire seizure. In those instances when a significant quantity is seized, the seizure should be measured by both gross weight and volume. It should be recognized that marijuana will lose some of its weight over time due to the evaporation of moisture.

Plant Material

Counts and area. When plant materials seized are few in number they should be counted. Large amounts of plant material should be photographed. If the plant material is growing at the time of seizure the dimensions of the grow area should be measured. For example, a 10 foot by 15 foot area equals 150 square feet of grow area. In smaller grow areas a count of the number of plants in a square foot or square yard may be determined and that count multiplied by the number of square feet or square yards in the total grow area. This results in an approximation of the number of plants in the grow area.

Weight. If the approximate weight of the plant material is desired, a sample of plant material from a pre-measured grow area is weighed. The weight of the plant material from this area is multiplied by the total area to determine the approximate total gross weight of all plant material contained in the area. The purpose of the weight and count is not necessarily to determine the true weight of the plant material, but rather to approximate the amount of plant material involved. This approximation is intended to serve as a control on the storage of the evidence and the basis for a future compliance audit of the property control system.

Packaging Evidence and Property

Almost any clean container is sufficient and various types and sizes of containers are available for the storage of property.

The property control officer can be innovative in adopting various types of containers. The primary consideration is the container is clean and does not contaminate evidence placed in the container. Figure 3.1 lists the various alternative containers, sizes and their recommended uses.

Polyester Bags

Clear polyester (plastic) bags are practical for documentary evidence. Placing a document into an appropriate size clear plastic bag reduces handling wear, eliminates the need to staple forms or identification tags to the document, seals the document, yet makes it readily visible for inspection.

Placing similar types, yet different size documents, into a standard size plastic bag creates a uniform size for the filing of documents in a file drawer. This reduces the potential of documents being lost or misplaced within the file. Paper has a tendency to curl over when stored on its side and the plastic bag reduces this tendency to curl. Property placed in plastic bags and properly tagged is identifiable immediately as evidence. This eliminates confusion regarding the nature of a piece of property and reduces the potential for the misfiling of evidence.

By affixing a plastic hook tab to the top of plastic bags, the bags can be hooked to a metal rod suspended from the top, inside a storage bin. This keeps the bags upright, in plain view and significantly increases storage capability.

A caution regarding plastic bags. Certain items should never be placed into plastic bags for storage. This includes any materials related to an arson investigation as well as wet and damp items. Since plastic is a petroleum by-product, arson evidence may become contaminated by the petroleum base of the plastic bag material. If physical evidence associated with a fire investigation is later analyzed for an accelerant, or to eliminate an accelerant as a consideration, a false conclusion may result. (Dietz, 1991)

Wet or damp items should never be placed in a plastic bag. Plastic does not allow transpiration of air in and out of the bag and wet or damp contents will putrefy in the sealed environment.

Container Type		Sizes	Recommended Uses
Bags	*Polyester*	Pouches 4' x 6" to 10" x 52" and and tubular stock 9 1/2" x 200' to 24" x 250'	Documents, any nonorganic/ nonbiological materials, dry clothing
	Brown Paper	Various sizes	Any dry materials, clothing. Tools, weapons to be printed
	Burlap	50 lb.	Marijuana plant material
Bottles	*Glass*	1 to 128 ounce	Most liquid and solid samples
Boxes	*Cardboard*	2 1/4" x 1 1/4" x 3/4" to unlimited size	Small dry items; bullets, hair, paint samples, fibers, etc.
	Gun Boxes	Pistol and long gun	Hand guns and long guns for storage, or to be shipped to laboratory
		15" x 12" x 10" to 24" x 15" x 10 1/4"	Large items; bagged or unbagged, large quantities of records (place hanging file folders over sides of box)
	Plastic	24' x 15 1/2" x 10" to 48" x 44" x 22"	Large items; bagged or unbagged
Cans	Metal with screw-on or pressure lids	Pint, quart, gallon	Flammable liquids, arson debris
Envelopes	*Paper*	Coin size to 4 1/2" x 9 1/2" to 9 1/2" x 15"	Bullets, hair, paint samples, biological samples
	Cellophane	4 1/2" x 9 1/2" to 9 1/2" x 15"	Used for long term storage of documents or, acid free paper envelopes

Figure 3.2
Evidence Packing and Storage Containers

Wet or damp items should be allowed to air dry for several days before being placed in a plastic bag.

Selection of plastic bags. A variety of plastic bags are available and careful consideration should be given to the quality, price, and quantity of bags purchased. Police agencies should consider contacting a crime laboratory or other police agency using plastic bags to determine their experience with the various manufacturers and suppliers of plastic bags.

The Los Angeles County Sheriff's Department tested plastic bags to determine if one brand could be found to safely contain PCP. Previously, deputies and laboratory personnel were suffering from exposure to the PCP they handled. The symptoms included dizziness, heart palpitations and psychological difficulties. The Sheriff's Department tested the polyester narcotics evidence pouch manufactured by Kapak Corporation and subsequently approved its use by department personnel. No reports of narcotics side effects have been noted since the Kapak® system was adopted. (Food and Drug Packaging, 1982) The United States Customs Service, Drug Enforcement Administration, and the Federal Bureau of Investigation use the Kapak Corporation's evidence pouch.

Paper Bindles

Paper bindles are useful for packaging small items such as narcotics, hairs, fibers and other items of trace evidence. Bindles should be created in such a manner that they will contain the item securely and are easily recognized as containing evidence. Figure 3.3 shows a preprinted 8 1/2 x 11 inch sheet of paper with instructions for converting it easily into a bindle.

Paper Bags

The brown paper bag commonly found in grocery stores is an ideal container for the storage of miscellaneous loose property as well as evidence. There are several advantages to using paper bags. They can be acquired very inexpensively and may be written upon with a felt tip pen to record case information; including case number, Property Control Number, type of offense, contents, officer's name and any other pertinent case information. Paper bags can be formatted with case information and content inventory through the use of a large rubber stamp

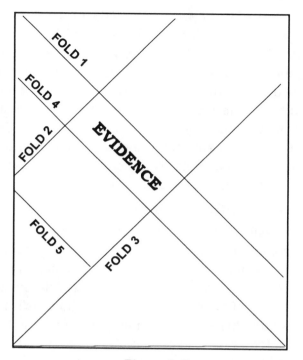

Figure 3.3
Paper Bindle

available in most stationary stores, or the use of computer generated inventory labels.

Bags should not be sealed with staples. Removal of the staples will allow access to the contents of the bag and the bag may then be restapled and give no indication that it had been opened.

The use of staples in the Property Control Room is not advocated due to the potential for skin cuts from staples and the bacteria and viruses that may be present in the Property Control Room. Evidence tape is the preferable alternative for sealing bags. Writing the investigating officer's name and identifying number or the Property Control Officer's identification across the bag flap and the evidence tape creates a tamper-resistant seal on the bag.

Disadvantages of paper bags. A disadvantage of paper bags is the contents of the bag cannot be readily seen without opening the bag. Also, unless paper bags are doubled-up, they tear easily and may spill their contents.

Window bags. Brown paper bags with a cellophane window are generally constructed of a heavier paper stock. Also, they may be ordered with a preprinted information format on the face of the bag. One major deficiency is the tendency of the cellophane to become brittle and crack over time. This may cause the contents to spill out of the bag. Cellophane window bags should be sealed with evidence tape, not staples, in a fashion similar to paper bags discussed above.

Storage Containers

Bags of evidence or other loose items may be stored on shelves in common cardboard boxes, records storage boxes, milk crates or plastic totes. These storage containers are useful for storing separate smaller containers associated with one case together, or for holding miscellaneous small items. If barcoding is used the storage container itself should be identified with a barcode label to record the location of the storage container and any items stored in the container.

Cardboard Boxes

The advantage to using common paper cardboard boxes is they are relatively inexpensive or can be obtained at no cost. The contents of the box or other case-related information can be easily written on the end or sides of the box with felt tip marker. A significant disadvantage to using common cardboard boxes is the sides and corners become frayed and weak from use. Eventually, the boxes may weaken, break open and spill their contents.

Records storage boxes. Records storage boxes are designed for ease of handling. Many are constructed with handles on the sides and removable covers or top flaps that serve as a cover. Storage boxes are available in several sizes, measured in cubic feet capacity, and have a 40 to 60 pound capacity. The use of storage boxes to store packages of evidence; from one or multiple cases, is an efficient way of maintaining orderly storage shelves or areas.

Gun Boxes

The use of gun boxes for the storage of handguns and long guns may result in a more efficient use of available storage space. This particularly true in the instance of handguns. Handguns consume a disproportionate amount of storage space if they are stored loose on shelves, in small individual shelf bins, or on wall mounted pegs. The use of gun boxes permits guns to be stored side-by-side on shelve units in a manner similar to books in a library. If the gun boxes are stored chronologically by case number, firearms in custody can be more efficiently "aged" and disposed of in a more timely manner. The additional cost of the gun boxes may be offset by the more efficient use of available shelves, more efficient location and retrieval of handguns when needed, and the fact that the boxes are reusable.

Gun boxes are constructed so as to allow the weapon to be secured in the box with a plastic tie. This is the preferred method of handling and shipping a firearm to the crime laboratory for fingerprint and other types of analysis.

An adhesive label can be placed on the end of the gun box on which to record pertinent case information. This will preserve the box for future reuse. As with any other adhesive labels, one must purchase quality adhesive labels to ensure the label will adhere to the box during the time the gun is in police custody; often a long period of time. The paper from which the label is constructed must likewise be a quality paper if it is to retain the ink impression of the recorded information over a long period of time.

Small, color labels can be affixed to the box to indicate the purpose of police custody of the firearm. A red color label could, for example, indicate that the firearm is being held as evidence; a green label to indicate a safekeeping firearm. The use of color-coded labels in this manner will make retrieval of firearms by nature of custody easier.

Plastic Milk Crates and Storage Totes

The plastic milk crate type container has significant advantages. They are very rugged and may be used for bulk property that is not packaged. The contents are visible through the milk crate design on all four sides of the container, the crates are light weight and, generally, can be obtained inexpensively. In addition, the crates can be easily tagged by inserting the string on the property tag through the milk crate openings. This allows an immediate review of the contents of the milk crate. Milk crate-type containers are reusable indefinitely since they are stronger and more functional than common cardboard boxes.

Plastic storage totes, similar to those used by the postal service, are available in sizes 48 inches x 44 inches x 22 inches, to accommodate most bulky items and 24 inches x 15 1/2 inches x 10 inches for smaller items. Smaller totes have a 150 pound capacity.

Color coding. Milk crates and totes can be purchased in various colors. The colors can be used to designate the various categories of property: red for Evidence, yellow for Lost and Found property and green crates for Safekeeping property.

Using a color-coded scheme eliminates the probability of misshelving property and expedites the reshelving of items. Using a color-coded storage system the Property Control Officer knows immediately the type of property in the crate and can reshelf it in its proper location.

Property Inventory Tags

Property inventory tags are used to distinguish evidence from other types of property. Several property and evidence tagging systems are available commercially. If commercially available tags are used, it is recommended that chain of custody entries not be entered on the tag. Such entries create an original entry and the card must be maintained as a permanent, original record of the chain of custody. This poses several problems. First, the space available for chain of custody entries on the back of 3 inch by 5 inch tags is often inadequate to record all of the movements of the evidence during the period of custody. This may require the use of several tags to record all chain of custody entries compounding the paperwork problem. Also, the filing of these tags is cumbersome since their size makes it difficult to later locate the tags in a file.

```
                              EVIDENCE
     Case Number _____ Property Control Number _____

     Case Name / Owner _____

     Evidence Description _____
     _____

     Location Recovered / Found _____

     _____
     Date and Time of Recovery            Evidence Recovered By
```

Figure 3.4
Evidence Tag

```
                        MISCELLANEOUS PROPERTY
     Safekeeping ☐      Found ☐         Abandoned ☐

     Case Number_____ Property Control Number _____

     Property Owner_____

     Property Description_____
     _____

     Location Found_____

     _____
     Date and Time of Recovery            Property Received By
```

Figure 3.5
Safekeeping / Found Property Tag

Property tags can be produced in-house through the use of a word processing or desktop publishing program. The tag format can be printed onto pre-punched, continuous card stock available at office supply stores.

Pre-Numbered Tags

Pre-numbered property tag systems should be avoided if possible. The use of these systems requires the tags be distributed to various organizational units and made available to agency personnel. The intended purpose of the pre-numbered tag is to introduce an audit trail within the property control system. In practice, however, the tags become lost, are discarded after an error in completion, or are used out of numerical sequence. Any one of the events defeats the intended purpose of pre-numbered tags. Loss of an unused property tag or a discarded tag creates a gap in the numerical sequence of control numbers entered in the property control log. The time and effort required to trace the tags and tag numbers not accounted for can be better expended on other duties. An alternative to pre-numbered tags is the introduction of a Property Control Number. The Property Control Number is assigned by the Property Control Officer when property is received initially.

Blank Card Stock

An alternative to preprinted property tags is the purchase of blank card stock drilled with holes for string. A customized information format can be developed to fit on the card. This custom format can be taken to any large stationary store and a large hand-stamp ordered to duplicate the card layout. The size of these hand-stamps is virtually unlimited. This permits both an unlimited size and information format on cards, envelopes and forms.

Another alternative is the use of continuous roll card stock that can be can be fed into a computer printer. A customized format can be created on a word processing or desktop publishing program and printed on the card stock.

Color-Coding

A color-coding scheme may be used also with the tags to identify the type of property. A red tag may be used to identify Evidence, a yellow tag Lost and Found property, and a green tag Safekeeping property. Tags may be purchased on colored cardstock or they may be created using a broad, felt-tip pen. By simply marking the top 1/4 inch of cardstock with a colored felt-tip pen the tag is color coded for ease of recognition. When the property classification changes the appropriate color can be applied to the bottom of the tag to indicate the new classification.

Nylon Tags

An alternative to the use of card stock tags is a heavy nylon property and evidence tag available commercially. These tags are available in various colors for a color-coded tagging scheme. Tags are also available with a writing surface on the face. The property control or case number can be written with permanent ink marker. These tags are affixed to the item of property by a tie-wrap strap. The strap is inserted in or around the piece of property and looped back through a one-way, tamper-proof locking mechanism.

Nylon tags are also useful to secure firearms that may be introduced in court. By inserting the strap of the tag through the frame of a revolver, or the chamber and down the barrel of a semiautomatic, and then through the tag locking mechanism, the firearm is rendered inoperable.

Property Inventory Report

In a clean, orderly property control system, the Property Inventory Report itself may serve as the property tag. The report is attached to the property container and is stored with the property. The advantage to using the Property Inventory Report as the property tag is the entire contents of the container are described on the Inventory Report.

This alternative has certain advantages. By affixing the Property Inventory Report to the evidence, it eliminates the need to store the inventory report in a file folder while the property is in custody. In addition, whenever there is movement of the property from the Property Control Room, the inventory form, and the chain-of-custody entries section, is available immediately for custody information update. In addition, the amount of paper work that must be completed and later filed is reduced. By affixing the Property Inventory Report to the property the purging of property can be made more efficient. Using the information on the Property Inventory Report the Property Control Officer can purge property by the date of custody, crime type, and type of property; Evidence, Lost and Found, or Safekeeping. This alternative should be considered only in a clean, orderly system. Otherwise, the Property Inventory Report will become damaged or separated from the property.

Property Control Number

It is strongly recommended that a Property Control Number (PCN) system be adopted. This number should include the current year followed by a sequential number. Either an E (evidence) or P (property) prefix may be used to differentiate the

PCN from a case number. This is generally not necessary however. An example of a PCN is the year (99) and sequential number (001); 99-001. This number indicates this is the first package of property received in the Property Control Room in 1999. If each individual item or package of property inventoried requires a separate inventory number—as required by law in some states—an alphabetical suffix can be used. The first item or package, for example would be numbered 99-001A; the second package 99-001B; the third package 99-001C.

The purpose of the PCN is to maintain control over property. Each investigated or reported case has an assigned case number, however, every case does not have property associated with it. This creates "gaps" in the case numbers associated with property in custody. When an audit is conducted it is difficult, and time consuming, to determine if the numerical gap is the result of property loss from the Property Control Room, or the missing case numbers never had property associated with them.

The PCN should be assigned *only* by the Property Control Officer at the time the property is stored in the permanent storage area. To allow patrol officers or investigators to assign a PCN will defeat the purpose of this control technique. Each PCN assigned should be entered in a Property Control Log to maintain the sequential assignment of numbers.

Chapter Notes

Dietz, William, R.; "Physical Evidence of Arson: Its Recognition, Collection and Packaging," *Fire and Arson Investigator,* (June, 1991), p. 34.

Food and Drug Packaging, reprint, May, 1982.

New York Times, Tuesday, December 12, 1972, p. 39.

Chapter 4

Preservation and Storage of Evidence

Whenever possible, evidence should be photographed and returned to the owner as an alternative to storage in the Property Control Room. This procedure will reduce the volume of evidence stored and demonstrate respect for crime victims' rights.

Photographing evidence must meet specific standards if the photographs are to substitute for the item itself as an exhibit in court:

- Permission has been received from the prosecuting attorney;
- The defense attorney has not requested the court to hold the item of evidence for production at trial;
- The defense has not requested an independent examination or analysis;
- Photographs will demonstrate the nature of the property;
- The photographs are retained by the police agency in lieu of the evidence, and;
- The property owner signs a receipt upon return of the property.

Preservation of Evidence

One of the primary objectives of the property control system is the storage of evidence to preserve the physical composition and quality of the evidence. While it is expected that biological materials will deteriorate with the passage of time, such deterioration can be minimized by promptly taking proper precautions. "Physical evidence may undergo change in the following ways:

1. Loss by leakage or by evaporation from an improperly stoppered container

2. Decomposition through exposure to light, heat, or bacteria

3. Intermingling of evidence from various sources and locations in a common container.

4. Alterations by the unwitting addition of a fresh fold or crease in a document; or a tear or cut in a garment

5. Contamination, bacterial or chemical, resulting from the use of unclean containers."

Precautions that should be employed to reduce or eliminate deterioration and contamination include:

1. Use only fresh, clean containers.

2. Use leakproof, sealable containers

3. Uphold the integrity of each item of evidence by using separate containers.

4. Keep evidence away from direct sunlight and heat. Refrigerate biological evidence when not being transported.

5. Deliver evidence as quickly as possible to the laboratory.

6. Handle evidence as little as possible." (Ward, 1993: 180)

Temporary Secure Storage

In order to maintain the chain of custody, it is necessary that all items be placed into temporary secure storage as soon as possible after initial custody by the police agency. Several alternative methods by which to secure the property are discussed below. In order for a temporary secure storage system to function effectively, the Property Control Officer must check the lockers daily and remove any items stored in them.

Temporary Storage Lockers

Temporary storage lockers should be considered a basic component of any property control system. Several alternative locking devices are commonly used.

Key drop. One of the most common, yet more expensive, systems is the key drop type. In this system the key is maintained in the locker door lock. The presence of a key in the door lock indicates that the locker is available for use. The officer unlocks the locker, places the property into the locker and then closes the door, removing the key. The key is then inserted into a drop slot in the door and falls inside the locker.

As the property custodian retrieves the property from each of the individual lockers, the keys are removed from the locker and replaced in the door lock. This system is similar to those used in bus and airline terminals. It may require the use of tokens as a mean of allowing the key to be turned to remove it from the lock. This method should be reviewed critically since it is an expensive system and is designed primarily for a payment-for-use type system.

Padlocks. An improved and less expensive system is a padlock system with key control. Open padlocks are maintained at some central location available to all patrol and investigative personnel; the watch commander or desk-sergeant area. When an officer requires a locker, a lock is obtained from this central source and placed through the lock hasps on the locker door.

The Property Custodian should, by policy and practice, maintain the only key to these padlocks in order to ensure an uninterrupted chain of custody.

Combination locks. Combination-type locks are not recommended for use in Property Control systems unless a master combination number is programmed in all the locks in use. This eliminates the need for the Property Control Officer to remember, or record, numerous combinations for the locks. With key-type padlocks, a master key padlock system may be purchased which negates the necessity for numerous keys to open the padlocks.

Pass-through lockers. Pass-through lockers allow evidence to be placed into a temporary storage locker and be retrieved by the Property Control Officer from the rear, or interior of the Property Control Room. These lockers eliminate the need to open one or several lockers to retrieve evidence and then carry it into the security of the Property Control Room. Removing evidence from the rear of the locker allows one locker to be cleared and processed at a time with greater security and efficiency.

The backside of pass-through lockers is secured by one or several doors that open to expose several storage bins. Other systems employ a single, overhead rollup door system that exposes all the storage bins at one time. A work surface counter at a suitable height and covered with a scrubbable surface should be located in the immediate area to the rear of the lockers for the initial processing of evidence.

Bank Lock Boxes

Bank lock boxes should be considered also as a potential source of secure storage of evidence with high value, or of a sensitive nature. In considering the use of bank lock boxes, arrangements should be made with a local bank prior to the actual need for a lock box. Policy regarding the use of lock boxes should state the specific purpose or reason for the use of such a storage location, individuals authorized to place items into a lock box, as well as procedures for notifying the bank and requesting the use of a lock box. Procedures should require also that all keys for the lock box, the depositor and bank's copy, should be inventoried and secured in the Property Control Room. These keys should be entered as evidence and maintained under double secure storage. This storage policy maintains not only the security of the evidence, but a double chain of custody since notations are made on the Property Inventory Log and on the bank's safety deposit box entry records.

Watch Lockers

The use of patrol watch or investigative team property control lockers should be discouraged. Such paired locker arrangements raise significant issues regarding the chain of custody. A patrol officer or investigator may place evidence into a locker after another officer previously placed evidence into the locker. This multiple access raises a question as to the chain of custody of the evidence first placed into the locker.

Personal Lockers

Officers should not be allowed to maintain property or evidence in their personal lockers. Such a policy not only raises issues regarding the chain of custody but also contributes to the loss, contamination, or unauthorized use or appropriation of property. This issue should be addressed directly by policy governing the property control function, and procedures addressing the proper temporary storage of evidence and other classifications of property.

Drop Slots

Securing small, unbreakable items such as documents is expedited through the use of drop slots. It is recommended that drop slots be located in the door to the Property Control area only if it is a solid core door. Two types of drop slots are available and can be constructed or installed with little effort.

The first type of drop slot utilizes the mail slot device commonly found in the front door of many homes. These may be purchased at a local hardware store and installed quickly with little effort. It is recommended that property placed in the drop slots not be allowed to fall onto the floor on the other side of the door. Instead, a basket container of some type should be affixed to the back of the door approximately 12 inches below the drop slot. Property placed into the drop slot will then fall into the basket and not onto the floor. This will eliminate the potential of the property being retrieved from under the door as well as expedite the retrieval of property by the Property Control Officer for processing.

The depth of the basket affixed to the back of the door should also be a consideration. The amount of property that can potentially be dropped into the basket should be considered and the depth of the basket sufficient to contain at least several days of property. This is to take into account long weekends when the Property Control Room may be closed.

Tray drops. Another type of drop slot operates on the principal similar to that of a public mail box. This device can be constructed by cutting a panel out of a solid core door. A tray-like device is then constructed and secured to the panel.

When the drop slot door is opened, the tray device affixed to it moves to an upward position. This eliminates access to the room inside but provides a flat surface on which to place the property. The article of property is placed on the tray and the drop slot door closed. This causes the tray to reposition to a downward angle. Property placed on the tray will slide off the tray and into the Property Control Room.

This method of securing property should be used only for small, light weight, unbreakable property. Provisions should be made for a box, preferably with a cushioned bottom, to be placed inside the door. When an article slides off the tray device and falls to the box, the cushion breaks its fall and prevent damage to the property or any property previously deposited in the drop slot.

U.S. postal boxes are a variation of the tray drop method. Some police agencies have acquired the large postal boxes found commonly in public places. These postal boxes can be secured to the floor and provide secure temporary storage of evidence. The same caveats regarding small, light weight property and cushioning mentioned above apply also to these storage devices.

Reverse locker. A common problem encountered is the return of evidence to an officer for court presentation at a time when the property room is not open, or the Property Control Officer is not on duty. A "reverse locker" may provide a solution to this problem. After an officer has requested evidence, the Property Control Officer places the evidence in a temporary storage locker and locks the locker. The key to the locker is placed into an envelope that is sealed with the Property Control Officer's signature across the flap and addressed to the officer requesting the evidence. An additional step, intended to maintain the written chain of custody, is a preprinted chain of custody format on the envelope. When the property officer places the locker key in the envelope a chain of custody entry is completed relinquishing custody of the key.

The envelope containing the key is slipped into the officer's personal locker, placed in the officer's department mail box, or other location that officers regularly receive written information.

The officer may then retrieve the key from the sealed envelope, open the locker and retrieve the evidence. At this time the officer completes a chain of custody entry on the envelope. The envelope containing the key is then deposited by the officer in a drop slot locker to secure it and return it to the Property Control Officer. Chain of custody issues are minimized through the use of the sealed envelope with the chain of custody entries on it. The officer can testify to receiving the sealed envelope containing the key as well as the chain of custody of the key and the evidence that was originally placed in the reverse locker.

When the officer returns the evidence the officer places it in an unused temporary storage locker for retrieval by the Property Control Officer.

Temporary Secure Refrigeration

To reduce the potential for lost, contaminated, or spoiled perishable evidence two refrigerators should be dedicated to the storage of evidence. One refrigerator should be accessible in the temporary secure storage area for temporary refrigerated storage.

The temporary storage refrigerator can be made secure, thereby maintaining the chain of custody, by constructing sheet metal compartments that can be installed and secured inside the refrigerator. Even the smallest bar refrigerator will accept up to eight of these compartments. A hinged door on each compartment with a lock hasp for a padlock will secure the evidence during temporary storage.

The second refrigerator should be located in the Property Control Room for longer term storage. The storage of personal food items in these refrigerators should be discouraged. Evidence placed in the refrigerators may contain bacteria, viruses or other contaminates. These may contaminate personal food items and cause illness.

One situation encountered by the author involved a small brick of cream cheese found on the kitchen table at the scene of a residential burglary. The burglar had removed the cream cheese from the refrigerator, opened the tin foil packaging and holding the cream cheese with his thumb and first two fingers bit off a piece of the cheese. This left three fingerprint impressions and a teeth bite pattern in the cream cheese. The investigating officer collected the evidence and transported it to the police station.

Because the department, at the time, had no secure refrigeration for evidence the cream cheese brick was placed in a refrigerator shared by all department personnel. Upon retrieving the evidence the next day to transport it to the crime laboratory for analysis, the officer found someone had developed a taste for cream cheese. The unknown eater had opened the still sealed end of the package and cut off a generous slice. In the process the fingerprints and teeth impressions were obliterated and the evidentury value of the cream cheese brick was destroyed.

Long-Term Storage

The first step in developing a property storage system is the determination of the classifications by which the property and evidence will be stored. All property entering the Property Control Room should be classified immediately into one of three categories: Evidence, Lost and Found (including Abandoned property) and Safekeeping property. This storage classification procedure should be supported by the packaging classification presented in Chapter 3.

Evidence

Evidence should be classified further as Evidence to be Forwarded to the Crime Laboratory or Evidence to be Retained (pending further investigation or trial). A further subclassification of "case solved" or "case unsolved" will also assist in storage decisions.

Lost and Abandoned Property

Lost and Found and Abandoned Property is recovered property with no evidential value. This property should be processed and stored separately from Evidence since purge, or disposal criteria differs for each property classification.

Safekeeping Property

Safekeeping Property is property for which the owner is known. In this case the law enforcement agency is merely storing it until the owner is notified and takes physical possession of the property.

Classifying property in the manner suggested above permits more efficient decision-making in the initial storage of the property.

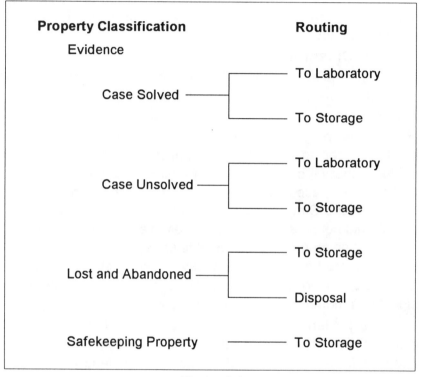

Figure 4.1
Classification of Property For Storage

Shelving Methods

Since the majority of property will be placed on shelves or bins within the Property Control Room it is essential that shelving methods be selected to maximize storage space and efficiency and allow ease of retrieval. The shelving system described takes advantage of the several methods by which property may be stored temporarily on shelves or in bins.

As the property classification changes over time it must be transferred from one classification shelf or bin to another as a means of maintaining this system. This policy will make it easier to maintain control, retrieve and purge property from the storage system. Five alternative shelving methods are available to accomplish these purposes. These include the Subject Classification, Matrix, Terminal Digit, Chronological and Sequential methods. Two or more of the shelving methods may be used together to create a storage system customized to the needs, resources, storage space availability and problems unique to each police agency.

Subject Classification

Using the subject classification method property is classified and shelved by type of property; Evidence, Lost and Found, Safe Keeping or, by the type of evidence.

In designing the property control system, consideration must be given to the various classifications of property and evidence that will come into agency custody and the procedures and storage space necessary to efficiently store these property classifications. Since certain types of evidence are incompatible and should not be stored with all types of evidence, the subject classification method can be used to store such property types. Examples are beer (which may have been opened), firearms, narcotics, United States currency and other evidence with significant monetary value such as jewelry.

The efficient, continuing operation of this shelving method requires property be moved and reshelved as its classification changes from time to time. For example, evidence no longer needed for court purposes, and the owner is known, must be removed from the Evidence shelves and placed on the Safe-keeping shelves. The same procedure applies to Lost and Found property. Once the property owner's identity becomes known the property is no longer classified as Lost and Found but is reclassified as Safekeeping property. Adhering to the storage classification method described above, the property is transferred to the Safekeeping shelves.

Advantages of subject classification method . The Subject Classification method segregates property by value; evidential and monetary, by purpose of custody; as evidence, pending owner identification or notification, retention time period, and sensitivity; narcotics, firearms and currency.

This segregation permits more frequent, and less time consuming, purges and dispositions of property. It also supports increased security over sensitive types of property and the conduct of audits. The Subject Classification method should be incorporated into all property storage systems. The advantages of this method far outweighs any actual or perceived disadvantages.

Matrix Shelving Method

The Matrix Shelving method assigns each column of shelves or bins a sequential alphabetical character. These characters range from A to Z depending upon the number of columns. When the number of columns exceeds the number of letters in the alphabet, a double letter address may be created; AA, BB, CC. Each row of shelves is then assigned a sequential number.

By assigning the columns a letter and the rows a number, a matrix is developed. Property stored in a bin is addressed by that bin's column and row designation. A piece of property in the upper left-hand bin, for example, is addressed as A-1. Property placed in the third column, third row, is addressed as C-3.

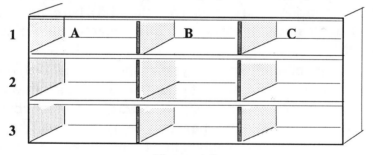

Figure 4.2
Matrix Shelving Method

Advantages of the matrix method. The Matrix method allows property to be placed on a shelf that is relatively clear of other property. The method is flexible since the number of bins created is at the discretion of the Property Control Officer. The method is easily adapted to very small as well as very large property control shelving systems.

The benefits of the Matrix method, incorporated into the Subject Classification approach, is property can be shelved evenly among available storage bins and only property with the same classification is stored together. This supports periodic purges of property by classification. The storage location is not constrained by the case numbers as is the case with the terminal digit method.

Disadvantages of the matrix method. The major disadvantage of the matrix method is the property storage address is an artificial address that bears no relationship to the case number, property control number, or other property identifier. To retrieve property stored by the matrix method the user must refer to property inventory records to determine the storage location.

Thus, while the major advantage of the matrix method is the flexibility in assigning shelf space to property for storage, the disadvantage is in the later retrieval of the property.

Terminal Digit Method

The term "terminal (end) digit" refers to the last number or numbers (depending on the size of the property storage system) of the assigned case number. All property having the same final digits (numbers) is stored together.

Each of the bins or shelves is assigned a number from zero to nine. A specific piece of property is stored in a bin or on a shelf whose address corresponds to the last number of the case number.

In larger property control systems the Terminal Digit numbering system may expand to the last two digits. Each storage bin or shelf space would be assigned a two digit number from 00 to 99. In very large systems there may be a need to use the last three digits of the case number. In a system of this magnitude there would be 1000 storage bins; 000-999.

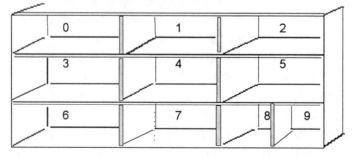

Figure 4.3
Terminal Digit Method

Advantages of the terminal digit method. A significant benefit of the Terminal Digit method is the property storage shelving system can be expanded almost indefinitely. As a small property control room grows, the shelving system can be expanded easily.

When property is to be retrieved the Property Control Officer need determine only the case or property control number associated with the property. Identifying the last two digits of the case number gives the address of the property on the shelving system. When an officer or investigator requests evidence for court or other purposes, they need to know only the case number. The case number will immediately identify the location of the evidence on the storage shelves.

Disadvantages of the terminal digit method. If the property control number is used to determine the storage address to be assigned to the property, property control records will have to be checked to determine the storage address. Since the investigating officer is not likely to know the property control number, the officer can not supply it to the Property Control Officer at the time of request.

Chronological Shelving Method

The Chronological method assigns each of the shelves or bins a month of the year, January through December. This method allows a determination of the month in which property may be disposed of while complying with applicable law. The property may be stored in a bin representing the month the property came into department custody or, it may be stored in a bin representing a future month when the property may be disposed of.

The Chronological shelving method is best suited for property that will be disposed of at a predetermined future time. If, for example, Lost and Found property must be retained for six months before disposition, the Chronological method will be beneficial in determining what property should be disposed of in a particular month. This is determined by placing the property in a bin or on a shelf corresponding to the sixth month of agency possession.

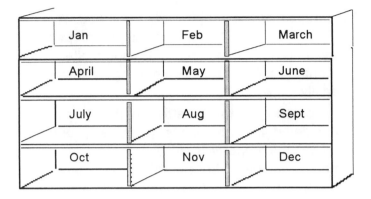

Figure 4.4
Chronological Shelving Method

The chronological shelving method is particularly useful for storing Safekeeping property. Safekeeping property, that which the owner is known, should be disposed of periodically; either by return to the owner or sale at auction if the owner fails to respond to requests to retrieve the property. The retention period for Safekeeping property after owner notification is established either by agency policy, ordnance or state law. At the end of the retention period the corresponding bin or shelf for that month is checked, and all property found on that shelf moved to a location suitable for storage until a mass property disposition is affected.

Advantages of the chronological method. The Chronological method is most advantageously used with Lost and Found and Safekeeping property. Where statutory or policy provisions require the police agency to maintain Lost and Found property for some specific length of time, the Chronological method is an ideal solution for maintaining control over the disposition of such property. Storing property in a bin by month of custody or disposition allows the property to be "aged." The easier it is to dispose of property the greater the reduction in the volume of property that is stored.

The Chronological method is also useful to separate property by the year in which it is taken into custody. This suggests the chronological method can be incorporated with the Subject Classification, Matrix, Sequential and Terminal Digit methods to create a more sophisticated approach to property storage.

Combined Matrix and Subject Classification Methods

This combined method incorporates the classification of property; evidence, lost and found, for example and stores property by its classification and matrix address. One shelving structure is dedicated to evidence only. Evidence associated with a specific case is stored in a bin or shelf adequate to contain the volume of evidence associated with that case. This method is also suited for use with abandoned, lost and found, and safekeeping property.

Sequential Shelving Method

This method stores property by the sequential case or property control number. Property is stored in a sequential order on shelves. The results is property is stored by the year it is taken into custody and in the sequence in which it is received.

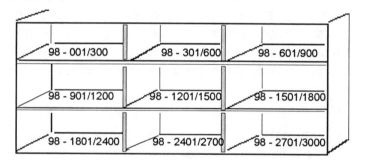

Figure 4.5
Sequential Shelving Method

Advantages of the sequential shelving method. A significant advantage of this shelving method is it supports the segregation and purging of property by year of custody. One of the major deficiencies in many property control systems is the inability to efficiently identify property that has been in custody for a long period of time and to assess the necessity of continued retention.

The sequential shelving method expedites the identification of the oldest property in inventory through the property's physical location. It also provides a rapid method of determining the amount of recoverable shelve space if a mass property disposition were to be effected.

Disadvantages of the sequential shelving method. A simple sequential shelving system requires potentially incompatible property types to be stored together. Since the storage criterion is the date the property came into custody evidence, found property and safekeeping property is stored side-by-side on the same shelf. In many police agencies currency, narcotics, lost license plates, open beer cans and a similar array of items are found stored together. Such storage practices obviously violate the principle of security levels for different types and classifications of property.

Storage of Evidence Subject to Judicial Appeal

Policies addressing the storage of evidence associated with criminal offenses should include the possibility of appeals from the trial court verdict. Consideration should be given to the designation of a suitable storage location for appeals cases. This should be a secure location, easily accessible, yet removed from the area designated for active case storage. Specific factors to be considered in the location and length of custody include:

- The statutory time limit for appeal
- Court orders for the retention of evidence pending the filing of an appeal, or an order for impoundment of physical evidence
- The frequency and immediacy of retrieval of the evidence
- The quantity and volume of evidence to be retained.

Questions and issues pertaining to the time and the potential for appeal and the retention of evidence should be directed to the prosecuting attorney.

Summary of Shelving Methods

The selection and development of a property storage system should be based on specific storage criteria. These criteria include the initial shelving of the property, locating property for future retrieval, purging for final disposition and separate storage of property of a sensitive nature; firearms, narcotics, United States Currency and jewelry.

The question often arises whether evidence from one specific case should be stored separately because of size limitations of the bins or shelves. The most appropriate response to this situation is to analyze two factors associated with the evidence in question; the amount of evidence associated with the case and, the exact nature of the evidence.

In those instances when large quantities or single, large items of evidence are entered into the property storage system a decision should be made regarding the assignment of a storage location. Ideally, the storage location should be large enough that all evidence associated with a specific case can be stored on one shelf or bin. This requires the property storage system be flexible enough to meet practical storage demands.

In order to maintain the described storage systems it is necessary that property be relocated when its classification changes. Evidence no longer required for court, for example, should be relocated to another storage bin due to this reclassification; either Lost and Found if the owner is unknown, or Safekeeping if the owner is known and is entitled to legal possession.

As ownership is determined for the property stored on the Lost and Found shelves that property should be relocated to the Safekeeping shelves. It is recommended the Safekeeping shelves be arranged chronologically similar to the Lost and Found shelves. This provides a system for maintaining control over Safekeeping property.

A property storage system should be designed and operated with due consideration given to operating flexibility. Day-to-day storage demands, in terms of quantity, bulk and length of custody should dictate the design of the storage system and the storage methods to be used. Security measures necessary to maintain the chain of custody and prevent cross-contamination of evidence should take precedence in the decision to separate evidence associated with one case and store it in different locations within the Property Control Room. Narcotics, weapons and United States Currency associated with a single case should be stored separately, however, in order to maintain the necessary level of security.

Biohazard Evidence Storage

All items of property that are known, or suspected to be contaminated with any pathogen should be stored in a separate, secure area. This may include evidence from homicides, sexual assaults, aggravated batteries, and other crimes against the person where a body fluid or other biological matter has contaminated clothing, a weapon, or other crime scene evidence.

Factors that should be considered in planning and operating a biohazard storage area are contaminates, air quality, offensive odors and rodent infestation. Additional consideration should be given to the availability of personal protective equipment (PPE) in the immediate vicinity of the biohazard storage area, handwashing facilities, or an approved hand cleanser, and the necessary supplies for cleanup of package spills. Disposable gloves, at a minimum, should be worn when handling any evidence that is in the biohazard storage area. An established routine should include handwashing after removing disposable gloves. All disposable protective clothing and equipment should be removed while in the biohazard storage area and deposited in an approved biohazard waste container located in the immediate area. This procedure will reduce the potential for contaminating other areas of the property control room as well as other property control personnel.

The storage area must not only be securable, it should remain locked unless their is an immediate need to enter the area; double-secure storage. Due to the nature of the evidence stored in this area, the entire storage area should be considered contaminated. Most often evidence that was stored initially under refrigerated conditions is no longer refrigerated after it has been analyzed by the crime laboratory. The amount of time spent in this area should be minimized due to the bacterial and viral contaminated air, unpleasant odors, and the potential for rodent and bug infestation.

Documentary Evidence

Documentary evidence and other types of documents should be stored, when practical, in sealed, plastic evidence bags. Documents should be maintained in a file cabinet employing a filing system that allows ease of storage, access, and retrieval. While the filing system for evidentury records and other property is dependent upon the actual needs of each department, there are several basic documentary evidence files that should be considered.

Questioned Documents

The first of these files is "Questioned Documents." This file contains all documents in which the authenticity of the document itself or signer's signature is questioned.

Drivers Licenses

The second file is driver's licenses and vehicle titles. This file contains documents that are to be returned to the licensing authority and is a temporary file only. In addition, other vehicle registration documents should be stored in this file.

Latent Fingerprints

An additional documentary file is one for latent fingerprints lifted at crime scenes. These fingerprints should be stored in file folders by the case number for future reference as needed. This assumes, of course, the department does not have access to an Automated Fingerprint Information System (AFIS).

United States Currency

United States Currency being kept for safekeeping while awaiting transfer, should also be maintained in a file folder. While it is not advisable to maintain non-evidentury United States currency in the Property Control Room, temporary storage arrangements should be made.

Non-Evidentury value. United States Currency having no evidentury value should be taken to the jurisdiction's finance or treasure's office as soon as possible and deposited in the jurisdiction's general fund. A receipt should be obtained for the amount of monies so deposited, and the receipt entered into the property control system in lieu of the currency. This eliminates the storage of currency while documenting the fact that the currency came into the department's possession. When the rightful owner is identified, the receipt should be given to the owner with instructions to take it to the jurisdiction's finance officer to exchange it for United States Currency.

Seized currency. Currency that has been seized pending forfeiture should be deposited in an interest bearing seizure account at a federally insured bank. The purpose of the interest bearing account to earn income on the seized monies as a means of increasing the forfeiture account. Should a court refuse to forfeit the monies, and order them returned to the owner, the court may order also that interest on the seized money be paid to the owner. With the monies in the interest bearing account the interest earned may offset the court-ordered interest payment.

Forfeited currency. Monies that have been ordered forfeited should be withdrawn from the seizure account and deposited in a forfeiture account. In most jurisdictions the forfeited monies may be expended only for those budgetary items that support the drug enforcement objectives of the jurisdiction. The withdrawal of these funds should be by check; requiring two co-signers and a clear statement of the purpose of the expenditure. These procedures are necessary to maintain a paper trail of the deposit, withdrawal and expenditure of the monies.

Evidentury value. United States currency of questionable value, i.e. counterfeit, should likewise be stored in a file folder until the United States Secret Service is notified and instructions received regarding the disposition of the questioned currency. In all cases, currency should be placed in an envelope and sealed with evidence tape. The intent of this policy is to eliminate any possible opportunity, or potential for funds to be used temporarily for purposes other than those associated directly with a counterfeiting investigation.

Narcotics and Dangerous Drugs

All narcotics and dangerous drugs should be stored in a separate locked file cabinet or safe to create "double-secure" storage. Because of the nature and sensitivity of this type of evidence, weight and count control should be maintained when receiving and destroying drugs. In addition, a substance test; in the form of a field test, should be conducted on a representative, random sample of the drugs before they are destroyed.

Prisoners' Property

Prisoners' property should be maintained with the same degree of care and security as other types of evidence. There are several reasons for an increased concern for the security of prisoners' property. First, the police agency is responsible for the safe keeping of a prisoner's property while the prisoner is in police custody. A higher degree of bailment is created with the seizure of an individual's property; as is the case with a prisoner. In addition, a prisoner's inventoried property may contain what is later learned to be evidence. If a complete chain of custody of a prisoner's property is not maintained, this newly discovered evidence may be inadmissible in court.

Bulk Property Storage

Consideration must be given to the location and procedures for the storage of large, bulk items of property that may come into the custody of the police agency. A bulk storage area should be identified in property control procedural statements.

Temporary Bulk Property Storage

A storage area must be available for immediate use upon taking large items or large number of items into custody. The temporary storage area can be any secure location available for use while the Property Control Officer is not on duty.

One potential temporary bulk storage area is an interrogation room or a cell. After property is placed into the interrogation room or cell, the room should be secured by a standard lock. Evidence tape should then be used to seal the door. The reporting officer's initials should be written on the evidence tape. The tape should span across the door to the door frame. This is necessary to indicate the door has not been opened and, therefore, the chain of custody has been maintained.

Notification of property control officer. When property is placed into the temporary bulk storage area the Property Control Officer must be notified. This can be accomplished by placing the Property Inventory Report in a temporary storage locker, depositing it in a drop slot or the officer's mail box, a notification placard in a conspicuous location, or by some other standardized method. Property in the temporary bulk storage area should be transferred to a permanent bulk storage area by the Property Custodian upon reporting for duty.

Permanent Bulk Storage Area

A permanent bulk storage area should be made available for bicycles, motorcycles, and any other large items taken into custody. Bulk storage areas should be indoors in a secured area. The use of outside bulk storage areas is not recommended since it subjects property to the weather and deterioration. A police agency, as a gratuitous bailee, has a responsibility to the property owner for only reasonable care of the property. It could be argued, however, that outside storage does not constitute reasonable care considering the nature of the property and the circumstances and conditions under which it is stored.

All property stored in a bulk storage area, regardless of its nature or location, should be secured adequately. This may necessitate the use of padlocks, steel security cable, chain-link fences, or other devices appropriate for securing the storage area and the property contained inside.

Bicycle Storage

Many municipal and county law enforcement agencies face a significant problem with the storage of recovered bicycles. The size, number and the length of time bicycles are keep contribute to the magnitude of this problem. The frequent disposition of bicycles is the most appropriate response to this problem. However, statutory retention periods may prevent such timely dispositions so as to prevent this problem. One solution is to maximize the use of space dedicated to bicycle storage. A hanging rack increases significantly the storage capacity of the bicycle storage area. Bicycles are hung from hooks placed through the front wheel with the underside of the frame readily visible. This allows a quick inspection and location of the serial number regardless of its location on the bicycle.

Planning and Equipping Property Control Systems

Planning for a new, or redesigned property control system should include public and restricted access, floor level, security levels and devices, evidence preparation and temporary storage areas, temporary secure storage equipment and dedicated storage areas. Construction materials, electric, water and sewer service, sprinkler protection, and the proximity of toilet and handwashing facilities should be considered also . Other considerations include the size and placement of evidence preparation work surfaces, office equipment, storage shelves and bins, efficient foot-traffic and workflow patterns, and air-handling requirements and equipment.

The Property Control Officer, or another person with a sound understanding of the property control function should be assigned to work with the architects staff in the conceptual design and layout of the new areas. The individual assigned should have a thorough understanding of the principles and practices associated with evidence packaging and processing, temporary and long-term storage methods, biohazard evidence, OSHA and EPA requirements and legal mandates. The individual should possess also some knowledge of the levels of security associated with the processing and storage of the various classifications of property, and the security devices that may be required to ensure these levels of security.

Evidence Preparation Area

Evidence preparation and processing areas should be physically located away from prisoner processing areas. This is for the safety of officers and the physical security of evidence being processed.

Preparation tasks should be done in a secure area, preferably immediately adjacent to temporary secure storage lockers and close to the biohazard drying area. Handwashing facilities should be available in the immediate, or nearby area to meet OSHA standards.

Equipment, including scales, temporary secure refrigerator and packaging supplies and materials should likewise be located conveniently in the preparation area. Biohazard personal protective equipment is a definite supply in this area.

Table Space

Sufficient table space should be provided for inspection and wrapping items. Ideally, evidence preparation work tops should be stainless steel with a rolled "lip" around the outer edge to prevent runoff should a spill occur.

A roll of butcher paper should be available to serve as a working surface to catch any trace evidence that may fall off evidence being handled and also to wrap items too large to fit into paper bags. The wrapping paper may also serve as a disposable surface on which wet items can be laid while air drying.

Contaminated evidence should not be placed in direct contact with table tops or other non-contaminated surfaces. Wrapping paper, paper bags, plastic drop cloths or other suitable covers should be used as table surface covers.

Other supplies that should be available in the immediate area include rolls of string and twine, reinforced tape, evidence tape, various types and sizes packaging materials and a suitable packing material; bubble pack, styrofoam chips and newspaper.

Drying Rack

A drying rack should be incorporated into the design of the Property Control Room. The purpose of this rack is to have a convenient, unobstructed area to hang wet or damp items so they may air dry before being packaged.

When air-drying contaminated evidence outside a drying cabinet, wrapping paper should be draped around the item in a manner that will allow air circulation, yet prevent contamination of nearby areas. A biohazard sticker should be affixed to the wrapping paper. Disposable gloves, eye protection and face masks should be worn when air-drying, handling and packaging contaminated evidence.

Ventilation

Proper ventilation of the Property Control Room must be given consideration. The air quality in storage areas and the office area is a composite of the narcotics, chemicals, bacteria, dampness, odors and all other substances stored in the room. The Property Control Room should be provided with adequate temperature control and ventilation devices. As a last resort, a portable fan should be used to maintain a constant air movement in the room while it is occupied and an electronic deodor-izer device installed to disinfect and mask unpleasant odors.

File Cabinets

Metal file cabinets should be present in sufficient quantity to contain all the property control files related to evidence and property currently in the Property Control Room. File cabinets should be available also for the storage of documentary evidence.

Useful measurements in assessing the need for filing space in relationship to the documents to be stored are:

- One file drawer will hold 24 inches of files; front to back
- A letter size file drawer holds 1.5 cubic feet of records; a legal size drawer, 2 cubic feet
- One four drawer file cabinet requires six square feet of floor space and an additional six square feet immediately in front of the file cabinet for aisle space

The architectural design, or rearrangement of the Property Control Office should consider the quantity of current records that must be stored as well as an estimate of future records storage requirements. A more accurate estimate of records storage space, and floor space required, may be calculated by reviewing the types of records identified in Chapter 6.

Lockers, Safes and Vaults

Metal storage lockers can be considered for double-secure storage of narcotics, handguns and other valuable or sensitive items. Care must be given to the quality (thickness) of the metal frame, door and sides of the cabinet. A secure locking device (other than the key handle-lock mechanism) should be installed on the locker if it to be used as double-secure storage. When only small quantities of narcotics are stored a floor safe should be considered. If the safe weighs less than 750 pounds it should be bolted to the floor or wall in such a way that it cannot be removed easily from its location.

A chain-link fence erected within the Property Control Room has been employed by some police agencies to create a double-secure storage area. The level of security that these barriers provide should be considered. One purpose of double-secure areas is to prevent unauthorized access to certain classifications of evidence. An unauthorized access to the Property Control Room may be further compounded if access to the secure area was made by the perpetrator cutting the chain-link with bolt cutters found in the Property Control Room.

A walk-in vault should be considered in the design of a new property control system. This vault should be located in a convenient location considering the workflow pattern and of sufficient size to hold the quantity of firearms, narcotics, money and jewelry the police agency has in custody as well as any projected future growth.

Refrigeration

Two refrigerators should be available for the storage of evidence that requires refrigeration. One should be located in the temporary storage area for immediate refrigeration of per-ishable items. A small, bar-type refrigerator is sufficient in size for agencies of several hundred officers. Compartments with hinged doors can be constructed from sheet metal and secured to the interior of the refrigerator. The compartment doors can be secured with padlocks to allow access to the refrigerator and still maintain the chain of custody.

The second refrigerator should be located in the Property Control Room and used for longer term storage. The size of these refrigerators may vary from a small bar refrigerator for the temporary storage area to a full size 14 cubic-foot refrigerator in the Property Control Room. No food stuffs, other than that which is evidence, should be stored in these refrigerators.

A freezer unit should also be considered for the long-term storage of evidence that has been analyzed by the laboratory, or for food stuffs that are being maintained as evidence. A thermometer; either built-in to the door or hung inside the freezer, should be available to permit periodic checks of the interior temperature. A power failure and temperature alarm should also be considered. Should the power supply be inter-rupted, or a mechanical failure cause the freezer to cease functioning, the alarm will provide sufficient notice to save the evidence from thawing-out and spoiling.

Determining Storage Locker Requirements

The number and size of temporary secure lockers required in any police agency can be calculated easily. By maintaining a count of the average number of items entered into the property system on a daily basis by approximate dimension: very small (envelopes), small (handguns), medium (tape decks, personal clothing), and large (long guns), the average daily demand by locker size can be calculated. These calculations should then be extended to cover the maximum length of time (in days) the Property Custodian is not on duty. This maximum time period should include a three day holiday weekend.

On a normal work day the Property Custodian is available for all or some portion of their tour of duty to receive property directly. This is followed by a sixteen hour period of time when the temporary lockers are used. During a three day weekend 88 hours will elapse during which the temporary storage lockers are available for use. For example, from 4 P.M. Friday to 8 A.M. Tuesday is 88 hours. Therefore, the number of temporary storage lockers required is approximately four times the average number of items stored on a daily basis. By maintaining a temporary record of the small, medium and large items of property placed in temporary secure storage on a daily basis, the number and size of these lockers can be then calculated.

Shelving Requirements

Scale diagrams can be used also to determine the required cubic feet of potential storage space. The length and width dimensions of a storage area are useful to determine, for example, the number of shelving units or bins that can be placed in an area. The height of the area will determine the maximum height of the shelve units and, therefore, the maximum number of shelves.

With this information the number of shelves, and the length and depth of the shelves, can be determined and the cubic feet of storage space calculated. For example; assume storage containers are twenty four inches deep, fifteen inches wide and ten and a quarter inches high (24" x 15" x 10.25", a standard legal size records storage box). This box displaces two and one half cubic feet of shelve space. Dividing the total cubic feet of available shelf space by the standard box size (2.5 cubic feet) yields the number of boxes that can be stored on the shelves. Consideration should be given to future increases in the volume of property and the shelving space required. Expansion flexibility and storage capacity must be considered in the initial planning design phase if the new property storage areas are to adequately serve long-term storage requirements.

An estimate of future expansion and flexibility requirements can be calculated. Maintaining records of monthly, quarterly and annual property dispositions: destruction, return to owner, auction, department appropriation, will support an estimate of the cubic feet of property disposed of. Records of property taken into custody can be used to calculate the average number of packages (cases) that will fit into a storage container. Subtracting the average volume of annual property dispositions from the average volume of property intakes produces an estimate of annual additional storage space used, or the amount of storage space reclaimed.

For example, if 900 cubic feet of property is disposed of during a year and 1200 cubic feet of property is taken into storage, the net result is an additional 300 cubic feet of shelve space consumed. Three hundred cubic feet is approximately 120 storage boxes. One hundred and twenty (120) storage boxes, each fifteen (15) inches wide, require 150 linear feet of shelve space.

Average annual property intake (cubic feet) 1200
Average property dispositions (cubic feet) ... . <u>900</u>
Additional annual shelve space required .... 300 [1]

Assume 2.5 cubic feet per storage box [2], then;

$$\frac{300 \, [1] \text{ cubic feet}}{2.5 \, [2] \text{ cubic feet / box}} = 120 \text{ additional boxes}$$

120 storage boxes x 15 inches wide = 150 linear feet of additional shelve space required on an annual basis.

Figure 4.7
Calculating Shelving Requirements

Alternative calculation. If the average number of annual property intakes and dispositions is known, and the average volume (in cubic feet) of evidence items per case is known, the calculation can be accomplished on a property case basis. For example, if the evidence associated with an average of three cases will fit into a storage box fifteen (15) inches wide, the evidence for each case requires an average of five linear inches of shelve space.

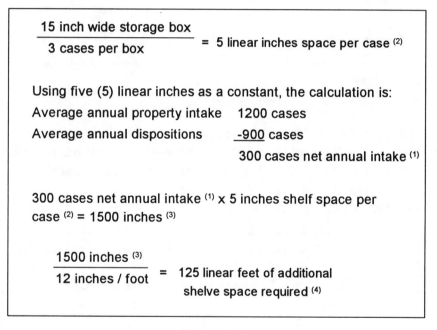

$$\frac{\text{15 inch wide storage box}}{\text{3 cases per box}} = 5 \text{ linear inches space per case [2]}$$

Using five (5) linear inches as a constant, the calculation is:

Average annual property intake   1200 cases
Average annual dispositions   -900 cases
                          300 cases net annual intake [1]

300 cases net annual intake [1] x 5 inches shelf space per case [2] = 1500 inches [3]

$$\frac{\text{1500 inches [3]}}{\text{12 inches / foot}} = 125 \text{ linear feet of additional shelve space required [4]}$$

Figure 4.8
Calculation of Shelving Requirements

Estimating Floor Area

After estimating the required shelve storage space, the next step is to determine the floor space that is required for the shelve units. This can be calculated as shown in the figure below.

Shelving unit floor area. Assume each shelving unit is 96 inches (8 feet) long, 86 inches tall, 15 inches deep with 14 inches vertical spacing between shelves. A total of six shelves are available on this specific evidence and property shelving unit.

6 shelves x 96 inches each = 576 linear inches per shelve unit [5]

$$\frac{576 \text{ linear inches }[5]}{12 \text{ inches / foot}} = 48 \text{ linear feet }[6]$$

125 linear feet of additional shelves required [4]
48 linear feet per shelve unit [6] = 2.6 or 3 additional shelving units [7]

3 units [7] x [8 feet (length) x 1.25 feet (depth)] = 30 square feet [8]

Figure 4.9
Calculation of Floor Space

Aisle floor area. The aisle space required between the shelf units is 2 to 2.5 feet (4 to 5 feet if shelves do not share an aisle with opposite shelve units). Aisle space for the three additional shelving units identified earlier requires 16 square feet per unit, or a total of 48 square feet.

8 foot length shelve unit x 2 feet aisle space = 16 square feet

3 shelving units x 16 square feet each = 48 square feet aisle space [9]

Figure 4.10
Calculation of Aisle Space

The total additional floor space required for the 3 shelving units necessary to store the net annual intake of 300 property cases is an additional 78 square feet of floor space in the property control room.

30 square feet for shelving units [8] + 48 square feet for aisle space [9] = 78 square feet total floor space required.

Figure 4.11
Additional Floor Space Required

Movable shelving systems. Where floor space is limited for the placement of shelving units, a movable shelving system may be an alternative to consider. These shelving units are secured to tracks on the floor, making it possible to move the shelving units laterally. Since the shelving units are moved back and forth easily this system eliminates the need for an access aisle between each set of shelves. In a three-shelf system, only one 36 inch-wide aisle space is required. This eliminates one 36 inch-wide aisle space that may be used for additional storage. In a five-shelf unit, four such aisles would be eliminated, saving a total of 12 feet of floor space that may be utilized for additional shelves. These movable shelving systems, available commercially, have the potential of saving up to 50 per cent of the floor space required by conventional, stationary shelving units.

Financing Property Control Room Equipment

Acquiring the funds to properly equip the Property Control Room is often cited as a major reason for not having adequate equipment. In those instances when the agency's budget appropriation does not allow the purchase of this basic equipment, serious consideration should be given to the use of drug asset forfeiture funds. Many state laws permit the expenditure of forfeited funds for purposes that further the efforts to prevent drug abuse and investigate drug dealing. Since the Property Control Room is the repository for all seized narcotics and dangerous drugs, some portion of forfeited funds should be made available to provide a secure, adequately equipped property control system.

Federal Surplus Property

The National Defense Authorization Act (P.L. 101-189) allows state and local government units to acquire federal surplus military equipment for use in anti-drug activities. This should be viewed as a potential resource for equipping the property control room.

1208 Program. The 1208 Program allows states to contact directly the Department of Defense (DOD) surplus depots to request surplus property. Any excess DOD property is available at no cost for transfer; including office furniture. The Defense

Logistics Agency (DLA) regional office should be contacted for further information.

1122 Program. This federal surplus property program allows state and local agencies to *purchase* law enforcement equipment for anti-drug efforts through federal procurement channels. A catalog of equipment items is available. Participation in this program is through a State Point of Contact (SPOC) in each state as established by the governor's executive order.

Relocating The Property Control Room

The opportunity to relocate the Property Control Room to a larger area or new facility provides significant opportunities and, at the same time, creates several problems that must be effectively addressed and resolved. Issues that need to be addressed include: design of the new property control storage areas, disposition of excess property, planning the relocation, and physical and procedural security. Other considerations include a new property classification system, chain of custody, and the packing and physical relocation of property and evidence.

Planning The Relocation

Planning should start as soon as it is known that the relocation is to take place. A written plan for the relocation should be developed, reviewed and approved by the supervisor in charge of the relocation and the command officer responsible for the property control function. The selection of a moving service to pack, transport and unload the property to be relocated, and the design of the new storage shelves, bins, lockers and double-secure storage must also be planned. The plan should include pre-move, move, and post-move tasks, priorities, personnel assignments and due dates. Time estimates should be calculated—and then doubled—to account for unexpected, yet inevitable delays.

Diagrams. Scale diagrams of the new property storage areas should be developed during the planning phase. These diagrams should include the width, length and ceiling height of the new storage areas, the location of doors, interior walls, light switches, heating and ventilation ducts, and other physical design elements. These diagrams will be useful later in determining the size and placement of shelving units and storage areas within the Property Control Room and other storage areas.

Planning for relocation is an opportune time to reclassify property: evidence, found, safekeeping, double-secure storage. Reclassification will aid also in identifying and designing storage areas for appeals evidence, electronic evidence and bulk storage to improve the efficiency of the storage system. Once property and evidence has been reclassified, and the volume estimated, scale diagrams of the storage areas, storage space and shelve designs can be developed.

Property disposals. Planning for Property Room relocation is an opportune time to dispose of property. The planning process should consider the disposition of unnecessary property and evidence that is currently being stored. Property that has languished in the Property Control Room for years, and for which records of initial custody are incomplete, or cannot be located should be targeted for disposal. If these property custody records have not been located in the past, it is highly unlikely they will be located in the future. The justification for these disposals is improved property system efficiency and reduced operating costs. Mass, planned dispositions of property prior to the relocation will require less time in packing, transporting and unloading and result in fewer trips between locations. This savings of time will result in a real savings of dollars.

A concerted effort should be made well in advance of the physical relocation to obtain property dispositions from officers and submit the necessary requests for property disposition. This task includes obtaining the required approvals for disposal: prosecutor approvals, court orders, and final approval by the chief of police or sheriff. An efficient property control system; a system free of the unnecessary property that is currently stored, is considerably easier to manage and maintain.

Based upon a reduction in the volume of property, a more exact estimate of shelves, shelve space, bins, lockers, and bulk storage space needs can be determined. This may in turn reduce the time necessary to design the new storage areas and result in further cost savings.

Security Considerations

Maintaining security over property and evidence during the relocation must be given priority if the chain of custody is to be maintained. Physical security must be considered during the packing, loading, transportation and unloading of the containers. If assistance is required during the packing phase, adequate supervision must be maintained at all times. This is especially true if non-department—contract—personnel are used to assist in packing. Non-department personnel should not be allowed in those areas that contain valuable or sensitive property; firearms, narcotics, jewelry and currency. It may be prudent also to conduct criminal background checks on the employees of commercial moving companies that will be engaged in the relocation.

Adequate security must be provided by sworn personnel during the loading, transportation and unloading of the moving van. Security will be improved if property and evidence containers are loaded and transported separate from any non–property room items; the moving van should contain only those containers originating from the Property Control Room.

Packing containers; boxes, drums, etc., should be marked with a consecutive number, i.e.; box 1 of 95 and sealed with evidence tape. This will permit a quick inventory of the containers upon arrival at the new location.

Physical Relocation

In addition to numbering the moving containers, the containers should also be color-coded to indicate their assigned shelve, locker, or storage area in the new Property Control Room. Moving containers can be marked with red stickers for evidence, green stickers for safekeeping and yellow stickers for lost property. Property to be placed in double-secure storage can be marked with two stickers. The sticker color indicates the general storage area for the container and the container number indicates the positioning of the container within the shelve or storage area.

The scale diagram of the new property control areas, developed during the planning phase, should be readily available in the current and the new Property Control Rooms. The diagram is helpful in marking the containers for identification and relocation to the new storage areas. As the containers are unloaded at the new location, the diagram is a useful reference to direct the containers to the proper shelf, bin or storage area.

Making a commitment to comprehensively plan the relocation of the Property Control Room will result in several benefits. These include minimizing the volume of property to be relocated, a savings in time and dollar expenditures, maintenance of the chain of custody during the relocation, and minimal disruption to the daily routine of property control operations.

Property System Security
Security Audits

Security audits of the Property Control Room should be conducted to ensure all methods of access are secure and adequately controlled. This includes all doors and windows, whether facing the interior or exterior of the building, ceilings, walls, floors, and the need for additional security devices. Audits should include also an examination of property control policies and procedures to assess their comprehensiveness, whether they are up to date; from both a procedural and security technology perspective, and adherence to policies and procedures by all department personnel.

Double Secure Storage

Sensitive or valuable items should be stored in a double secure environment. Storage devices used for double secure storage include: vaults, safes, file cabinets with locking devices, and wall lockers. A "strong room" built into the Property Control Room is considered a basic necessity.

Double secure storage should be planned and regularly used for all narcotics and dangerous drugs, firearms, valuable jewelry and United States currency. Access to this storage area or cabinet should be restricted at all times. These secure areas, safes and cabinets should be unlocked only when there is an immediate need to enter for evidence storage or retrieval.

Door Locks

All door locks installed on the Property Control Room should be the dead-bolt type to prevent the lock from being slipped, thereby allowing an unauthorized entry.

Key control. Control over the Property Room key must be maintained at all times and addressed by agency policy. An ideal situation is one in which only two Property Control Room keys exist. One key is maintained in the custody of the Property Control Officer, the other key is maintained in a sealed envelope stored in a key control cabinet with limited access.

The key stored in the key control cabinet should be stored in an envelope secured with evidence tape bearing the initials of the Property Control Officer and one other individual. This procedure is intended to control access to and use of the key. If the key were to be used it will become evident immediately by the broken seal on the envelope.

If the second copy of the key is used to gain entrance into the Property Control Room the individual entering the Room should be required, by written policy, to initiate and complete a report. This report should contain the date and time of entry, the purpose and authorization for the entry, and the specific description of any property removed from, or deposited in the Property Control Room.

The Property Control Room keys in the possession of the Property Control Officer should also be subject to security measures. Keys should not be carried on the same key ring containing the Property Control Officer's house and car keys. Should these personal keys be lost the Property Control Room key would be lost with them, creating the possibility of a compromise of the security of the Property Control Room and its contents. This procedure also reduces the potential for an impression of the Property Control Room key being made while the keys are temporarily out of the possession and control of the Property Control Officer.

The keys to the Property Control Room, and other secure property storage areas, should be non-duplicatable keys. Locks on these secure areas should be changed in the event the keys are lost or misplaced, or when the Property Custodian is reassigned or replaced.

In summary, the keys to the Property Control Room should be carried separately from other personal keys, remain unmarked as to their identity and be stored in a secure location when not in the direct possession of the Property Control Officer.

Electronic locks. Electronic locking devices are an alternative to key locks and should be considered in new construction or major remodeling. Card keys have a magnetic strip that allows the card to be programmed for specific locks as well as specific days of the week and hours when the card will activate the lock.

Key pads are another alternative. Located at an entrance door, these devices can be programmed to allow access only if the code number for that door is entered in the correct sequence and within a predetermined time. These locking devices can also be programmed to limit access to certain days of the week and hours, and record the times when access was attempted.

Pass-through lockers. If pass-through temporary storage lockers are used consideration should be given to installing a steel security bar across the inner doors. The latches on these doors have been compromised allowing entrance to the property control room through an unlocked locker, or reaching through a locker to an adjacent locked compartment.

Walls And Ceiling

In addition to assessing the security of doors and windows, the security audit should be directed to the walls and ceiling of the Property Control Room.

Walls. Thin plasterboard walls are an invitation for unauthorized entry. Plasterboard can be cut open or forcibly broken allowing entry into the Property Control Room. Whenever possible, the walls should be constructed of reinforced cement building block to prevent the possibility of intrusion. If cement block walls are not feasible double layers of 5/8's inch plasterboard should be installed on both sides of the wall studs.

When the Property Control Room is located in an out of the way location particular attention must be given to both interior and exterior walls.

Ceilings. Ceilings are a potential security problem from several respects. Dropped, suspended or other types of false ceilings often can be accessed from outside the Property Control Room. Ceiling panels can be removed, access gained and the panel replaced; without an immediate visible indication that access has been gained. A secure barrier device should be installed between the permanent ceiling and the dropped ceiling to prevent access.

Heating and ventilating ductwork must also be considered a potential access point. In some cases the ductwork is wide enough to crawl through. The location where ductwork goes through a wall is a weak point in the wall. This may provide a convenient point of attack on an otherwise secure wall.

Alarm Systems

In those instances were the Property Control Room, or access doors, is located in an isolated area consideration should be given to the installation of an alarm system. The alarm system should protect the doors, walls and ceiling. The interior of large storage areas should be protected with a motion sensor. Exterior storage areas may warrant visual surveillance through the use of video cameras and monitors.

Factors to be considered in the decision to alarm the Property Control Room or use video surveillance equipment include:

- The type of property stored in the area
- The sensitivity and value of the property
- The location of the storage area within the police facility
- Potential internal and external threats to the storage area and its contents
- The potential for uninterrupted attempts to gain access to the storage area

Security of the Property Control Room and auxiliary storage areas must be afforded the high priority it commands. A security audit, based upon the issues and concepts presented, should be on the agenda of every Property Control Officer.

Chapter Notes

Osterburg, James W.; and Ward, Richard H.; *Criminal Investigations: A Method For Reconstructing The Past,* (Cincinnati: Anderson Pub. Co., 1992) p. 180.

Chapter 5

Managing Electronic Evidence

Electronic recording devices are increasingly being used to record information for short- and long-term storage and fast and efficient retrieval of that information. These devices, and others modified for an illegal purpose, are being used to surreptitiously record the activities and communications of others. The widespread use of electron devices increases the potential that police agencies will seize, inventory and store electronic recording devices, equipment and data that have been used illegally. This chapter addresses the types of electronic devices that may be seized and be used as evidence. To ensure the future admissibility of this evidence at trial, these devices, equipment, and the data they may contain must be properly managed while in police custody; the management of electronic evidence.

Electronic Evidence

Electronic evidence consists of devices that use the flow of electricity through transistors to store, manipulate and manage data. These devices have evidentury value when the device, or the data stored within it, can provide an answer to the questions regarding the elements of a crime, the identity of the offender or a victim, and other basic evidentury questions addressed in an earlier chapter.

Many of the evidentury issues associated with nonelectronic evidence apply to this modern, and highly technical, approach to criminal investigations. Issues associated with the seizure and storage of electronic evidence include: the originality of the evidence, the chain of custody, and the reproduction of the stored data. Also, the identification of the individual depicted, or whose voice is recorded, storage conditions and disposal. A major distinction between nonelectronic and electronic evidence, however, is the manner in which the evidence is hidden—not unlike biological evidence—and the volatility of the data that are stored in the electronic device.

Admissibility as evidence. Due in part to the increasing use of digital technology, courts are becoming more open to the use of electronic technology for evidentury purposes. This increased availability and use of electronic recording devices brought about the beginning of forensic audio, video and computer specialists. These forensic specialists employ a variety of electronic equipment, scientific tools, computer programs and practical knowledge to determine the likely history and legal significance of electronic evidence.

As the use of electronic technology in criminal investigations increases so will the judicial scrutiny of the technology employed and the persons associated with electronic evidence. The judiciary will want to keep the quality of electronic evidence high. The increase in use of electronic evidence may cause some people to cut corners; to use short cuts in the application, storage and introduction of the electronic evidence in court. This raises questions regarding the admissibility of the evidence at trial and the credibility of the electronic data and those associated with the evidence through the chain of custody. This will result in greater demands upon forensic experts and Property Control Officers.

A potential major problem is ensuring the integrity of electronic evidence and defending it against allegations that the evidence was altered in some unseen, or unobservable manner. The trend toward conversion to full-digital technology, the rapid growth in power, capabilities, and the overall availability of computer-based, digital editing systems, may create issues relating to the editing, alteration, and the potential fabrication of digital data, and digitized audio and video recordings.

Writing on the issue of falsification of electronic evidence the author of one textbook, directed to attorneys, states there is disagreement whether potential falsification "... presents a problem that is different in kind from the problems associated with forgery of paper documents, tampering with paper documents, or with witnesses who lie. Many ... under estimate the potential for the manipulation or falsification of all types [of electronic evidence], especially as the switch-over to full-digital technology continues". (Gruber, 1995) This potential raises new issues regarding the collection, storage and chain of custody that defense lawyers may raise, and the procedures police agencies should adopt to further ensure that electronic evidence is admissible in court.

The potential for allegations of evidence alteration should be recognized within the context of the proper inventorying, sealing and storage of electronic evidence. Case law in this area of physical evidence can be expected to appear unexpectedly. Therefore, investigators and Property Control Officers should familiarize themselves with growing number of technical, forensic, legal and other evidentury issues associated with electronic evidence.

The Digital Revolution

There is a continuing trend toward a conversion to digital and laser technology from magnetic data storage. Tape recordings can now be recorded on nontape and nonmagnetic media. A video segment recorded on a computer hard disk, for example, is stored on a magnetic-, not tape-based medium. An audio or video recording made on an optical disc is stored on a medium that is neither magnetic nor tape-based. Proper storage of electronic evidence requires some knowledge of the recording medium and its susceptibility to its immediate environment.

As the computer and digital revolutions proceed, it may become necessary to incorporate additional terms that relate to the specific recording format and equipment into the lexicon of property and evidence management. These terms include: "digital audio tape (DAT) recordings," "mini-disc," "multimedia", and "erasable compact disc" (CD-E). Also, terms such as "WORM", "optical discs" and "data encryption". The types of physical evidence that can be anticipated in the future include: computers, audio and video recordings, E-mail, digital photographs, cellular telephones, pagers, digital answering machines and other, yet to be developed, electronic data storage and communications applications.

The various methods that have been, and are being, used to store data electronically are shown in Figure 5.1. It is important that the investigator and the Property Control Officer be familiar with these methods since evidence handling and storage conditions differ with the type of storage media.

Method of Information Coding	Magnetic Tape	Tapeless Magnetic	NonMagnetic
Analog	• Cassette Recorder • Microcassette Recorder • Reel to Reel Recorder • Eight-Track Player • Camcorder • Answering Machines	obsolete	obsolete Vinyl Phonograph Record
Digital	• Digital Audio Tape Recorder (DAT) • Digital Compact Disk Recorder (DCC) • Stationary Head Recorders (DASH) • Camcorder; audio •Computer Tape Backup	• Microcomputer or Digital Audio Work Station using: - floppy disc - hard disc - removable cartridge - floptical disc - magneto-optical cartridge	Audio Recorder Computer, or Answering Machine (using memory chips) Optical Laser Units - CD-ROM - CD-Interactive - CD-Worm - CDR (recordable) - Mini Disc - Magneto-Optical Cartridge

Figure 5.1
Information Storage Medium

Based on: Gruber, *Electronic Evidence*, 1995: 152

Data encryption. Data encryption is the scrambling of information to keep it from the eyes and ears of those who have neither a need or right to know the information. The debate over encryption software programs has raised many issues of a practical legal, constitutional, national security, personal privacy and investigations nature. Strong encryption codes; those that can not be broken quickly, or not at all, have received particular attention. Federal investigative agencies, and particularly the FBI, have asserted that the availability of strong data encryption programs to the general public and to foreign governments could seriously hamper criminal investigations and could pose a threat to national security. Currently, there are commercial and free versions of encryption software available on the Internet.

As the private lives of citizens move increasingly to data networks questions about personal privacy arise. Personal information pertaining to medical history, employment, family relationships and personal habits is increasingly being digitized, stored and transmitted from one location to another. This raises questions relating to the constitutionally implied right to personal privacy. In a recent potentially precedent-setting case a U.S. District Court judge found that the 1st Amendment appears to protect data encryption as a form of free speech. In this case the judge ruled that a software program that contains a strong encryption code could be distributed by the developer without procuring a federal license. (Gillmor, 1998: 5)

These issues, and the availability of data encryption software, can be expected to have some significant impacts upon the ability of criminal investigators to retrieve electronic evidence and on the practical evidentury value of seized electronic evidence.

Admissibility of Scientific Evidence

The standard for the legal admissibility of new, or controversial scientific evidence in federal and state courts since 1923 was the *Frye* Standard. (*Frye v. United States,* 1923) This Standard, often referred to as the "general acceptance theory", addressed the reliability of the evidence in terms of its general acceptance within the relevant scientific community.

A 1993 unanimous decision by the United States Supreme Court in the *Daubert* case lowered the standard for admissibility of scientific evidence in the federal courts. The *Daubert* decision modified the federal standards for scientific evidence by overturning the long-established standard established in *Frye*. (*Daubert v. United States*, 1993) The Daubert decision mandates that a judge conduct a preliminary assessment of whether an expert's testimony is scientifically valid and can be applied in the case at hand. In one case subsequent to the Daubert decision the court said: "elimination of formal barriers to expert testimony has merely shifted to the trial court the responsibility for keeping 'junk science' out of the courtroom". (*Wilson v. West Chicago*, 1993) Because the *Daubert* case was decided on federal statutory interpretation, and not constitutional grounds, state courts are not required to follow the *Daubert* decision.

An application of the *Daubert* decision, with respect to electronic evidence, is the case of estimating a bank robber's height from bank surveillance photographs. An FBI agent testified that the robber's height was calculated from the photograph by means of photogrammetry. The Federal Appellate Court upheld the conviction stating that this height estimation process did not involve novel or questionable scientific techniques. (*United States v. Quinn*, 1994)

Over time we are certain to hear about, or become involved in, cases involving the reconstruction of erased computer data files, decoding of encrypted data files, photographs reproduced from electronic files, and similar issues brought before the courts to question the management of electronic evidence while in police custody.

The federal *Electronic Privacy Act of 1986* should be studied to determine the potential for violating an innocent person's right to privacy with respect to computer information on electronic bulletin-board operations. When accessing a target on a networked system, issues related to personal privacy and wiretapping should also be considered.

Quality Control Issues

In addition to the requirements of materiality and relevance to the issues before the court, electronic evidence must generally meet several quality control standards before it may be admitted as evidence. Regardless of the type of electronic device being considered, three basic questions must be addressed, and satisfactorily answered, before the results of electronic or digital evidence may be admissible. The questions that must be addressed are:

- Was the device working properly?
- Does the device's hardware and software actually do what it purports to do?
- Is the output of the device a fair and accurate depiction of what it purports to demonstrate?

An example of the application of these questions is the use of electronic imaging. The conversion, for example, of photographs to digital images for enhancement. In this example the input device(s)—digital camera, film scanner, or flatbed scanner—would be subjected to these qualifying questions:

- What proof is there that the device was checked by, and satisfactorily completed, a diagnostics routine without any indication of malfunctioning?
- What proof is there that the software program enhances an image without altering substantially the essential characteristics of the image?
- What proof is there that the enhanced image that is produced by the output device—a printer, for example—is essentially the same as the software program that produced it?

The same issues apply if the device is an analog or digital voice recording, computer generated data, or other form of electronic evidence. These issues relate, in part, to the proper handling and storage of electronic evidence. Handling and storage in such a manner that the device functions properly when it is submitted to forensic analysis.

The remaining sections of this chapter address the various types of electronic evidence that may be encountered and the many issues associated with the proper management of this evidence.

Inventorying Electronic Evidence

Inventory descriptions. Most of the legal references and case law reviewed use the terms "audiotape" and "videotape" to refer to audio and video recordings. This is because magnetic tape was, in the past, the predominate use for both recording formats. There is now an evolving transition from magnetic tape recordings to recordings made on nontape and nonmagnetic media. A video segment recorded onto a computer hard disk, for example, is stored digitally on magnetic, not tape-based medium. An audio or video recording made on an optical disc is stored on a medium that is neither magnetic nor taped-based. The term "audio recording" or "video recording" should, therefore, be used when describing electronic evidence on an evidence inventory. This may avoid confusion and possible objections to the admissibility of evidence that is described in one manner, yet it exists in a different format, e.g.; tape versus disk.

Computer Evidence

Computers have become increasingly involved in, and associated with, criminal offenses. Virtually all the traditional crimes investigated by law enforcement; drug trafficking, gambling, homicide, prostitution, burglary, harassment, counterfeiting, etc., have been associated with the use of a computer. The wide spread availability of powerful personal computers, computer networks and the Internet has resulted in new variations of traditional crimes as well as several new criminal offenses. The computer is the essential tool of the techno-criminal. Telephone toll fraud, credit card theft and copyright infringement are but a few of these technology-based crimes. Pedophilia, distribution of pornography, pyramid schemes and other offenses have escalated with availability of the Internet and video technology. Computer video technology provides a mechanism for elegantly and conveniently cross-referencing, indexing, retrieving, and displaying documents.

Computers are being used increasingly by criminals to store, index, access and manipulate data and as a means of hiding data in the forms of information, photographs, voice recordings and computer generated motion and still videos.

Computers themselves have become the objects of attack. Theft of computer based information, digital image fraud, and theft of computers and computer chips would not exist but for the adoption of electronic information management.

Computer technology includes CD-ROM, laser and optical discs. These medium can be used to store, index, cross-reference, randomly access and present enormous amounts of information. Entire boxes of documents, once imaged, can be reduced to a single disc and indexed for rapid, random access. Large numbers of documents may involved; over several thousand, hundreds of thousands or possibly millions of documents. The use of video imaging technology for information-storage purposes is one of the single largest economic growth area in electronic technology. An entire support industry has developed in this area providing numerous software and hardware solutions.

Computer evidence tends to be volatile; especially magnetic-based storage medium, and can be damaged through negligent handling and storage. Because of the complexity of many computer-related crimes, computer equipment may have to be stored for long periods of time. To meet this need, planning should be done to identify a secure, dedicated area for the handling and storage of computer and other types of electronic evidence.

When raiding a site, and seizing a computer operation, the possibility of explosive, incendiary and other self-destructive devices built into the computer equipment should be considered. (Laska, 1997)

- Computer crime investigators should consider the possibility that a seemingly innocent computer system can be intricately involved in a criminal offense. Computers that control building security systems, corporate business computer systems, and other controllers may be used to support a computer crime.
- The crime scene, as well as the cabling and operation of the computer equipment, should be photographed and video recorded prior to seizing

the system.

- Prior to removing a computer from its original location at the crime scene, the area and the path to exit the scene should be checked with a magnetic compass to detect any "degaussing fields" that may have been created by the suspect to erase the data from hard drives and discs.

- Computer evidence should not be transported near magnetic fields. This includes the trunk of squad cars or other transporting vehicles. Since the radio transmitter emits an electromagnetic field, a wise precaution is to turnoff the radio while transporting computer evidence.

- When transporting computer evidence in hot or cold climates, the transporting vehicle should be cooled or heated prior to the computer evidence being loaded into the vehicle.

Inventorying Computer Systems

The initial step in inventorying a computer system is to take photographs of the system while it is in its original location and before it is disassembled for transportation. If video recording and inventory is to be conducted, still photographs of the system should also be taken. The still photographs will serve as a backup should the videotape experience some mishap such as erasure or tape breakage.

- Computer evidence should not be placed into plastic bags for transport or for storage. Plastic bags can generate static electricity. If available, computer components should be packed, transported and stored in their original packing boxes.

- Magnetic discs should not be photocopied to produce an inventory. The magnetic field generated by a photocopier may damage, or erase the stored data. Photographing should be adopted as the standard procedure for recording information on disk labels.

- Prior to disassembling a computer system for transportation each wire, cable and power cord should be tagged or labeled to identify the port to which it is connected. Cables that are not in use (connected) should likewise be identified with a notation that they were not connected to any device when they were seized.
- The cable diagram should be inventoried and stored with the evidence to facilitate the reconstruction of the computer system in the future.

A sample cable diagram is shown below in Figure 5.2

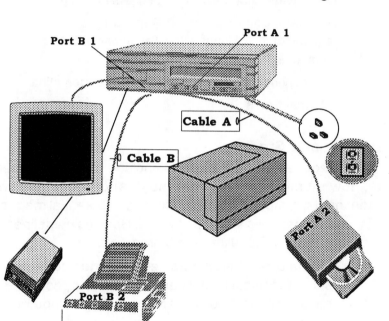

Figure 5.2
Computer System Cables Diagram

The physical inventory should include all input, processing and output devices; including the cables and cords, as well as computer disks and documentation of every kind. The computer system and related items that could be expected to be entered onto a Property Inventory Report form include those listed below.

- CPU
- Keyboard
- Monitor
- Fax Machines
- Modem
- Cables and
  Connectors
- Tapes
- External Hard Drives
- Document Scanners
- Hardware, Software
  and Instruction Manuals
- Computer Related
  Correspondence
- Informal Notes

- Memory Dial Telephones
- Printer
- Tape Storage Units
- Circuit Boards and
  Other Components
- Optical Discs
- Floppy / Compact Discs
- Cartridges
- Cables Diagram
- Ledgers and Logs
- Repair Bills
- Telephone and Address
  Books
- Other Documentation

Handling and Storage

The requirements for this area include a stable temperature, low humidity, free from dust and other airborne contaminants, removed from any existing or potential magnetic fields, and nonmetallic storage shelves. Specific guidelines for computer evidence handling and storage are:

- No one other than the trained, assigned computer crime technical investigator should stop, commence or interfere with any operating computer equipment.
- Computer evidence should not be stored near magnetic fields. This could alter or destroy the data stored on hard drives or discs. Large stereo speakers and electric motors should not be stored, or used in the area of magnetically stored evidence. The magnetic field, even when they are not in use may be strong enough to damage stored data.
- Computer components that are not in their protective cases and exposed should not be handled

with bare hands to avoid the potential of skin oils contaminating the storage medium. Prior to handling computer components the handler should "ground" his or her body to dissipate static electricity

- Computer evidence should be stored in an area that maintains a temperature between 60 and 90 degrees Fahrenheit. This storage area should be away from heating and cooling ducts that may cause wide fluctuations temperature.
- All computer evidence from a case should be stored together to maintain system integrity and facilitate reassembly of the system in the future.

Computer-related evidence requires special care be taken with respect to handling and the environmental conditions under which the evidence is stored. The primary hazards to diskettes are dust, temperature extremes, electromagnetic interference, liquids and vapors.

Diskettes. Magnetic disks (floppy-diskettes) may be stored horizontally or vertically but they must be protected from compression or sagging. Disk packs should be stored flat on shelves. Care should be taken not to drop, squeeze, or bend the disk, or touch the recording surfaces of the disk.

Diskettes should be transported, handled and stored in hard cover containers. Dust is a major factor in the loss of data on diskettes. Dust particles, smoke and paper particles in the air will deposit particles on the surface of the diskette. Later, when the diskette is examined, the read/write head of the disk drive may scratch the disk surface. This will damage the diskette and contribute to data loss.

Disks should not be stored on or near any magnetic field as this may cause the data on the disk to be erased. Magnetic fields surround many common office equipment including telephones, electric pencil sharpeners, telephone answering machines, and other equipment that has electric motors or electromagnetic coils.

Magnetic disks should be stored at temperatures between 40 and 90 degrees Fahrenheit. At these temperatures the expected storage life for data retention and retrieval is approximately three years. A diskette that has been subjected to a significant difference between indoor and outdoor temperatures should be allowed to sit for 24 hours to equalize with the indoor temperature before being used.

Care should be taken to prevent liquid spills on diskettes, diskette jackets and envelopes. The residue from the spill may damage the surface or contaminate the diskette. Vapors from solvents, adhesives, nail polish and chemicals stored in the Property Control Room may affect the magnetic coating of a diskette.

Hard disks. Hard disks are make of metal and covered with a magnetic recording surface. They are both faster and have greater storage capacities than floppy disks which are also magnetically recorded. For a considerable period of time a hard disk of 20 or 40 megabytes was considered impressively large. Today, a 2 to 3 gigabyte hard drive on a personal computer is not uncommon.

Hard disk drives can be internal, with the mechanism built into the microcomputer, placed into an expansion slot in the computer in the form of a "hard card," or plugged-in externally for portability.

The storage requirements for hard disks are more stringent than those for diskettes. Because of the high rotational speed and the higher data density, hard disks are more susceptible to inadvertent damage or data loss. All the rules for diskettes apply to hard disks. Hard disk drives, and computers with hard disks, should be moved only after the read/write head has been "parked." Some fixed disks have a program that automatically parks the hard disk when the system is turned off. If the investigator or Property Control Officer is not familiar with the specific computer equipment to be moved, the operator's manual should be referred to.

Removable Cartridges. Removable cartridges are essentially hard disks enclosed in a plastic or metal cartridge so that they are portable and removable from their attendant drive mechanisms like floppy disks. Removable cartridges are a poplar variant on hard disks since they combine the speed and storage capacity of the hard disk with the portability of floppy disks.

The storage size of a removable cartridge ranges from 20 megabytes to well over 200 megabytes, with typical sizes currently including 44 megabytes, 88 megabytes, 105, 200, and 270 megabytes. Both the drive mechanisms and the individual cartridges are somewhat expensive, but because these devices are portable and rugged, have fairly large capacities, and can be used as the "disk" in direct-to-disk recording, it is likely that they will eventually be available for audio recording.

Magneto-Optical Cartridges. Magneto-optical cartridges; also referred to as thermo-magneto-optical cartridges, or erasable optical cartridges, are a relatively new form of storage medium. They can presently store either 128 or 230 megabytes per cartridge. Since this technology relies on a combination of magnetic, thermal laser and optical laser technology magneto-optical data are impervious to normal magnetic influences.

Data are stored on the cartridge through the use of a laser that heats small sectors of the cartridge to a temperature of about 300 degrees Fahrenheit. These sectors are then charged with a plus or minus magnetic polarity by an electromagnet. The differences in polarity, which are read by a lower powered laser, constitute the 9s and 1s of the binary code. While the drives are expensive, the cartridges are inexpensive, compact and reliable. Magneto-optical systems are also becoming faster, and in some cases are being used as the primary storage device. As cartridge capacities increase their use in the future will increase also.

Computer printouts. Computer printouts should be stored out of direct sunlight to avoid fading. Printouts should be stored on flat surfaces between computer printout binders. If continuous form computer printouts are to be bursted, a positive page sequence, or numbering should be assured prior to bursting to assure correct page sequences. (SRI, 1989)

Computer Recoveries

If seized software or data files are to be run on the agency's computer, the potential for computer viruses and pirated software should be considered. While the dangers of computer viruses are well known, seized pirated software can be a cause of substantial problems to a computer system. Seized or pirated software may have been accidentally or intentionally contaminated with viruses, or may have been intentionally booby-trapped. Pirated software programs are often incomplete. A missing software component could possibly crash a system, destroy data, and preclude the use of the agencies computer.

Pirated software. The passage of the federal *No Electronic Theft Act* (NET) in December, 1997 amended the copyright law to protect copyrighted works, including computer programs, on web sites. The *Act* clarifies the law to include the infringement of a copyright by reproducing or distributing during any 180 day period, one or more copyrighted works with a total retail value of more than $1,000. The Act provides for monetary fines and five years in prison for felony violations.

Several organizations can provide assistance if software is thought to be pirated. These organizations include:

- Software Publishers Association (SPA). The Association offers telephone, web site and e-mail information sources on pirated software. They can be contacted at 1-800-388-7478, http://www.spa.org, and e-mail at piracy@spa.org.
- Business Software Association. (BSA) This Association has downloadable programs to find licensed and unlicensed software installed on a computer system; http://www.bsa.org.
- Microsoft offers an on-line guide to licensing and software management on the Web and on a toll-free hotline. Web addresses are: http://www.microsoft.com/licenses and http://www.microsoft.com/piracy. The hotline number is 1-800-R-U-Legit.

Locating equipment owners. Recovered stolen computers can be traced to their owners if the computer equipment was reported stolen, or if they appear at a recovered property showing. A third method is examining the files and folders to determine a name, an address or a telephone number that had been stored in a file. If the thief has not reformatted the hard drive there is a potential that a comprehensive file manager or utility program will provide a means of searching directory trees, file lists and ZIP archives. From these "erased" data sources the owner may be identified and the equipment returned.

Computer Forensics

Computer forensics is a speciality that addresses the use of computers as a tool in the commission of criminal offenses, or are the target of the criminal. This includes the discovery, collection, processing, examination and documentation of computer evidence, and the safe storage of electronic evidence. Forensic computer specialists employ traditional investigative methods as well as computer programs, fuzzy logic analysis, encryption, and other electronic tools to discover and preserve computer evidence.

One of the primary goals of computer forensics is to recover information that is related to an investigation and to assist in the prosecution of the criminal. This information may be evidence that a particular computer is stolen or, for example, that an individual engaged in child pornography.

Forensic tools. The tools of the forensic computer specialist include a variety of hardware and software to access, recover, view and document the information present on the storage medium. As computer hardware technology advances, increasingly more sophisticated software programs are necessary to efficiently scan the storage medium and recover information. In the recent past a 500 megabyte (MB) hard drive was considered extremely large. Today, a 1 gigabyte (GB) hard drive is standard on most personal computers, 2 gigabyte hard drives are widely available, and larger capacities will be possible with existing advances in system architecture.

Software serves as the essential tool of the computer forensic investigator. These programs include the various operating systems that may be encountered, various software applications that are commonly used, and software programs that can access operating systems and applications. These include utility, imaging and viewing programs.

Utility programs allow the analyst to go behind what one typically views on a computer screen. Utility programs delve into the sector—hidden—level of information storage where files, slack and unused storage areas can be examined. Scattered sectors of data can be located, and possibly joined together, after they have been deleted by the suspect. Utility programs are used also to circumvent password-protected data, manage files, write-protect hard drives and perform file searches using key words.

Imaging programs are used to replicate, or make mirror images of, the data on a computer system. When the data on a suspect computer a copied to another computer for analysis only the intact and logical files will be copied. This leaves behind a significant amount of data that may be essential to the investigation. An imaging program will make an exact copy of all the physical sectors on the suspect computer disk. After this copy is made available the intact files can be examined and the deleted files can be undeleted and sector searches conducted.

Viewers are the final software tool. Because of the myriad of applications programs available commercially it is impractical for the computer investigator to have available each of these programs. Viewers are used to view the contents of the files and disk sectors that have been recovered previously. An effective viewer program will display the file contents in their native format and allow that data to be printed for closer analysis.

One computer program available to law enforcement, for example, was developed to assist forensic computer specialists to assess laptop and personal computer hard-drives to identify the frequency and identity of Internet Web browsing and a suspect's e-mail activity. This program was developed originally for investigating child pornography cases, but can be used in other crimes involving the Internet. This program, IPFILTER, can be downloaded from the Internet at http://www.secure-data.com.

Audio Recordings

The voice can be used as a weapon in numerous ways, and voice identification evidence may be associated with a number of crimes including: extortion, obscene calls and bomb threats, kidnapping, robbery, murder, and narcotics trafficking. When an unknown speaker has committed a crime and other evidence of identity is sparse, voice identification may become particularly important.

The use of audio recording evidence will become increasingly more important with the further development of new and existing technologies. One author points out in a recent text: "The use of audio recordings as evidence has been and will continue to be greatly affected by the convergence of four important historical trends. The trends include:

> • A steady, society-wide increase both in the number of audio recordings being made and in the variety of situations and contexts in which such recordings are being made, as well as an increase in the variety of evidentury and other legal uses to which such recordings are being put;

> • A progressive relaxation of the evidentury requirements applied to audio recordings for the purposes of authentication and admission;

> • A rapid growth in the power, capabilities, and overall availability of computer-based, digital editing systems that will enable both professionals and laypersons to edit, alter, and even fabricate audio recordings;

> • The beginnings of forensic audio, a new forensic specialty ...." (Gruber, 1995: 10)

The use of audio recording devices for evidentury purposes can be classified in several ways. One classification is the source of the recording; the organization or individual who caused the recording to be made. The source of the recording can be further classified into four broad categories: law enforcement agencies, other governmental agencies, businesses and individuals. Another classification is the time the recording was made in relationship to the original event being investigated. Categories within this classification include: contemporaneous, immediately subsequent and retrospective.

> • Law enforcement agencies

This includes audio recordings made by, or at the direction of, a law enforcement agency as a proactive strategy to investigate a crime. Included also are those audio recordings that have been made and are then seized as evidence.

• Other governmental agencies

This includes recordings that are made in the daily operations of the agency and later are identified as having evidentury potential. An example is the recordings made on a fire department 911 system reporting a bomb incident, a false report of a fire, or other intentional false reporting.

• Corporations and small businesses

These recordings include answering machines and voice-mail recording false reports, bomb and extortion threats, and corporate espionage. Audio recordings are routinely made in the private sector including: hospitals, airlines, security firms, educational institutions, telephone companies, and the entertainment and information industries. Voice mail, digital audio messages in personal electronic "mail boxes" is another source of potential electronic evidence.

• Individuals

Many recordings are made by individuals in a private capacity. The increasing use of audio technology greatly increases the probability that an audio recording of a conversation will be made and that the recording will surface later as evidence. The widespread use of telephone answering machines and voice mail systems sponsored by telephone companies provide a consumer an individual electronic "mailbox". These include threatening telephone messages received and recorded on an answering device, or messages sent by an individual and received by others.

The ability of answering machines to record both sides of a conversation also increases the probability that they may become electronic evidence. These recordings are often made with ordinary cassette tape recorders; with or without the consent of all the parties to the conversation. The use of "high-tech" surveillance equipment by private citizens has increased due to the availability of electronic surveillance devices on the consumer market. Wireless communications devices in use today; portable telephones, cellular telephones, pagers and CB radios, make it possible for anyone with a suitable radio frequency scanner, an audio recording device, and a little knowledge to surreptitiously record personal conversations. (Taylor, 1987)

Law Enforcement Recordings

A growing number of criminal investigations include audio recordings as evidence in criminal cases, in part, because of the federal *Racketeer Influenced and Corrupt Organizations Act* (RICO) and other similar state statues. The increasing use of voice recorders to take statements from victims, witnesses and suspects also increases the probability that audio recordings will be submitted as evidence. Many investigators use a voice recorder when interviewing victims and witnesses but do not have a transcript created unless the transcript later becomes necessary.

Voice recordings also furnish observable proof of the fairness of an interview and the specific questions that were asked and answered. The recording may eliminate the possibility that the witness will claim they did not read a statement they made to the investigator. The most important criterion for admissibility as evidence, however, is that the audio recording accurately reflects the conversation which it purports to record. In a California case the court allowed the audio recordings of conversations with the defendant shortly after an accident. The recording was not admissible for its content, but rather the defendant's pronunciation and manner of delivery. (*People v. Young*, 1983) These common investigative practices require a high degree of care in the handling, storage and security of the audio tapes.

Law enforcement audio recordings may be further characterized as contemporaneous, immediately subsequent, or retrospective recordings.

Contemporaneous recordings. Audio recordings made at the time the original event was actually occurring are referred to as contemporaneous evidence. Contemporaneous evidence is referred to also as "live", "actual", "original", or "real" evidence. While this type of evidence was once relatively rare, the wide spread use of recording devices has made contemporaneous recordings much more common. Examples of contemporaneous audio recordings include in-car audio/camera and electronic eavesdropping.

Immediately subsequent recordings. Recordings made a very short time after the event in question, such as voice recordings made by officers and investigators for field reporting purposes, are included in this category. Because jurors have a strong tendency to believe that audio recordings are "true", as well as a tendency to believe that all assertions in any way supported by such recordings are also true, there is a possibility of allegations of prejudice, unfairness, or distortion associated with such evidence. Objections to the admissibility of the evidence as a result of allegations of fabrication, alteration, or unfair editing of audio evidence may be sustained if the evidence is not properly managed. Consequently, it is not unreasonable to expect that stricter standards will be applied to the admissibility of contemporaneous and immediately subsequent audio recordings as evidence.

Retrospective recordings. Retrospective recordings are those that are made substantially after the events and occurrences that are under investigation. Most of the audio recordings made by police investigators fall into this category. Admissions, confessions, and other relevant after-the-fact statements are considered retrospective recordings.

Seizure and Inventory

The *Biggins* criteria—addressed later in this chapter—are considered guidelines for the introduction of audio evidence in court. One of these criteria is the identification of the relevant speakers on the voice recording. Property inventories of voice recordings should document the identity of the speaker(s), if known. The term "voiceprint" should be avoided in referring to the recording and the term "voicegram" used instead. The safety tabs on the container should be removed to prevent any accidental over-recording. The fact that the tab was removed should be recorded on the Property Inventory Report for future reference as necessary.

The importance of a complete seizure and inventory of audio recordings and related equipment can be realized through a review of the advice given to attorneys in a recent text on electronic evidence:

> "• Gather all information with respect to the purported protocol by which the questioned recording was made. Such information includes environmental details (type of room, number of people present), technical details (type of tape used, power supply used), and operational details (how were record and erase functions, and tape transport functions, used). This is an extremely important step and should never be shortchanged as it provides the essential background information necessary to formulate all other [forensic] analysis decisions and strategies.

> • Obtain all information to date with respect to the chain of custody of the particular audio storage unit on which the recording exists.

> • Determine if attorney, attorney's client, or other witnesses have already listed to recording, and if so, gather all their impressions as to the content and anomalies.

> • Request all maintenance or damage records with respect to audio recorder, peripherals, and accessories.

> • Request all technical manuals, specifications, and other available literature and information from the manufacturer of the tape recorder, and from manufacturers of other peripherals or accessories (for example, microphones) if applicable. If no literature or manuals exist, repair technicians are frequently an excellent source of detailed, valuable information.

> • If defending a recording, gather any testimony and allegations as to illegal acts by witnesses for any side, making all information as complete as possible.

- Obtain preexisting transcript(s) of recording, if available.
- If a copy, not the original, is being examined, obtain all information with respect to the making of that copy.
- Assist attorney in formulating discovery plan to gather more relevant information." (Gruber, *Electronic Evidence*, 1995)

Sealing and Storage of Recordings

Audio recordings that are obtained by means of court ordered electronic surveillance are subject to several statutory requirements relating to the delivery, sealing, and storage of the recordings. Every state has statutory such requirements and the law of one's own state should be consulted for specific requirements. State statutes are modeled essentially upon the federal *Wiretap Act* which may be useful as general guidelines for the handling and storage of electronic surveillance recordings.

The federal *Crime Control Act of 1968* requires that immediately upon expiration of the period of an electronic search warrant, recordings must be delivered to the judge issuing the warrant and sealed at the judge's direction.

Delivery. The purpose of the delivery requirement introduces the concept of judicial control by giving the judge, not the investigating officer, decisions about the storage and access to the originals of the audio recordings pending trial; and thereby avoiding completely secretive surveillance. To avoid the risk of defense allegations of tampering, and the uncertainties of later challenges to their introduction into evidence, courts have required officers to deliver the recordings within a short period after they have been made. This period of time has been interpreted variously by the courts: within a day or two by a federal court, and within ten days after the termination of the surveillance according to Arizona statutes. The New York Court of Appeals held that a delay of two days in the delivery of the tapes resulting from inadequate police procedures was not explained adequately. *(People v. Gallina, 1985)*

The most useful advice on the subject of delayed delivery was offered in the courts decision in *United States v. DePalma,* (1978) wherein the court stated: "In most circumstances ...

procedures should include restricted access to the monitoring area, *records indicating who held custody of the tapes at all times, and storage of the tapes under lock and key pending a judicial order sealing them"*. [emphasis added] A Rhode Island state court has held that sealing [of the tapes] by the officers and opening and resealing by the court [upon delivery] has been expressly sanctioned.

When the police have failed to keep the tapes secure until their delivery to the court, it has the burden of showing that the loss was not intentional, deliberate, or in bad faith, and that earnest efforts were made to find the tapes. *(United States v. Kincaid,* 1983) It has been held that, in addition, the police should be required to show that it has promulgated, enforced, and attempted in good faith to follow rigorous and systematic procedures designed to preserve all discoverable evidence. *(United States v. Bryant,* 1971) This court opinion is further support for the adoption of comprehensive, sound evidence management policies and procedures prevent loss, alteration and physical deterioration of evidence. If loss or inadvertent destruction of evidence does occur, the police agency may be able to demonstrate "good faith" by providing its written policies and procedures to the court.

Sealing. Strict compliance with the sealing provision has been required. It has been ruled that the sealing requirement was not met by the officer's sealing the tapes, and storing them in the police department evidence room, without first presenting the tapes to the issuing judge. *(United States v. Gomez,* 1995.) The sealing requirement does not, however, apply to consensual recordings that not made pursuant to a court order since there is no identifiable judge to direct the sealing.

The presence of the seal, or a satisfactory explanation for its absence, is a prerequisite for the use or disclosure of the contents of the recording. According to the Supreme Court the purpose of the delivery and sealing provision "is to ensure the reliability and integrity of any evidence obtained by means of electronic surveillance" by limiting the opportunity for the government "to tamper with, alter, or edit the conversations that have been recorded". *(United States v. Ojeda Rios,* 1990) Thus, the government has the burden of proving that the integrity of the tapes was not compromised. In this regard, it has been said that the purposes of sealing are to reduce the risk that skillful editors might make undetectable alterations, to establish a chain of custody, and to protect the confidentiality of the tapes. The sealing requirement may serve also to preserve the confidentiality of an ongoing investigation. It has been stated generally that if the government desires to postpone the sealing of the tapes, for whatever reason, it must seek court authority to do so immediately.

Storage. Under state and federal court decisions judges are given a wide latitude in ordering the custody and storage of surveillance records. In one case a state court judge ordered the tapes placed in the custody of the defendant's attorney (*State v. Seigel*, 1971) In another case a federal court judge ordered the tapes sealed and kept by the court clerk. In every instance the tapes should be stored in a location that will protect them from physical deterioration. The Sixth Federal Circuit has prescribed procedures to be followed by district courts in considering storage of audiotapes. These procedures include:

- If the plastic safety tabs are removed from the housing of a recording this information; as well as the identity of the person removing the tab, if known, should be noted on the Property Inventory Report form.
- Any existing scratches, pry marks, tool marks, signs of tampering, or damage to the housing seal should also be recorded on the property inventory to preclude any future allegation that the recording was tampered with, or altered while in police custody.
- Tapes should be sealed individually. Placing unsealed tapes in a cabinet or locker which is then sealed may be insufficient.
- Tapes should be sealed in such a manner that breaking the seal will be detectable.
- A log should be kept to record the movement and transfer of custody of the tapes.

- Access to stored tapes should be allowed only upon court order.
- Sealed recordings should be opened only with prior approval of the court.
- The court order for unsealing tapes should specify procedures and the timing for resealing the tapes.
- If the tapes are unsealed with a court order the prosecution will be required to prove that the unsealing and use of the tapes did not result in alterations or tampering.
- When tapes have been unsealed for a permissible purpose they should be resealed to preserve their integrity.

The federal requirement is that tapes shall be destroyed only on the order of the issuing judge, and in any event shall be retained for a period of 10 years applies only to tapes made on the basis of court ordered wiretaps and not to consensual recordings. Even if interception by a clone pager of numbers transmitted to the pager of a narcotics defendant constituted electronic surveillance, the sealing requirements would not apply because recording the contents of the communications intercepted was not possible.

Chain of Custody

A more stringent chain of custody is required for nonconsensual (surveillance) recordings to comply with federal or state statutory sealing regulations. (*United States v Mendoza*, 1978)

The importance of chain-of-custody of audio surveillance evidence depends upon both the jurisdiction and the specific circumstances of the case. If the court determines that a more stringent chain of custody evidence is necessary, the absence or insufficiency of such a chain of evidence can result in the exclusion of the audio recording. One legal analyst states: "[t]he party offering the tape should be prepared to demonstrate the chain of custody of the tape from the time it was used to the date it is offered in evidence. (Fishman, 1978: 309) Case law has established, however, that "it is not necessary to account for 'each minute' between those dates; it is sufficient to show a chain of custody which establishes the reasonable probability that no tampering occurred. (*Gwynn v State*, 1986). In another case the judge ruled that the chain of custody requirement has been satisfied by the fact that a law enforcement official has been in possession of the recording from the time it was made. It was presumed that police officials properly discharge their duty and do not tamper with evidence. *(United States v McCowan,*1983) It has been recommended that witnesses be present during any examination of tapes by either the defense or the prosecution to maintain an unbroken chain of custody. Fishman states that "police officers be present at all times to preserve the chain of custody and the integrity of the tapes". (Fishman, 1978)

Custody challenges. Any break, or any possible break, in the chain of custody of a recording may subject the recording to more rigorous defense challenges and, if the accuracy and authenticity of a recording is challenged, the chain of custody criterion may take on a larger role in the issue of admissibility of the evidence. [Accuracy is defined as signifying that a "recording has not been altered, distorted, or changed, and that aside from problems of inaudibility, the recording in fact contains what was said".] As a court wrote in one case, "When a colorable attack is made as to a tape's authenticity and accuracy, the burden on those issues shifts to the party offering the tape, and the better rule requires that party to prove the chain of custody. Moreover, not only is a strong showing as to chain of custody the "most effective method of demonstrating that a tape is the original recording," but in case the original recording "has been lost through no fault of the party offering the tape, a previously recorded duplicate may be introduced so long as the custody and integrity of the duplicate is properly established." (*United States v. Starks*, 1975)

Incomplete chain of custody. An incomplete chain of custody, or an inability to show that the recording in question was properly 'preserved' since the time of its making or discovery, suggest the existence of an opportunity to falsify the recording.

Although the presence of an unbroken chain of custody is today not typically a strict requirement for admissibility, its absence helps to defeat the presumption of "official regularity" and increases the probability that the evidence may be ruled inadmissible.

Transfer of custody. The safest method for transferring custody of electronic evidence; one that assures the chain of custody and the integrity of the physical evidence itself, is the personal delivery of the evidence to the other party. This includes placing the recording in its case and packaging it in three inches of packing material on all sides. When express shipping services are used specific instructions should be given to avoid magnetic fields. Forensic audio experts state that the United States Postal Service should not be used to transmit recordings. If the Postal Service must be used the package should be sent Registered Mail.

Audio Forensics

Audio forensics software enables criminal investigators to engage in sound editing and is commonly available. This technology allows the investigator to suppress undesirable signals in recordings; whether generated by electrical equipment, machinery, office or traffic noises, or other background noise sources. This software "cleans-up" low level background noise that may obscure the recorded evidence, or that causes distractions to the listener. One software program analyzes a portion of the recording that has no source material—silence—and creates a noise-print based upon that portion of the recording. The software is then able to distinguish between "noisy" and "clean" signals to eliminate the unwanted signals. According to the software vendor the "unwanted noise is eliminated with *minimal effect* on the source material". [emphasis added]

A consideration associated with this "clean-up" is that the recording has been modified; despite the "minimal effect" claimed. The evidence, therefore, is not in the same condition as when it was originally recorded, or when it came into police custody and may raise questions regarding the accuracy of the recording.

Identification of Speakers

One of the major purposes for making, or seizing evidentury audio recordings is to identify the person(s) speaking. Persons of the same sex have voices that are neither aurally, nor spectrographically similar. Obtaining appropriate exemplars requires finding person of the same sex, age, and size who also possess similar voice characteristics in terms of pitch, accent, and socioeconomic class. Ideally, voice spectrograms should be created from a number of people whose voices are similar to the voice of the suspect. These spectrograms are then evaluated and only reasonably close spectrograms become part of any voice lineup. The process requires that someone who is familiar with speech and acoustic phonetics, The individual also has to have a solid understanding of the difficulties with, and the purposes behind, creating a voicegram voice lineup. The cost to create an effective voice lineup can easily exceed several thousand dollars.

Speech exemplars. Speech exemplars are an audio recording speech sample used in performing an aural, or spectrographic voice comparison. There is generally an unknown exemplar; a previously recorded audio recording; such as an answering machine message, or a 911 call, and the speaker's identity is unknown. One or more known exemplars may be taken from the individual suspected of having made the unknown exemplar. If a voice lineup is used, 36 additional known exemplars may be taken from other individuals whose voices sound similar to the suspect's voice. Legal requirements associated with the taking of known exemplars from suspects are fairly well-settled. The U.S. Supreme Court has rejected conclusively all objections to a court order compelling the production of voice exemplars as violating the Fourth and Fifth Amendments. (United States v Dionisio, 1973)

Voice lineups. One use of audio recordings is a voice lineup. A "voice lineup" occurs when the examiner is presented with more than one known exemplar (voice), or, more precisely, when known exemplars are produced by both the suspect and at least one other person whose voice is not the voice recorded on the unknown exemplar.

Closed and open lineups. In a "closed" voice lineup, the examiner knows that the suspect's known exemplar is definitely included in the group of exemplars with which he or she has been presented. In an "open" voice lineup the examiner does not know, with certainty, whether the suspect's voice exemplar is included.

A modified form of open voice lineup, known as a "sequential" voice lineup, is considered preferable for voice identification protocols. This method forces the forensic audio examiner to consider more than just a single known exemplar produced by the suspect. A well-executed voice lineup attempts to reduce the possibility of detrimental effects that may be caused by examiner bias. The examiner is informed that any specific voice exemplar may have been produced by a person who is not a suspect. This is done to eliminate the possibility that an examiner may, consciously or unconsciously, make inferences about the likelihood that the known voice is the same as the unknown voice.

Introduction of Audio Evidence

The usual way of laying a foundation for the introduction of evidence at trial and the playing of a recording is to call one of the participants, or a monitor, to testify that the conversation was recorded accurately. The term "foundation" refers to the preliminary questions asked of a witness in order to establish the admissibility of evidence.

A federal court wrote in a major case ruling: "... [R]equirements may justifiably be imposed on the party seeking to introduce sound recording into evidence only when the party introducing it carries its burden of going forward with foundation evidence demonstrating that the recording as played is an accurate reproduction of relevant sounds previously audited by a witness. As a general rule... [the foundation] requires the prosecution to go forward with respect to the *competency of the operator, the fidelity of the recording equipment, the absence of material deletions, additions, or alterations in the relevant portions of the recording, and the identification of the relevant speakers".* [emphasis added] (*United States v. Biggins*, 1977)

The *Biggins* criteria are considered guidelines and not a rigid test. Some of the elements of the *Biggins* criteria that may satisfy the authenticity requirement would include, for example, a person who is in a position to hear a conversation testifies that he made an audio recording of that conversation. Also, that he had listened to the recording and found it to coincide with what he heard the parties say. From this one may infer that the recording device was "capable of taking testimony" and that the "operator of the device was competent."

A nonparticipant, but who overheard the conversation as it occurred; either through physical presence or electronic monitoring, may listen to the recording, identify the relevant voices, and testify to the recording's accuracy. Accuracy of a recording signifies that the recording has not been altered, distorted, or changed and that the recording in fact contains what was said. (Carr, 1991: 7.5b) One procedure that can ensure the accuracy of cassette recordings is to remove the small plastic tabs found on the top of cassettes and microcassettes.

In one criminal prosecution audio recordings of telephone calls to a victim's telephone were admitted as evidence to prove the caller was the kidnapper, as well as other details of the kidnapping. The introduction of the tapes, however, was not necessarily to prove that the caller was the defendant. *(Durns v United States*, 1977).

Forensic audio experts. Case and statutory authority indicate that, the scientific necessity of access to the original recording notwithstanding, it is the discretion of the trial judge as to whether an original recording must be provided for examination since it is generally legally sufficient if only a copy of the recording is provided. ". it was within the trial court's discretion to deny the defense access to the original recording". *(Johnson v State,* 1983)

A strategy suggested for use by defense attorneys to gain access to the original of a recording incorporates three steps:

- Make it clear why and how the evidence is believed to have been falsified,

- A forensic audio expert should explain to the

judge the scientific necessity for examining the original recording,

- The admission into evidence of a copy should be challenged on the grounds of the "best evidence" rule.

Considering the steps above, the proper handling, preservation and chain of custody of a recording can undermine this strategy at the first step.

The willingness of a police agency to release an original recording to a particular forensic audio expert may depend, in part, on the reputation of that expert and any past experience the agency has in dealing with that expert. Consequently, investigators may wish to make inquiries with respect to the expert's professional history when such issues arise.

There are several reasons why a forensic audio expert must have access to the original recording device. Without the original recorder, exemplars of known record events cannot be produced. Such exemplars are at the heart of the waveform analysis of recording event signatures and also play a key role during magnetic development. Without the original recording device, the expert cannot investigate the physical characteristics, and idiosyncrasies, of that recorder and their effect on the questioned recording.

Copying audio tapes. It is not recommended that copies of audio tapes be made on high-speed, less expensive cassette tape decks or "boom boxes". These devices do not produce high quality copies and the added stress from high-speed copying can potentially damage an original recording. After copying, a segment of the copy should be compared directly to the original recording to ensure that the copying process was successful.

Forensic Audio

There are two main reasons why a forensic audio expert must have access to the original recording device.

1. Without the original recorder, exemplars of known record events cannot be produced. Such exemplars are at the heart of the waveform analysis of record event signatures and also play

a key role during magnetic development.

2. Without the original recorder, the expert cannot investigate the physical characteristics and idiosyncrasies of that recorder and their effect, if any, on the questioned recording.

Handling procedures. Officers be present at all times to preserve the chain of custody and the integrity of the tape.

Audio Recorder Checklist

In order to ensure the admissibility of audio evidence in court routine maintenance procedures must be periodically conducted on the recording devices. In some police agencies the Property Control Officer is responsible for maintaining such equipment. In other agencies, while this responsibility may have been assigned to someone else, the Property Control Officer should have a basic familiarity with these requirements.

If a police agency has more than one audio recorder, these routine procedures should be applied to each machine.

- The audio recorder is generally clean, well-maintained, properly functioning and safely stored.

- The audio recorder's record and erase heads have been properly cleaned on a regular schedule in accordance with the manufacturer's recommendations (if any)

- The entire machine has been lubricated, calibrated, and otherwise maintained according to the manufacturer's recommendations (if any)

- All functions on the audio recorder (rewind, fast forward, stop, pause, record, voice activation, etc.) have been tested on a regular (although perhaps infrequent) basis

- All accessory equipment (microphones, surveillance equipment, etc.) has been regularly maintained, tested and safely stored.

- Each audio recorder and piece of accessory equipment has been permanently labeled and identified for record-keeping, admissibility, and storage purposes.

Video Recordings

Video recordings, in general, have a much greater potential of uses than audio recordings. Studies indicate that most people remember up to 87% of information that they hear and see at the same time. Only 10% of the same information is retained if it is presented orally, without visual illustrations. (Sekuler, 1990)

The term "video recording" describes a recording that primarily, or solely, focuses on visual rather than aural (sound) information. The term "video recording" generally, but not always, refers to both the visual and aural components; the visual picture as well as the spoken word. It is essentially nothing more than a motion picture synchronized with a sound recording. Video recordings are classified in the same manner as are audio recordings: contemporaneous, immediately subsequent, or retrospective recordings. It should be recognized that video recordings that contain audio, as well as visual, information are subject to the considerations presented in both the video and audio recordings sections in this chapter.

Video recordings have numerous potential and actual uses in law enforcement. These uses include views of crime or accident scenes immediately after the event ("immediately subsequent recording"), the reenactment or reconstruction of crimes and traffic accidents (retrospective recordings), the condition of real property, an individual's physical or medical condition, and surveillances (contemporaneous recordings). Other potential uses include children's testimony in child abuse cases, the description and condition of a crime victim's body, admissions and confessions, intoxicated drivers, lineups, booking procedures, crime reenactments by a suspect, sexually explicit recordings, unruly crowds or strikes (mob action), and violation of restraining orders, or orders of protection in domestic cases.

The case law with respect to surveillance recordings has frequently commented on the poor quality of video evidence due to the use of inexpensive video recording equipment, or the improper placement of surveillance cameras. Recommended procedures for improving video evidence include:

- If only a video recording—no audio—is desired, a miniature phone plug can be inserted in the external microphone input jack on the camcorder. This will prevent the recording of sounds and conversations at the crime scene.

- After video recording has been completed, the break-away tab on the cassette should be removed to prevent anyone from recording over the tape and destroying the evidence.

- A backup copy of the recording should be made immediately and marked clearly "COPY".

- The original of the recording, marked ORIGINAL, should be entered into the evidence control system and not be viewed again until it is entered into evidence at trial.

- The backup copy should be used to review the video evidence that has been collected. If any mishap occurs the original recording will be available.

(Pointer, 1997)

Video Recordings and Children

Video recording, or closed-circuit television systems, are increasingly being used to take statements from children who are witnesses to, or victims of crimes, abuse, or neglect. A majority of states provide by statute for the testimony of a child to be taken by means of a video recording, by closed-circuit television or from another room, in appropriate circumstances (for example, when the child is the victim of physical or sexual abuse).

State statues vary considerably as to the ages of the children involved, the types of investigative proceedings in which they are applicable, whether a child may be compelled to testify later at trial, and the presence of the defendant.

The U.S. Supreme Court held that if a trial court makes a case-specific finding of necessity [for video recording], the Sixth Amendment's confrontation clause does not prohibit the use of a closed-circuit television system for receiving testimony from an alleged child abuse victim. Justice O'Connor pointed out that the majority of states allow videotaped testimony of child abuse victims, that almost half of the states allow the use of one-way, closed-circuit television, and approximately one dozen states allow the use of two-way, closed-circuit testimony in such cases. *(Maryland v. Craig*, 1990)

Video E-Mail

The evidentury implications of video mail transmissions should not be underestimated. Video e-mail transmissions may be recorded, or saved for long-term storage. If unsecured transmission channels are used, it may be possible to intercept privileged, or otherwise important messages. This same technique can be applied to communications by fax. It is likely that, in the future, a substantial amount of video evidence will begin as video mail. As police investigators begin thinking of video mail as a potential source of electronic evidence, the property control function must begin planning for the handling and storage of these recordings.

Document Conferencing

Documents can be viewed on computer screens and exchanged electronically through document conferencing. Current systems allow those at each end of a call to annotate and exchange documents, either through the use of keyboard commands, a mouse, or a light pen. The document actively being worked on is typically displayed in a window on the computer screen. It is possible at any point, to send documents that are being worked on to a distant fax machine.

Whiteboards present a greater level of collaborative work. Electronic whiteboards resemble commonplace wall-mounted whiteboards. When information is written on the whiteboard, however, it can be seen simultaneously on another whiteboard, or on a computer screen at a distant site. With some advanced systems, it is possible to display still video images in a window on the board and to annotate the displayed images with a wireless light pen. These types of electronic documents may be saved to a computer file and, therefore, potentially become electronic evidence.

Contemporaneous Video

Contemporaneous photographic video evidence is a record of the actual facts, or original events and occurrences in controversy. Because this is substantial evidence of what occurred at the time of the event, this type of evidence may come under more rigorous attack by defense attorneys.

In the case of immediately subsequent photographic video evidence, it is an accurate record of facts, events, occurrences, or statements that bears directly on the controversy in the case and is, therefore, substantial and relevant.

In the case of retrospective photographic video evidence, it is a substantive portrayal. For example, a video confession, or the reconstruction of relevant and essential facts, events, or statements.

Anticipated contemporaneous video evidence, verification of what has been recorded by a surveillance camera, can proceed under the "silent witness" theory if no eyewitness is available and can take place in any number of ways sufficient to demonstrate the integrity of the video evidence. The investigator must, however, know what is expected of them as testimony.

The single most important factor necessary to satisfy the authentication requirement is the testimony of a witness that what is depicted in the video recording is a fair and accurate portrayal of what the proponent claims it to be. The foundation for gaining admission of video tapes into evidence hinges on testimony that the video represents a fair and accurate portrayal of the event in question.

Photographic Evidence Theories

Pictorial communication theory. The "Pictorial Communication" theory of photographic evidence considered visual evidence, including video recordings, to be merely illustrative or corroborative, and not substantive. That is, photographic evidence did not prove the issue in question but only supported other direct evidence introduced at trial.

Silent witness theory. Under the newer and rapidly gaining acceptance "silent witness" theory, video evidence may be

considered to be substantive, and therefore, much more important. An example of the application of the "silent witness" theory
is a surveillance camera video recording which is admissible as
probative evidence; rather than simply illustrative evidence that
supports a witnesses oral testimony.

Contemporaneous video evidence, recorded by a surveillance camera, can proceed under the Òsilent witnessÓ theory
if no eyewitness to the event is available and admissibility can
be proven in any number of ways sufficient to demonstrate the
integrity of the video evidence.

An example of the application of the silent witness theory
applied to video evidence as both contemporaneous and substantive evidence is the case below. (See for example *United
States v Bynum,* 1978)

> Videotapes of union members' conduct in viola-
> tion of a restraining order issued against the union
> were admissible as substantive evidence of the mem-
> bers' misconduct under the *silent witness theory of
> admissibility*, even though the employer's witnesses
> had not personally witnessed the events because the
> employer showed that its video camera system which
> taped the events was reliable, and thus the *tapes
> spoke for themselves.* [emphasis added] *(Midland
> Steel Products Co. v International Union,* Ohio, 1991*).*

More jurisdictions are expected to adopt the "silent witness"
theory in the future and police investigators must know what is
expected of them in terms of court testimony. It has been said
that the single most important factor necessary to satisfy the
authentication requirement for the introduction of video recordings is the testimony of a witness that what is recorded on the
video recording is a fair and accurate portrayal of the events. In
this context, the immediate sealing of video recordings, and
longer-term chain of custody of the video camera, may be
important issues. One legal scholar argues for stricter criteria for
the admission of video evidence: "Given the potential to falsify
video evidence using various digital systems ... evidence should
be evaluated with respect to the likelihood of technical image
alteration and manipulation". (Gruber, 1995: 381). This state-

ment reflects the quality control issues related to electronic evidence that were presented at the beginning of this chapter.

Video Evidence

When deciding whether to use or create video evidence, the investigator should consider the following advantages and disadvantages.

Advantages

- Extremely powerful, persuasive, and potentially stimulating nature of video evidence;
- Can be one of the most important items of evidence in a case
- Has positive effect on most jurors' attention span, retention capabilities and comprehension;
- Greatly improves means by which accuracy of detailed visual and aural information can be directly communicated to a judge or jury;
- Can communicate evidentury information that cannot be communicated in any other way;
- Contemporaneous photographic video evidence is a record of the actual facts, or original events and occurrences in controversy;
- Subsequent photographic video evidence is an accurate record of facts, events, occurrences, or statements that bear directly on the controversy in the case and is, therefore, substantial and relevant;
- Retrospective photographic video evidence is a substantive portrayal (e.g., a video deposition), or a reconstruction of relevant essential facts, occurrences, or statements;
- Fulfills expectation by finder-of-fact, whether justified or not, that video evidence is appropriate or expected in a particular case;
- Video stills enable fast, organized access to a virtually unlimited number of imaged documents;
- In the case of video stills, increasingly enables

"treatment" of virtually unlimited number of imaged documents;

• Enables framework around which each item of supporting evidence can be organized, whether photographic, computer-generated, still, or motion.

Disadvantages

• Time and financial costs in preparing video evidence;

• Time and money spent in presenting video evidence;

• Overly polished, "slick" video evidence can have negative impact on jury;

• Poorly produced, poor-quality video evidence can have negative impact on jury;

• On an individual basis, individual jurors may simply dislike video evidence.

There is no particular methodology required to authenticate video evidence. As long as the witness's testimony provides satisfactory proof of the video recording's integrity, strict foundational requirements "are now almost universally rejected as unnecessary." (Scott, 1991)

Video and Audio Components

Lawyers offering, or opposing, video evidence are directed by one text to consider separately the evidence's video and audio components. (Heller, 1990: 305-06). If there is anything peculiar or unusual with respect to either the video or audio component of the recording, a stronger foundation may have to be laid by the prosecution to introduce the recording as evidence in court. From a defense viewpoint a stronger objection to the introduction of the video evidence may be made.

The distinction between the video and audio components of a video recording to be used as evidence, therefore, becomes an important consideration. This distinction, and the evidentury considerations are:

• On every type of video recording format, the audio and video information are recorded as separate and distinct—although linked—electrical signals

- Certain technological functions; such as digital sampling and editing; and the possibility of malicious alteration and outright fabrication that may result from these functions, are recorded in the audio, rather than the video, component
- Potential evidentury objections will most likely attack either the audio or the video component of the recording. During the playback of video evidence to a jury, for example, it may be necessary to exclude segments of either the audio, or the video portions of the recording, but not both. This is accomplished by editing or, much less satisfactorily, turning off the picture or the sound.

Cellular Phone Fraud

Illegal activities associated with cellular telephones and related electronic communication devices make use of several technologies that potentially may be seized and inventoried. These illegal activities include: cellular phone cloning, tumbling, call selling operations and electronic pager cloning. This section briefly addresses the methods and tactics cloners use to commit electronic fraud.

Cloning

Cellular telephone fraud through cloning involves modifying the microchip in a cellular phone so that both the electronic serial number (ESN) and the mobile identification number (MIN) correspond to those from a bona fide cellular phone user. This is analogous to surreptitiously altering the VIN on an automobile--the ESN--and the license plate number--the MIN--to make the automobile appear as if it is identical to the original automobile. Hence, the term "cloning".

Cloners will often carry both a cloned phone and a pager. They will receive calls via the pager and return calls on the cloned phone. The charges for telephone calls made with the cloned phone appear on the monthly statement of the bona fide customer resulting in a fraud.

Cellular phone cloning operations make extensive use of electronic devices to determine the ESN and MIN of innocent victims' cellular phones. These electronic devices include the cloned cellular telephone, pagers, laptop computers, ESN readers and modified radio frequency scanners. The scanners are often modified to make possible a cable connection to a laptop computer. This connection allows ESN and MIN numbers obtained via the scanner to be entered directly into a computer data file rather than manual data entry. Therefore, cellular phones seized with computers is indicative of a cellular phone cloning operation. Because these devices are used to perpetrate the fraud they are contraband and may seized as evidence.

Tumbling

This method uses counterfeit chips in a legitimate, or stolen cellular phone. The phone.s internal logic system matches an MIN programmed by the fraudulent user with an ESN. The "tumbled" phone thereafter appears to be continually making its first call. Tumbling operations are most effective if the calls are placed by a "roaming" phone, or in those geographic locations where the communications carrier uses "post-call validation". This type of fraud may involve the use of phones that were stolen from some distant location.

Call Selling Operations

These are operations and locations at which customers used cloned, and often stolen cellular phones, to place long distance and international phone calls of an unlimited duration for a flat fee. Many of these operations are located in apartments, in automobiles, and many otherwise legitimate locations.

Fraudulent cellular services are often associated with other criminal enterprises such as drug trafficking and money laundering operations. If the investigator "recalls" the last number dialed on a cloned phone there is a possibility the investigator will identify another criminal.

Pager Cloning

A cloned pager is a device that intercepts numbers transmitted to another pager from various telephones. The interception of encrypted messages—such as those directed to personal pagers—is prohibited by the federal *Electronic Communication Privacy Act* (ECPA).

A major east coast news paging company was shut down by federal agents after the owners were indicted on charges of violating the ECPA. The company service is to transmit messages to their fee subscribers with information about news events such as police actions and fires. The federal indictments allege that the company used cloned pagers to intercept pager messages sent to New York City's Chief of Police. These cloned pagers mimicked the pagers carried by police officials. When messages were sent to the Chief the same messages were received on the cloned pagers. The indictments allege that the company then broadcast the pager information to its subscribers as news tips.

The company used scanner-computer equipment to monitor the transmissions of the City's pager service provider to determine what pager identification codes were assigned to various City officials. The indictment alleges that the news paging company then programmed its own pagers with the codes; allowing them to receive messages intended for police officials. While the software is legal to possess, the use of the software to intercept pager transmissions and reuse the transmissions or information is illegal. (Dispatch, Oct, 1997)

Associated Criminal Statutes

The United States Secret Service has jurisdiction for the investigation cellular phone fraud that is in violation of federal statutes. The federal statutes applicable to cellular phone crimes are listed below:

Telephone Disclosure and Dispute Act. The federal *Telephone Disclosure and Dispute Act* makes it illegal to manufacture scanner radios that are capable of receiving frequencies allocated to cellular radio telephony, capable of being readily altered to receive these frequencies, or equipped with decoders that convert digital cellular transmissions to analog voice audio. (Telephone Disclosure ... Act)

Counterfeit Access Device and Computer Fraud and Abuse Act. This Act makes it a federal crime to engage in interstate or foreign commerce, with the intent to defraud, in relationship to:

- Produce, use or traffic in one or more counterfeit devices;
- Possess fifteen or more counterfeit or unauthorized devices;
- Produce, traffic in, control or possess device-making equipment.

(*Counterfeit Access Device ...Act*)

Communications Assistance for Law Enforcement Act. This Act amended the earlier *Counterfeit Access Device ... Act,* §1029, and added the prohibition of the: "use of altered telecommunications instrument, or a scanning receiver, hardware or software, to obtain unauthorized access to telecommunications services for the purpose of defrauding the carrier". (*Counterfeit Access Device ...Act*)

Chapter Notes
Texts and Articles

Anderson, *Tape Recordings As Evidence*, 17 Am Jur POF 1, 1966.

Carr, J., *The Law of Electronic Surveillance*, (Clark Boardman Callaghan, 1991).

Counterfeit Access Device and Computer Fraud and Abuse Act, 18 U.S.C. § 1029

Dispatch Monthly Magazine, "News Pager Shut Down, ECPA Violation Alleged", October, 1997, page 9.

Federal Wiretap Act (18 USCS) § 2518 (8) (a)

Fishman, C., *Wiretapping and Eavesdropping* § 310, n. 17 (1978).

Gianelli and Imwinkellied, *Scientific Evidence*, 2d, (The Mitchie Co., 1985, 1994 Supp.).

Gillmor, Dan, "Decoding positions on encryption policy", Chicago Tribune, § 4, Page 5, January 19, 1998.

Gruber, Jordan, *Electronic Evidence,* (Lawyers Cooperative Publishing, Danvers, MA, 1995).

Laska, Paul, "Computer Crime, Investigations for the Twenty-first Century", *Law Enforcement Technology*, (April, 1997).

Leeds, M., "Desktop Videoconferencing", *MacWorld* 87, (November 1994) p. 115.

McCormick on Evidence, (West Publishing Company, 1984).

No Electronic Theft (NET) Act, H.R. 2265, December, 1997.

Omnibus Crime Control and Safe Streets Act of 1968, Title III.

Owen, J., *Forensic Audio and Video-Theory and Applications*, Audio Eng. Soc., Vol. 36, No. 1/2, 34. (Jan/Feb, 1988).

Pointer, Robert, "Videotaping Tips", *The Daily Hound*, (Lynn Peavey Company, Lenexa, KS, October, 1997), p. 4.

Scott, C, *Photographic Evidence,* 2d Ed § 1297, (West Publishing Company, 1969, 1991 Supp.).

Sekuler, "New Demonstrative Evidence to Help Your Clients," *Lawyers Alert* (August 6, 1990) p 31.

SRI International, *Computer Crime: Criminal Justice Resource Manual,* (United States Department of Justice, 1989). p. 196.

Taylor, L. Jr., *Electronic Surveillance*, F. Watts, 1987.

Telephone Disclosure and Dispute Act, 47 U.S.C. § 302 a. subd. (d).

Tosi, "Voice Identification", in E. Imwinkelllried, *Scientific and Expert Evidence*, 2d ed., (Practicing Law Institute, 1981).

Court Decisions

Bergner v. State, 397 NE2d 1012 (Ind App., 1979).

Brooks v. State, 141 Ga App 725, 234 SE2d 541 (1977).

Daubert v. Merrell Dow Pharmaceuticals Inc, 113 S Ct 2786, 125 L Ed 2d 469, (1993).

Durns v. United States, CA8 Mo, 562 F2d 542, 2 Fed Rules Evid Serv 462, cert. den. Durns v. United States, 434 US 959, 54 L Ed 2d 319, 98 S Ct 490, (1977).

Fisher v. State, 7 Ark App 1, 643 SW2d 571 (1982).

Frye v. United States, 54 App DC 46, 293 F 1013, 34 ALR 145, (1923).

Gwynn v. State, Ala App, 499 So 2d 802, (1986).

Johnson v State, Tex Crim, 650 SW2d 784, reh den, (1983).

Maryland v. Craig, 497 US 836,111 L Ed 2d 666, 110 S Ct. 3157, 1990.

Midland Steel Products Co. v. International Union, United Auto, etc., Local 486, 61 Ohio St 3d 121, 573 NE2d 98, reh den 61 Ohio St 3d 1432, 575 NE2d 219, (1991).

People v. Gallina, 66 N.Y. 2d 52, 495 N.Y.S. 2d 9, 485 N.E. 2d 215, 220, (1985).

People v. Heading, 39 Mich App 126, 197 NW2d 325 (1972).

People v. Young, 224 Cal App 2d 420, 36 Cal Rptr. 6.

Shaw v. State (730 SW2d 826,828, petition for discretionary review ref (Feb 10, 1988) and habeas corpus granted (CA5 Tex) 5 F3d 128, 38 *Fed Rules Evid. Serv.* 343 (Tex App. Houston,14th Dist. 1987).

State ex rel. Lucas v. Moss, 66 ALR3d 630 (Mo, 1973).

State v Cannon, 2 NC App 246, 374 SE2d 604, 609, app dismd, review gr, in part 324 NC 249, 377 SE2d 761 and review den, motion den 324 NC 249, 377 SE2d 757 and revd in part on other grounds, 326 NC 37, 387 SE3d 450 (1988) (videotape admitted after police officer testified to having had exclusive care and custody of video camera since night of robbery).

State v. Seigel, 13 Md. 444, 285 A.2d 671, 685, (1971).

United States v. Biggins, CA5 Fla, 551 F2d 64, 1 Fed Rules Evid Serv 710, (1977).

United States v. Bryant, 142 U.S. App. D.C. 132, 142, 439 F.2d 642, 652, (1971).

United States v. Bynum, CA1 Mass, 567 F2d 1167, (1978).

United States v. DePalma, 461 F. Supp. 800, 827, S.D.N.Y. (1978).

United States v. Dionisio, 410 US 1, 35 L Ed 2d 67, 93 S Ct 764, (1973).

United States v. Gomez, 67 F. 3d 1515, 1523-24, 10th Cir. (1995).

United States v. Kincaid, 712 F.2d 1, 2-3, 1st Cir. (1983).

United States v. McCowan, CA8 Ark, 706 F2d 863, 13 Fed Rules Evid Serv 769 (1983).

United States v. Mendoza, CA5 Tex, 574 F2d 1373, 3 Fed Rules Evid Serv.

United States v. Ojeda Rios, 495 U.S. 257, 263, 110 S. Ct. 1845, 1849 (1990).

United States v. Quinn 18 F.3d 1461, 1465, 9th Cir. (1994).

Wilson v. West Chicago, 6 F.3d 1233, 1238 7th Cir. (1993).

Chapter 6

Handling and Disposal of Property

The handling, transfer and disposal of property occurs under several circumstances. The first of these circumstances is the return of property to the owner. Other transfers may include: transportation or shipment to a crime laboratory, introduction in court or review by prosecuting or defense attorneys, and loan of evidence to another law enforcement agency. Policies and procedures for these activities are necessary to ensure uniformity in the handling, external storage and return of evidence. Other property handling issues involve auctions, appropriation for agency use, and the handling and disposal of hazardous materials.

Preparing Evidence for Laboratory Analysis

The purpose of this section is to address the several considerations in making the decision to package and forward evidence to a crime laboratory. It is not intended to be an exhaustive presentation of marking and packaging procedures. These procedures are more adequately addressed in the procedural guidelines available from the FBI and local crime laboratories.

Two special notes should be kept in mind while reading these considerations. Where it is stated that evidence should be dried before being packaged, the items should be air dried at room temperature. Hastening the drying process with heat or sunlight may damage or alter the evidence. Refrigerated items should be stored at a temperature of approximately 40 degrees Fahrenheit; in most situations they should never be frozen.

Drugs/Controlled Substances

Generally, only those items to be used as the basis to file criminal charges should be submitted to a crime laboratory for analysis. Many crime laboratories have issued specific instructions to law enforcement agencies not to submit syringes and will reject any that are submitted. The physical handling of syringes is governed under OSHA blood-borne pathogens regulations. Any attempt to remove the needle from a syringe; through cutting or breaking, creates the potential for an accidental wound. Syringes, therefore, are generally processed as contraband to be destroyed; not as evidence to be analyzed by the crime laboratory.

Marijuana. Marijuana should be air dried before placing it in a suitable container. Using a plastic bag only encourages the development of mold and, in the case of both marijuana and peyote, may cause decomposition of the evidence. Large amounts of marijuana, in excess of that which can be contained in paper bags, can be stored in burlap sacks. The sacks can be suspended from hooks, or arranged on the floor in a manner that will allow air circulation around the sacks. If marijuana sacks are piled one on top of another they should be inspected and rearranged frequently to prevent heat buildup in the middle of the pile. Drying marijuana may generate enough heat to create spontaneous combustion. These procedures address both the container and air-drying problems.

Water should be removed from water pipes and the pipes air-dried before packaging. Drug evidence should be packaged separately to prevent cross-contamination of the collected samples.

Paint Fragments

Paint is one of the most common types of physical evidence available to be collected. Paint chips should be wrapped in folded paper bindles. Small glass vials with screw caps and cardboard pill boxes with tight fitting lids are also acceptable containers for paint chips. Plastic bags should be avoided if possible. Static electricity causes paint chips to stick to the plastic and makes removal of paint chips difficult. If a plastic container must be used the paint sample should first be placed in a paper packet and then placed into the plastic container.

Tools containing paint traces should be wrapped in paper bags and sealed with evidence tape. Paint samples should be packaged in separate containers and should not be placed under plastic tape. The adhesive on the tape may contaminate the sample and interfere with certain instrumental analyses. Paint samples should not be placed in cotton to protect them during transport. The paint becomes imbedded in the cotton and makes it difficult to separate it from the cotton.

The clothing of suspects or victims will frequently contain microscopic quantities of paint. Clothing should be handled to the minimum extent possible, air-dried if necessary, and each article of clothing wrapped separately in paper or placed in a paper bag.

Glass Fragments

Loose glass fragments should be placed in a sealed paper bindle or plastic bag. Packages should be sealed completely, leaving no holes or open seams through which glass fragments can escape. Glass containers should not be used to package glass fragments.

Automobile Lights

In order to properly conduct and interpret the results of lightbulb filament examinations, it is often necessary for the laboratory technician to review the accident report and any pertinent photographs. Reports and photographs should be submitted to the crime laboratory at the same time as the physical evidence.

Hair and Fiber Evidence

Fibers or objects containing fiber evidence should be air dried before being placed into airtight containers. The surface of the packaging table should be cleaned thoroughly before placing the evidence, or the wrapping paper on the table. This is to prevent contamination of the evidence by foreign fibers or hair. Clothing with fibers or hair attached should be packaged separately in new paper bags or layers of clean wrapping paper. Plastic tape or glue should not come into contact with the evidence while it is being packaged. After the individual packages have been securely wrapped, items from the same person or source should be placed in a larger container for transportation to the crime laboratory.

Documentary Evidence

Questioned documents, handwriting specimens and type-writer exemplars should be enclosed in clear plastic covers. Documents should be preserved in their original condition. This requires that documents not be stapled or affixed with plastic tape to reports.

Arson Debris and Volatile Flammables

A primary concern with arson evidence is the prevention of contamination of volatile flammables. To ensure the integrity of the arson sample it should be placed in an unused, unoiled, wide-mouth, sealed paint can for transportation. Screw-top glass jars and coffee cans may be used if paint cans are not available.

Containers should be filled only one-half to two-thirds full. Containers previously used to hold any volatile flammable, solvent or oil should not be used. Plastic bottles or bags (polyethylene) should not be used since they are permeable to the hydrocarbon vapors of volatile flammables.

Explosive debris evidence such as metal fragments from pipe bombs should be placed in paint cans. Building materials and soil samples should be packaged separately to avoid contamination. Any containers suspected of containing sub-stances initiating an explosion should be placed in a separate package to avoid potential contamination problems.

Blood Samples for DNA Profiling

Blood samples submitted for DNA examination by the Federal Bureau of Investigation (FBI) are subject to several policy restrictions. In general, the FBI will accept such samples from current, violent crimes where appropriate standards for comparison are available. This policy limits analysis for state and local cases to homicide, sexual assault and serious aggra-vated assault cases in which a suspect has been identified. Exceptions are serial homicide/sexual assault cases and sexual assaults on young children.

Blood samples from living or dead subjects should be collected in a red stoppered, preservation-free vacutainer. The blood sample should be stored under refrigeration until it is to be transported to the laboratory. These blood samples should not be frozen.

Body fluid stained evidence submitted for analysis should be completely air-dried before packaging and submitted promptly. These blood samples should be frozen if there will be a delay in submission. (Washington State Patrol, 1993)

Latent Prints

A major concern with latent print evidence is the contamination of the evidence by subsequent handling. A secondary concern is shifting or damage to the object bearing the fingerprints. Items believed to have latent prints should be packaged securely to prevent contamination or damage during transit.

Firearms Evidence

The safe handling of firearms is of paramount importance. Weapons should always be rendered safe prior to handling for examination or packaging. A cocked revolver should be cautiously uncocked using the knurled area on the hammer. The chamber in the firing position should be identified by placing two marks on the cylinder, one on each side of the top strap. Fired and unfired cartridges should be removed from the weapon, noting the location of each in the cylinder, and individually packaged.

Semiautomatics. Semiautomatics should be inspected before handling to determine the status of any manual safety devices. The magazine should then be carefully removed and the chamber checked for a cartridge or casing. The weapon should be packaged with the slide locked to the rear. If this is not possible the slide should be closed with the manual safety device engaged.

Rifles and shotguns. Gun boxes, paper bags or heavy envelopes may be used to package long weapons. Plastic containers should not be used if the weapon is to be examined for latent prints or trace evidence. A firearm should never be unloaded by running the rounds through the action of the weapon. In addition, the weapon should never be cleaned, fired, repaired or modified if it is to be submitted as evidence.

Rifles and shotguns should be unloaded prior to packaging and submission to the laboratory. If the magazine is not removable the weapon should be unloaded in the same manner it would be loaded.

If for some reason a weapon can not be unloaded the packaging should be marked conspicuously to indicate it contains a loaded weapon. The direction of the muzzle should be indicated clearly on the packaging through the use of an arrow. Gummed-back safety stickers shown in Figure 5.1 should be available and be affixed to any package containing a firearm.

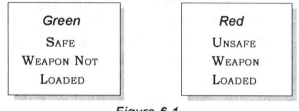

Figure 6.1
Firearms Package Labels

Postal regulations prohibit shipment of explosive materials through the U.S. Mail. Live ammunition and loaded weapons must be delivered personally to a crime laboratory.

Firearms tracing. The Bureau of Alcohol, Tobacco and Firearms (ATF), National tracing Center has the capability of tracing firearms back to their original point of sale upon request of a police agency. This information is helpful to the police agency in identifying suspects, proving ownership, establishing stolen status of a firearm, and providing additional evidence for prosecution. The ATF cannot, however, trace firearms manufactured prior to 1968, many surplus military weapons, imported firearms without the importer's name, and those not having a legible serial number. For additional information the Property Control Officer or investigator should consult the *Firearms and Explosives Tracing Guidebook* available from the ATF.

Bullets

Bullets can be placed in small pill boxes or plastic boxes. Cotton or tissue packing should not be used as these materials may adhere to blood on the surface of the bullet. The wadding and pellets from shotgun shells can be placed into cardboard pill boxes or plastic boxes.

Shoe and Tire Impressions

In most cases track impressions are submitted to the laboratory in the form of plaster casts and photographs. Plaster or photographic impressions, however, must be compared to reference tracks. Attempts to make reference tire tracks in the field, using ink or fingerprint powder, usually provides unusable tracks since the impressions do not pick-up accurately wear marks. This may necessitate the Property Control Officer preparing automobile tires for transportation to a crime laboratory. The tire(s) should be marked for wheel position on the auto prior to their submission to the laboratory.

Soil Samples

Soil samples must be air-dried before packaging. Soil samples and other organic materials should not be placed in plastic bags. After air-drying, the sample can be placed into a paper bag or other similar container, sealed and labeled. Loose soil or sand should be placed on a piece of clean paper which may then be folded to enclose the specimen. When the specimen has dried completely, it should be sealed in an appropriate shipping container and labeled to identify its source.

Toolmark Evidence

Toolmark evidence should be packaged in such a manner so as not to subject it to damage, loss or contamination of trace evidence (paint, soil, metal, glass). If the actual toolmarked item cannot be submitted for analysis a cast or mold of the item can be taken with a special material marketed for this purpose. The completed cast or mold should be placed into a paper or cardboard container and secured. The tool should be secured with soft cotton or tissue and placed into a paper bag. Plastic containers are not suitable for toolmark evidence. Plastic tape should not be used to protect the acting edge of a tool.

Sexual Assault Evidence

The evidence most frequently collected in sexual assault cases includes semen, hairs, fibers and blood. These specimens should be treated as a separate specimens for handling and packaging purposes. It is important that the chain of custody be maintained. This necessitates a policy that evidence should be handled by as few persons as possible and the trail of persons that have handled or kept the evidence be capable of being traced easily.

Particular care should be exercised in the receipt of victim's clothing collected by hospital personnel. In the urgency to provide medical attention to the victim clothing is often placed into plastic bags and given to the investigating officer.

Items should be allowed to air-dry and then be packaged separately in paper bags. Care should be taken not to loose hair or fiber evidence that may be on the clothing. Saliva samples should be taken on filter paper, air dried and placed into a paper envelope.

Entomological Evidence

Forensic entomology is the study and identification of insects associated with corpses to assist in estimating the time of death, or the death site. Carrion insects--those that feed on decaying flesh--form a sequence of arrival associated with each stage of body decay. An identification of the various kinds of insects found at a death scene, and their rates of development, can provide an indication of the time interval since death. The information that these insects can provide, however, is useful only if the insect samples have been collected and packaged properly.

Blow flies are generally the first insect to arrive at a decaying body and are considered the most important insect in establishing the time since death. Both live and preserved insect evidence is essential for this analysis and these samples must be collected, preserved and packaged properly to maintain their evidential value.

Live insects. Approximately fifty fly larvae (maggots) should be kept alive for positive identification.

- These should be packaged in non-airtight containers allowing sufficient space so they do not suffocate;
- Damp paper toweling should be included in the container to prevent drying;
- A label recording the time, date, and location of collection should be affixed to the container;
- If their is to be a delay in forwarding the samples they should be refrigerated;

- If refrigerated, the length of time refrigerated and the refrigerator temperature should be recorded on the label;
- The sample should be sent to the entomologist by overnight mail.

Approximately fifty fly pupae should be collected and kept alive.

- These should be kept dry and placed in non-airtight containers;

Preserved insects. Maggots of all sizes should be killed by placing them in boiling water for one to two minutes immediately after collection to stop their growth.

- This sample should be preserved in a 70 percent ethyl alcohol (ethanol) solution;
- The sample must be packaged and shipped in a leakproof container.

Live adult flies, beetles and beetle larvae should be collected and killed.

- These specimens may be placed directly into ethyl alcohol to kill and preserve them;

Dead adult flies, beetles and insect parts found at the scene should be packaged in a separate, dry container. They should not be placed into alcohol. (Cervenka, 1998)

Labeling containers. Each container should be either labeled with specimen collection information or numbered. If numbered the collection information should be recorded on a separate sheet of paper. Collection information should include:

- The time and date of collection;
- The location of the samples collected--both on the body and at the crime scene area;
- The investigator collecting the sample;
- The case number

Property Disposal

Department policy should be clear that responsibility for the final disposal of property and evidence taken into custody remains with the officer originating the Property Inventory Report. An officer's court related responsibilities includes notifying the Property Control Officer of the final disposal of evidence after the trial is concluded. If property is taken into custody for

---

Property Disposition Tracer

To: Investigating Officer
From: Property Control Officer
Date:

The property listed below was taken into custody by you and is being held in the Property Control Room.

Enter the appropriate status/disposition code next to each item so the property may be reclassified or final disposition can be made.

This Tracer must be returned to the Property Control Officer within five (5) calendar days from the above date.

If not received by that date a second notice will be forwarded to your shift commander.

Complaint Number	Offense Type	Suspect/ Victim	Property Description	Property Control No.	Disposition Code

DISPOSITION CODES:
- Return to Owner (RTO)
- Hold For Investigation (Hold)
- Warrant Outstanding (W/O)
- Destroy (Destroy)
- Court Ordered Disposition (COD); specify type of disposition ordered, judges name and date
- New Case Investigator (Name)
- Other Disposition _____

Figure 6.2
Property Disposition Tracer

safekeeping; the owner is known, the reporting officer should state a specific property release date.

The Property Disposition Tracer, Figure 6.2, is intended to expedite the final disposal of evidence and other property. This form should be completed periodically by the Property Control Officer and a copy sent to the investigating officer. A copy of the form should be filed in a suspense file, by due date, in the Property Control Room to maintain control over disposition of unnecessary evidence and property.

Property Return To Owner

The failure to return property to crime victims promptly is an issue that has received a great deal of attention. Victims' rights advocacy groups have demonstrated that this failure is a major deficiency in many police property control systems.

The President's Task Force on Victims of Crime has stated:

"The victims property belongs to the victim, not the system. Victims repeatedly tell of property ranging from family heirlooms to an invalids television set being held for months or years while the case moves slowly through the courts: in some cases, property has been mislaid or lost. Victims should have their property restored to them at the earliest date possible without compromising the prosecution of the case.

Police should cooperate with local prosecutors to develop procedures in which the prosecutor evaluates the evidentury value of the property, notifies the defense, arranges inspection if necessary, then releases these items to their owners as expeditiously as possible. Departments must devise a system that will notify the victim's family when property has been recovered, where it is being held, when it can be reclaimed, and what documents must be presented when a claim is made. Before items are returned they should be photographed in a manner that clearly identifies the property and will allow substitution of the photograph for the item itself as an exhibit in court." (President's Task Force, 1982)

In many cases the evidence retained in police custody is the tools with which the victim engages in their trade or occupation or a necessity of daily life; a toaster, dinner ware. In other instances the evidence in police custody is an amenity to their relaxation such as stereo components, a VCR or a television set.

The International Association of Chiefs of Police passed unanimously a *Crime Victims Bill of Rights* policy in 1983. The policy states, in part: "Crime victims are entitled: ... To a quick return of stolen or other personal property when no longer needed as evidence." (IACP, 1983)

Owner Notification

Notification letter. Upon conclusion of a court case, and a court-ordered final disposition of evidence, the recovery of lost or stolen property and other similar circumstances, a notification letter should be sent to the property owner requesting they retrieve the property from the police agency. In the case of valuable property the letter should be sent via certified mail, return receipt requested. A sample notification letter is shown in Figure 6.3.

The case information in the letter is important for the prompt retrieval and return of the property when the property owner claims it. The owner is encouraged to have the letter in their possession when claiming property since the notification letter contains all the information necessary for rapid retrieval of the property.

Telephone notification. Telephone notification to property owners is proper when the reporting officer initially takes property into custody. The telephone notification should be entered on the Property Inventory form as a means of documenting the fact that an attempted or actual contact was made with the property owner. This documentation notifies the Property Control Officer that such a contact was made, the officer involved and the date of the telephone contact. Notifications by the Property Control Officer should be primarily by telephone. The exception to this policy is when the property has significant value or when the owner no longer resides at the last known address and attempts are made to determine a forwarding address.

Ms. Mary Smith
123 Main Street
Yourtown, Ohio   Complaint Number:
                         Property Control Number:
Date: Date of Custody:
                         Items:

Dear Ms. Smith:

   A recent audit of our Property Control records shows the Police Department is in possession of property belonging to you.

   Please call the Property Control Officer; (555) 555-1234, and make arrangements to pickup your property.

   Property not picked-up within _ days of the date of this notice will be disposed of in accordance with applicable state laws and department policy.

   Property room business hours are from _ A.M. to _P.M. Monday through Friday. If you must pick up your property after scheduled office hours arrangements can be made at the time of your telephone call.

   Please bring this letter and personal identification with you when you pick up your property.

Sincerely

Property Control Officer

Figure 6.3
Property Owner Notification Letter

Return of Pathogenic Contaminated Items

   When a property owner or representatives insists upon the return of property suspected of being contaminated with pathogens the Property Control Officer should take all necessary precautions to protect himself from the contaminated items and inform the recipient the items may be contaminated. If the recipient wants to take possession of the items having this knowledge, a signed liability waiver statement should be required of the recipient. The signing of this statement should be witnessed by a supervisor and the waiver maintained in the case file. State laws pertaining to hazardous materials should be consulted as well as the department's legal advisor prior to the return of suspected pathogenic contaminated items.

Request for Return of Suspected Pathogenic Contaminated Property

       I hereby request the return of property to me now in the custody of the _____ _____Police Department.

       I have been informed that the property requested may be contaminated with body fluids that contain the HIV, AIDS or Hepatitis virus(es). Understanding this, the potential for possible contamination of my person and /or others, and the potential risk associated with the receipt of this property, I desire to take possession of the property.

       I hereby hold harmless the _____ Police Department, the City of _____, its employees and agents now and in the future of any adverse consequences of any kind associated with the receipt and possession of the requested property.

       I hereby acknowledge receipt of the following items of property now in the custody of the _____ Police Department:

List of specific items of property returned

Recipient's Printed Name: _____

Recipient's Signature: _____Date: ____

Property Custodian: _____ID:_____

Figure 6.4
Return of Contaminated Property

Return of Valuable Property

When valuable property is to be returned to the owner, a notification letter should be sent via U.S. Mail, return receipt requested. Since unclaimed property will eventually be disposed of; destroyed, auctioned or taken-up by administrative or statutory action, the agency should reduce any potential liability to the property owner. This is accomplished by maintaining documentation that the property owner had in fact received notification to retrieve the property. The return receipt notice will fulfill this requirement and should be filed in the appropriate property file for future reference.

Return of Firearms

Positive personal identification should be required upon the return of firearms. The identification source; a drivers license or other photo bearing identification, as well the identity of the person receiving the firearm should be recorded on the property control record. In those states requiring firearm owner's identification or permits, the production of such identification or permit is required before the return of firearms or ammunition. In certain circumstances an inquiry should be made with the National Crime Information Center (NCIC) prior to the return of the firearm.

Many departments have adopted the policy of not returning firearms and ammunition at the same time as a safety and security precaution. If a court order is to return a "firearm" this could be construed as a tacit approval to destroy the ammunition. In no case should a loaded firearm be returned to the owner. A prudent procedure may be to secure a nylon tag through the frame so the cylinder can not be closed, or through the chamber and barrel to deactivate a semiautomatic.

Sample forms for the request and return of firearms in police custody are shown in Figures 6.5 and 6.6 . These forms provide space for collecting sufficient personal information on the requestor to conduct a criminal history background check to determine their eligibility to possess a firearm. These forms should be modified to meet the criteria for possession under a state's laws. The completed forms should be retained indefinitely for future reference purposes.

Request For The Return of Firearm

This form must be completed and submitted to the Police Department's Investigation Division This procedure must be completed prior to the release of a firearm. You will be contacted within 15 days of the date this form is received. If the firearm(s) was seized from another person, you must provide notarized written proof of ownership, or owner permission, to receive the firearm.

Name (Last, First, MI)_____Date Of Birth:_____

Other Names Used: _____

Current Address:_____

Place Of Birth: _____ Soc. Sec. NO. _____

Driver's License Number:_____

Home Telephone Number:_____ Work Number:_____

I hereby certify that the above information provided by me to the _____ Police Department is true, accurate and complete. I understand that the Police Department relies on this information to make a determination as to my legal rights to possess a firearm.

Signature:_____

This section to be completed by the Police Department Investigations Division

CaseNumber:_____

Description of Firearm:
     Make:_____   Model:_____Serial #_____

     Caliber: _____   Handgun: ____Rifle: ____ Shotgun: ___

The owner, or other person entitled to possession is:
     Eligible_____ Ineligible____ to receive and possess a firearm under the laws of this state.

     Comments:

Releasing Officer's Name:_____ BadgeNo.:__ __ Date:_____

Figure 6.5
Request For Return of Firearm

Declaration of Receipt of Firearm

I, _____hereby acknowledge receipt of the above described firearm(s) from the _____ Police Department.

I understand that under State law I may not sell, deliver, or otherwise transfer a firearm or ammunition to anyone I know, or reasonably should know:

Enter ineligibility criteria for possession of firearm under state law.

1. Is under 18 years of age;

2. Is under 21 years of age and has been convicted of a misdemeanor, or has been adjudged delinquent;

3. Has any outstanding felony warrant for arrest;

4. Is a narcotics addict;

5. Was a patient in a mental hospital within the past five (5) years;

6. Is mentally retarded.

Dated this _____ day of _____ 19____ .

_____

Name of Person Receiving Firearm(s)   (Print Legibly)

_____

Signature of Person Receiving Firearm(s)

Figure 6.6
Declaration of Receipt of Firearm

Property Showings

Returning crime victim's property is an opportunity to establish good community relations. The President's Task Force recommended that police agencies: "...devise a system that will notify the victim's family when property has been recovered, where it is being held, ... and what documents ... when a claim is made." (President's Task Force, 1982) Property showings must be planned and conducted, however, according to established procedures to prevent this opportunity from turning into a major problem.

When there is a large recovery of stolen property it is not unusual that property owners will remain unidentified. This may be due to thefts, burglaries and robberies that occurred in other jurisdictions, or unreported crimes in one's own jurisdiction. In order to identify the owners' of such property it may be necessary to conduct a public showing of recovered property.

Publicity and Notifications

It is generally a better practice to plant a newspaper or television news story than to place a public notice of the property recovery. The news story should be timed about ten days before the public showing will be held. Crime victims should be informed to contact the police agency for specific information.

Owners of recovered property known to the police agency should be notified individually and be required to retrieve their property before the public showing. This will reduce the volume of property to be displayed and the number of viewers present at the public showing.

A special viewing for the television news media immediately before the property showing will be an opportunity to display the nature of the recovered property, publicize the arrest and recovery of the property. When crime victims call the police department inquiring about how the property can be reclaimed specific instructions should be available to provide to the caller. These instruction should include:

- The date, time and location of the showing
  - Documentation required: crime report on file with your department, or a copy of the crime report from

another jurisdiction

It should be stressed to the callers that only crime victims that have previously reported their loss to a police agency will be allowed to view the recovered property. This will reduce the number of "lookers" and expedite the process.

- Proof of ownership of the property: receipts with detailed or serialized descriptions, photographs, insurance appraisals, etc.

A count of the number of inquires received from claimants should be kept. This will provide an estimate of the number of people that can be expected to attend the public showing. If a large number of viewers are expected it may be prudent to stagger the viewing times. For example, five viewers may be told to appear on Saturday at 9 AM; another five at 9:15; and another group at 9:30. This will allow for the previewing screening addressed later.

Planning The Showing

The Auction Planning Checklist shown in Figure 5.4 can be used to plan the showing. In addition to the questions contained in the Checklist, consideration should be given to the following points:

- Only those viewers that have reported the loss of property, have a copy of the police report, proof of identity, and proof of ownership should be allowed into the viewing area.

This will reduce the number of viewers to those that are potential claimants. It should be kept in mind that this procedure will require a waiting area commensurate in size with the number of viewers expected.

- If a large number of viewers are expected a Viewers' Pass form should be created.

As the viewers provide the documentary proof outlined above they should be given a Viewers Pass that will allow them access to the actual viewing area. It should be kept in mind that the immediate purpose of the viewing is to distinguish those that can positively identify property and provide proof of ownership from those that may be crime victims but cannot identify property or provide proof of ownership.

Viewing Area

The viewing area must be large enough to display all the recovered property in an orderly and systematic manner. Property identified as originating from other jurisdictions can be separated from property from your own jurisdiction. There should be no visible indications as to its origin. This procedure will, however, allow viewers to be directed to specific areas first.

Viewers should be escorted by an officer into the viewing area. The property should be displayed under secure conditions and viewers should not be allowed to handle any item. Property that is identified should not be released at the time it is identified. This will only slow down the viewing process and add to the workload.

After each viewer has finished their view of the property they should be escorted out of the viewing area through a separate exit. Those that have claimed property as theirs should be informed their claim will be presented to the prosecutor and with prosecutor approval the property will be photographed and returned to them. The standards for photographing evidence should be reviewed to assure that the photos of the property are admissible as evidence.

Property Auctions

Property not returned to the owner, destroyed or appropriated for agency use (where permissible by law) is generally required to be disposed of at public sale. Property identified for auction must have first surpassed the statutory time limit for retention. Auctions of unclaimed property should be conducted as often as required and at least once each year. This policy will keep the Property Control Room clear of unnecessary property making storage and audit easier.

In most jurisdictions state law requires property to be sold at public sale to the highest bidder and the net proceeds deposited in the jurisdiction's general revenue or some other specified fund.

Preparation for Auction

The steps taken in preparation of the auction will determine the ease by which the auction proceeds. The initial step is the identification of property to be included in the auction. If the property storage system presented in an earlier chapter is adopted, property to be auctioned will be located easily in the Safekeeping and Lost and Found property storage bins.

Identification of auction property. Property designated for auction should be placed in a pre-designated, secure location awaiting the time of auction. Property control tags should not be removed from the property at this time. Removal of any property identification tags will frustrate future attempts to relate the property back to property inventory records. Chain of custody and property disposition entries should not be made at this time either. Final property dispositions should be recorded only after the property has, in fact, been disposed of at auction. This procedure will ensure the actual current status of the property will be reflected in the agency's official property records.

Property not sold at auction as scheduled should be held for the next auction. Statutory requirements should be reviewed to determine if the property need be again described in the public notice of auction. Property not sold at a second auction should be identified as "non-salvageable" and disposed of by destruction.

Record of property to be auctioned. The inventory of property items to be offered at auction should be compiled into an Auction Inventory, Figure 6.7. The Request For Property Disposition form in a later chapter may be used for this purpose. The inventory should consist of a sequential auction number, a description of the property, the case number and property control number.

Property should be identified by serial number and general description, or a complete description if it is unserialized. Entries on the inventory should be in sequential order by auction and case number. This sequencing of entries will allow any property item to be located quickly in the future. Since all three of these numbers are in sequential order, a property lookup can be accomplished by either auction, case, or property control number.

Space should be reserved on the Auction Inventory form for use during the auction. A copy of the inventory, with space allocated for auction entries is convenient to record the bidder's identification number and selling price.

Constructing the property inventory in this manner allows it to be used for two purposes; an inventory of property to be auctioned and the property that is actually sold at the auction. The Auction Inventory should be directed to the chief executive officer of the agency for final approval of the auction and the disposition of the property.

Auction Inventory				
Auction Number	Description	Case Number	Property Control Number	Bidder # Bid ($)

Figure 6.7
Auction Inventory

Auction approval. Upon receipt of the Request for Property Disposition by the agency chief executive, a Property Disposal Order—By Auction (see Chapter 6), should be prepared and directed to the Property Control Officer. The Property Disposal Order references the original request by date and directs the Property Control Officer to proceed with the next steps in the auction process.

Publication of legal notice. Statutory requirements generally require publication of a notice of auction in a newspaper of general circulation in the jurisdiction at least ten days prior to the auction. Publication serves as the official public notification of the auction. This notice must contain a general description of the property to be auctioned and the date, time and place of the auction. Additional requirements may include the authority for the auction, method and time of payment for purchases, and whether it is a reserve or non-reserve auction.

NOTICE OF POLICE AUCTION
UNCLAIMED PROPERTY

SEPTEMBER 24, 199X

Assorted unclaimed property in the possession of the Yourtown Police Department will be sold at auction on September 24, 199X, at 10:00 AM at the Yourtown Police Department, 1234 Main Street, Yourtown, MI

These items may be inspected one hour prior to the start of the auction. Items will be sold individually and in lots. Purchased items must be removed from the premises on the day of the auction. A ITEMS MUST BE PAID FOR IN CASH AT THE TIME OF THE PURCHASE. NO CHECKS OR DEPOSITS ARE ACCEPTED. For further information contact Property Control Officer at (313) 555-5555

By Order of John B. Law, Chief of Police

Figure 6.8
Notice Of Public Auction

The removal of purchased items and payment conditions in the Notice should be restated at the start of the auction. Depending upon the size of the jurisdiction, and the amount of property to be auctioned, it may be advantageous to post "Notice of Auction" posters and distribute flyers in various public locations.

In-House Versus Professional Auctioneers

Often a decision must be made to conduct auctions by the agency, using agency personnel and other resources, or employ a professional auctioneer. A cost/benefit analysis is helpful in analyzing the two alternatives. To conduct such an analysis one must first collect or estimate the time and effort required to conduct the auction in-house. If auctions are conducted during evening or weekend hours to attract a sufficient number of buyers the workhour estimates above should be calculated at the agency's overtime rate; generally time and a half.

Auction Planning Checklist / Cost Estimator

Site Planning

❏ Is an adequate site available for the auction

❏ If an outdoor auction is planned, have provisions been made to hold the auction indoors in case of inclement weather

❏ Is adequate parking available for those attending the auction

❏ Are sufficient public toilet facilities available

❏ Can adequate security be maintained at entrances, exits, parking facilities and within the auction area

Cost Estimate

Workhours estimated to place auction tags on property _____

Workhours estimated to set-up auction site _____

Workhours required to register potential bidders _____

Number of security personnel and workhours at the auction _____

Number of cashiers and workhours at the auction site _____

Number of runners and workhours at the auction site _____

Estimated workhours required to complete accounting and _____ other administrative paperwork after auction

Workhours required to pack and transport property to auction site _____

Workhours required to repack and transport unauctioned property _____ back to the property storage area

Total Estimated Workhours _____

Total Estimated Auction Costs* _____

* Workhours X Average Hourly Rate X Overtime Rate = Cost

Figure 6.9
In-House Auction Checklist

Professional Auctioneers

Professional auctioneers generally take a percentage of the gross proceeds of an auction as their profit and to cover expenses. Questions that should be asked of potential auctioneers are included in the Professional Auctioneer Checklist.

Professional Auctioneer Checklist		
	Department	Auctioneer
• Who is responsible for transporting the items to the auction site	☐	☐
• Is department or auctioneer responsible for tagging the property with an auction item number	☐	☐
• Who is responsible for providing adequate security during the preauction display and during the auction	☐	☐
• Who will transport unsold property back to the department property storage area(s)	☐	☐
	Yes	No
• Does the auctioneer provide detailed accounting reports to the department upon completion of the auction	☐	☐
• Does the auctioneer account for unsold property and dispose of unsaleables after the auction	☐	☐

Figure 6.10
Professional Auctioneer Checklist

During the pre-auction display a member of the public may recognize property that was previously lost or stolen. Officers handling the auction should be made aware of the potential for these situations and be prepared to handle citizens' demands for the return of their property.

A pre-auction display is generally allowed to permit the public to inspect the property to be offered at auction. The purpose of this display is two-fold; to allow potential bidders to inspect items prior to bidding and permit those that have lost property to inspect the items offered for sale.

It is generally accepted that the rightful owner to property has the right of title and possession any time until the property is actually sold. To avoid confusion, and to respect the rights of the person claiming title to the property, the property should be removed from the auction and set aside in a secure location. Upon conclusion of the auction the person claiming ownership must provide documentation that will substantiate their claim of ownership.

The name, address and telephone number of each potential bidder should be recorded and a Bidder's Identification Number assigned. This number is displayed on a card, approximately 8 1/2 inches by 5 inches, is used to identify the bidder during the auction process.

Appropriation for Agency Use

Where state statute or competent authority allows law enforcement agencies to appropriate property for agency use, the appropriation process should be documented thoroughly. The Request For Property Disposition form is intended to be used for this purpose.

Documentation should include a complete description of the property, including serial number, make and model, style, color and other identifiers, the reason for the need to appropriate the property and the unit or section to which the property is to be transferred. The property should also be entered on the agency's Permanent Property Inventory and inventory labels applied.

Upon transfer to the appropriating section or unit a chain of custody entry should be initiated by the Property Control Officer and signed by the commander of the unit or section receiving the property. A final property disposition, "Appropriated For Agency Use", is recorded on all applicable property control records.

Firearms

All firearms appropriated for agency use should first be verified for current status through NCIC. This verification should be conducted in addition to the NCIC check conducted when the firearm first came into the possession of the law enforcement agency. This second check is to ensure the firearm was not reported stolen subsequent to the time it was originally entered into the property control system.

National Firearms Act. Certain firearms and destructive devices come within the purview of the National Firearms Act. If any of the firearms or devices come into the possession a police agency through seizure or abandonment, and are to be retained by the police agency for official use, they must be registered with the Bureau of Alcohol, Tobacco and Firearms (ATF). (National Firearms Act) These firearms include:

- Sawed-off shotgun

    Barrel less than 18 inches in length, or overall length less than 26 inches.

- Sawed-off rifle

    Barrel less than 16 inches in length, or overall length less than 26 inches.

- Machine guns: including the frame or receiver, any combination of parts intended to convert a weapon to a machine gun and, any combination of parts from which a machine gun can be assembled

- Silencers

    Any device that will silence or muzzle the noise of a firearm discharge

- Destructive devices: including any explosive, incendiary, or poison gas; grenade, rocket, mine or similar device

These firearms and devices must be registered with the ATF by the police agency. An ATF *Form 10* is available for this purpose. Subsequent disposition of these firearms and devices can be only to another bonafide law enforcement agency or they must be destroyed.

Managing Seized Assets

Police agencies periodically seize the physical assets of criminals under various state and federal laws. These assets include real estate, vehicles, boats, aircraft, currency, jewelry and other valuables. Seizures are often effected without adequate planning for the continuing management of the assets while awaiting the order of forfeiture, or for the final disposal of the seized property.

Planning For Property Seizures

Packing and transportation. In the case of a seizure of large quantities of property, a commercial moving company may be the most economical method of packing and transporting the seized property. If real estate is seized there may be a problem with the furniture and other personal property located on the property. If the personal property is not subject to seizure and forfeiture the defendant/owner should be notified that they are responsible for moving the personal property. If this is not done the police agency may find that it has assumed the responsibility to properly secure the personal property. In these instances the defendant/owner should be advised, in writing, that a failure to remove the property within thirty days will be considered an abandonment of the personal property and subject it to sale by the police agency.

Storage and appraisal. Pre-seizure planning is important for the efficient management and storage of the assets seized. Issues that should be considered include a thorough inventory of the property, storage space requirements, storage location and adequate physical security. Storage fees must be considered also since they become the responsibility of the seizing agency. In most situations, animals and furniture may be too expensive to maintain or store. Consideration should also be given to an appraisal of the fair market value of the property in order to maximize the income from the eventual sale of the property.

Managing Seized Assets

Jewelry. The wholesale value of jewelry is generally 25 - 50 percent less than the retail sales price. Jewelry with a significant market value should be stored in bank vault ideally, or minimally, in double-secure storage in the property control room.

Aircraft. Seized aircraft can be expensive to maintain properly. Factors that should be considered in the planning and management of aircraft include the amount of the owner's equity and any liens on the title. Engine and airframe log books are important documentation to acquire and provide later to a potential purchaser. Aircraft repair facilities in possession of an aircraft may retain the log books until they are paid for any outstanding repair or storage charges. The amount of unpaid charges by the owner should be considered in the decision to seize and forfeit any aircraft. The Federal Aviation Administration (FAA) can provide the history of an aircraft from the time it was manufactured.

Boats. Boats and other types of watercraft should be placed in dry dock storage pending forfeiture and sale. This is to increase security and reduce the potential of damage while the boat is moored at a dock or buoy. In colder climates the boat should be winterized to prevent damage from freezing water in the engine or the hull.

Vehicles. Police agencies too often are improperly storing seized vehicles and finding themselves subjected to civil lawsuits for conversion or trespass. Vehicles must be stored in a secure location and in a manner that will preserve the value of the vehicle. It is not unheard of for the individual from whom the vehicle was seized to "steal" the vehicle, or strip it of accessories while it is in police storage.

The lack of adequate secure storage of vehicles creates a losing situation for the police agency in many respects:

- If the forfeiture is not perfected, and the vehicle is ordered returned to the owner, the police agency may have to reimburse the owner for loss or damage that the owner, or others, caused.
- If the vehicle is forfeited the agency will not realize the income that it otherwise may have gained from the sale.
- If the vehicle is forfeited and the vehicle has, or had, some potential use to the agency the police agency will have to expend the money from its budget to place the vehicle in operating condition.

The innocent lienholder on any property is generally protected to the monetary value of their recorded lien. Since the lienholder has an economic interest in the vehicle it is in their interest also that the vehicle is stored in a secure location and in a manner that maintains its value. When dealing with lienholder therefore, it may be advantageous to advise the lienholder that they owe the police agency repossession, towing and storage charges. This may cause them to want the vehicle returned for sale as soon as possible due to the depreciating value.

Depreciating property. Property of any nature that depreciates in value results in a decrease in benefits to the police agency while it is maintained in storage. Depreciating property should be turned into cash and the money deposited in an interest bearing bank account as soon as it is legally and practically feasible.

Contractors. Competitive bids should be solicited from companies that tow, transport, maintain, or store seized property. In many jurisdictions this is required under purchasing laws. The practical effect, however, is to identify the lowest cost bidder and maximize the return from the sale of the property. Background investigations on bidding companies and their employees that may have access to the property should be conducted. It is not unusual to find that many individuals employed in low paying, manual skills jobs have significant criminal histories. One of the primary purposes of using a contractor for the transport and storage of property is the increased physical security it can offer. Contractors should also provide proof of current insurance coverage to pay for any loss, damage, or destruction to property while it is in their possession.

Management of Real Property

Prior to seizing real estate the amount of equity the owner has in the property should be considered. The seizing agency can lose money if there is not sufficient equity to manage the property prior to its sale. A *Lis Pendens* should be filed with the Recorder of Deeds Office as soon as possible after the seizure of real property. This legal document provides public notice that there is a pending legal matter against the property. Should the property owner attempt to sell, or otherwise convey an interest in, the property after the seizure the filing of the *Lis Pendens* may nullify this action.

A professional real estate manager should be hired to manage seized real property. The day-to-day operations of real estate may be beyond the interest and the capability of the asset seizure officer, particularly when residential or commercial tenants are in place, or agricultural property must be maintained. Generally, property leases in force at the time of a seizure must be honored until the lease termination date, or event. In managing commercial property a percentage lease should be sought (monthly rent plus a per centage of gross profits) to maximize the cash flow to maintain the property.

An appraisal of the property should be acquired as soon as possible after the seizure. This appraisal should be independent of any Realtor that may be used eventually to sell the property. Fee negotiation with an appraiser should, if possible, include provisions for the payment of an appraisal fee only if the property is forfeited. The appraisal must include comparative properties that have sold within the last 6 months. This will ensure that the appraisal reflects current market value.

Each property that has been seized should be treated, and managed, on an individual case-by-case basis. A plan for the maintenance and management of each property should be developed.

Seized property should never be left vacant. This is to prevent vandalism and theft, squatters, and other problems that arise on a day-to-day basis. If the owner is allowed to remain on the premises during the pendency of the forfeiture process an occupancy agreement (lease) should be executed. Allowing the owner to remain places the police agency in the position of a landlord with all the rights, obligations and duties associated with that status. If the owner is to be removed an attempt should be made to have the court declare the property vacant (forcible detainer and eviction) and then advertise the property for rent. In return for maintenance of the property by a responsible tenant it may be beneficial to consider leasing the property rent free or at a reduced rent if the occupiers are not the owners.

The lease agreement should name the seizing police agency as loss payee for insurance purposes. The agency's insurance company should be notified of the seizure. The seizing agency should be named as loss payee if the property is damaged or destroyed. A copy of lease agreement should be provided to the lienholder to place them on notice. In some jurisdictions it may also be prudent to record the lease agreement with the court, or with the recorder of property deeds. This provides public notice that the property interest is encumbered by a tenant.

Property tax payments on the property should be checked to determine if they were paid by the owner up to the expected time of the forfeiture. If they are in arrears steps should be taken to ensure the property is not listed for a tax delinquency sale. In some jurisdictions property is considered technically tax exempt at the time of seizure.

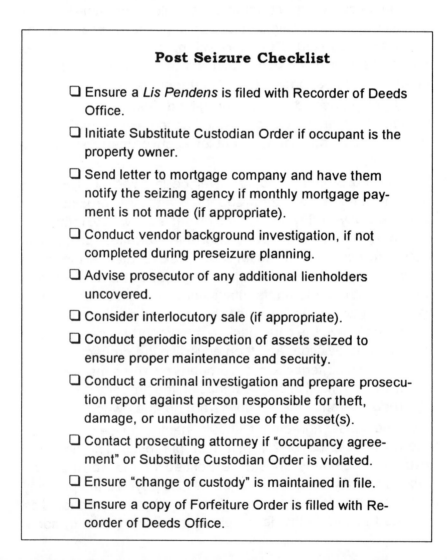

Post Seizure Checklist

❑ Ensure a *Lis Pendens* is filed with Recorder of Deeds Office.

❑ Initiate Substitute Custodian Order if occupant is the property owner.

❑ Send letter to mortgage company and have them notify the seizing agency if monthly mortgage payment is not made (if appropriate).

❑ Conduct vendor background investigation, if not completed during preseizure planning.

❑ Advise prosecutor of any additional lienholders uncovered.

❑ Consider interlocutory sale (if appropriate).

❑ Conduct periodic inspection of assets seized to ensure proper maintenance and security.

❑ Conduct a criminal investigation and prepare prosecution report against person responsible for theft, damage, or unauthorized use of the asset(s).

❑ Contact prosecuting attorney if "occupancy agreement" or Substitute Custodian Order is violated.

❑ Ensure "change of custody" is maintained in file.

❑ Ensure a copy of Forfeiture Order is filled with Recorder of Deeds Office.

❏ At the time of forfeiture, contact local property tax authorities, supply with a copy of the forfeiture order, and advise that the seizing police agency will pay taxes only up to time of forfeiture. Request a written tax exemption letter.

❏ Periodically check the County Recorder's Office for liens, attempts to transfer, or any other abnormalities which may have occurred during the forfeiture proceedings

Figure 6.11
Post Seizure Checklist

Hazardous Materials

A hazardous material is defined by the United States Department of Transportation as any "substance or material in any form or quantity which poses an unreasonable risk to safety and health and property". This raises questions as to what substance, what form, how much, and a definition of "unreasonable risk". Another, albeit, informal definition that may be helpful is that hazardous material is a "Substance that jumps out of its container at you when something goes wrong and hurts or harms the thing it touches". Regardless of the definition one adopts, the essential purpose of hazardous materials regulations is to protect public health and environmental quality.

Health hazards include: breathing irritating or poisonous gases, burns to the skin or eyes, radioactive poisoning and pollution of air, soil or water as a result of improper storage, transportation, disposal or fire control attempts. These materials also present hazards of fire and explosion under various circumstances. Because of the potential harm to property control personnel, the handling of hazardous substances is regulated extensively by health and safety agencies.

In the context of the police property control function, hazardous materials include any of the following items since they often pose a risk to health and safety, can effect the environment, and often "jumps out of its container at you".

- Weapons (firearms, knives, sprays, etc.)
- Ammunition
- Explosives
- Narcotics and Dangerous Drugs
- Flammables
- Hazardous Waste

    Biohazard Materials (blood borne / airborne pathogens)

- Water and Air Pollutants
- Corrosive Materials
- Tampered (Adulterated) Products

    As defined by the *Federal Food, Drug and Cosmetics Act*

Steps In Managing Hazardous Materials

Step 1 ... Identification or definition of material or substance

- Is it subject to regulation?

    Consult "Classifications of Hazardous Materials" below

- What are the potential hazards of handling or storing this material?

    Consult Material Safety Data Sheet (MSDS)

Once these basic material or substance identification questions are answered satisfactorily then packaging, storage and disposal questions can be readily answered. Steps 2 and 3 pose these additional questions.

Step 2 ... Packaging and Storage of Material

- Can this material be legally and safely stored?
- What quantity can be stored and for what length of time?
- What is the proper storage method and storage location for this material?

Step 3 ... Transportation and Disposal

- Can I properly dispose of this material myself, or
- Must this material be delivered only to a qualified disposal facility
- What precautions, or preliminary steps must be taken before the material can be transported, shipped, mailed?

Progressing through these three steps and answering the questions raised in each step will help ensure that hazardous materials are safely handled.

Classification of Materials

The United States Department of Transportation has classified hazardous materials by their nature and hazard. These classifications include: explosives, compressed gases, flammable and combustible liquids, flammable solids, oxidizers, organic peroxide, poisonous and irritating material, etiologic agents, radioactive materials, corrosive material and Other Regulated Materials (ORMS). Those classifications most frequently encountered by law enforcement officers are addressed below.

Explosives

Explosives includes materials with a mass explosion, projection or fire hazard.

Class A explosives. Explosive materials such as dynamite, TNT, black powder and military ammunition are considered Class A Explosives. These materials or devices present a maximum hazard through mass detonation.

Class B explosives. Often encountered by law enforcement officers, Class B Explosives include those materials or devices that present a flammable hazard and function be deflagration. These include display fireworks, rocket motors and military ammunition.

Class C explosives. These contain a minimum quantity of Class A or Class B Explosives. This division includes: detonation fuses, common fireworks and small arms ammunition.

Explosive Devices. While explosive devices do not fit neatly within the DOT classification they present, non-the-less, a significant hazard to law enforcement officers. The Bureau of Alcohol, Tobacco and Firearms (ATF) has reported that, in the five year period from 1989 to 1993, there were 7,716 bombings, 1,705 attempted bombings, 2,2242 incendiary bombings, 4,929 recovered explosives and 2, 011 hoax devices throughout the United States. This information may be highly representative of the United States but it should not be considered all-inclusive. In all probability many more explosives related incidents occurred than were reported to ATF or through the national UCR/NIBRS data collection system.

Bomb making instructions have become commonplace on computer bulletin boards. As a result there is a greater potential for homemade explosives to be seized and appear in property control rooms. Explosive devices consist of three basic components: the container, an explosive and a denotation device. Examples of homemade bombs that have been seized by police agencies include: muriatic acid and tin foil in a bottle, gasoline/any acid (separated) in plastic bottle and dry ice/water in plastic bottle. The interaction of chemicals produces a gas that increases in pressure until the container's strength is exceeded. An explosion results as the container bursts and fragments are projected for some distance.

Gases

This includes hazards from flammable, poison and corrosive gases. Poisonous and irritating materials include tear gas projectiles which are often found stored in property control areas.

Flammable Liquids

Liquids with various flashpoints; below -18C (0F), -18C and above but less than 23C (73F) and flashpoint of 23C and up to 61C (141F). This includes commonly encountered liquids such as gasoline, paint thinner and naptha.

Flammable Solids

This includes spontaneously combustible materials and materials that are dangerous when wet.

Poisonous and Etiologic (Infectious) Materials

Etiologic agents are living microorganisms that may cause human disease. These include viral or biological specimens including those associated with AIDS, hepatitis, and tuberculosis. Infectious materials are addressed comprehensively in a following section.

Miscellaneous Hazardous Materials

A number of other, nonclassified hazardous materials are known to come into the possession of law enforcement agencies because of their illegal possession, or use in illegal activities.

Disposal of Hazardous Materials

Hazardous materials to be transported over the highways must meet U.S. Department of Transportation (DOT) procedures regulating the packaging and transportation of hazardous substances. These regulations may be found in 49 *Federal Regulations*, Parts 170-172.

The disposal of hazardous substances is governed by the Environmental Protection Agency (EPA) under the *Comprehensive Environmental Response, Compensation and Liability Act of 1980*. These regulations are found under 42 USC 9601 et seq.

Biohazard Materials

Biohazard materials are those contaminated with human disease-causing organisms. The most frequently encountered infectious organisms found today are those associated with bacterial diseases; tuberculosis, syphilis, and gonorrhea, viruses; associated with AIDS, hepatitis and herpes and fungi; associated with candidiasis, AIDS, hepatitis B and tuberculosis.

Bloodborne Pathogens

Basic guidelines that should apply to all officers include: do not drink, smoke, eat or chew gum at a crime scene. Don't use the telephone at a crime scene. In addition to obscuring the "last number called" feature, the telephone might have blood on it, or you may breathe in some other type of contamination. Experts in the field of bloodborne pathogens believe a calm, rational view of infection control is the only one to take.

The statistics indicate that an officer's chances of contracting a bloodborne pathogen are slim, especially with regard to the AIDS virus. The Centers for Disease Control (CDC) do not maintain statistics on the incidences of law enforcement officers contracting the HIV virus through job-related exposures. An FBI study conducted from 1981 to 1991 reported that fewer than 10 officers contacted the disease on the job. The majority of these exposures were through the absorption of contaminated blood through cracks in the skin or open sores, or through accidental or intentional needle sticks.

The FBI surveyed law enforcement agencies and asked them to report any incident of an officer contracting any infectious disease. While the FBI study is not statistically or scientifically reliable, the FBI feels it safe to conclude that an officer's chances of contracting any disease on the job; including, hepatitis B and AIDS, are extremely small. These conclusions should not, however, be interpreted to mean that there is no potential for infection. In an FBI informal survey of 70 police agencies, it found that 61 percent did not have a policy regarding bloodborne diseases, 60 percent did not provide training on bloodborne diseases, and 71 percent did not know that OSHA requires agencies to provide protective equipment and HBV vaccinations to employees at no cost.

In late 1997 medical researchers identified a disease associated with World War I "trench fever" which was spread through the trenches by germs. Today the disease, bacillary angiomatosis, is spread through lice and effects homeless AIDS patients; particularly those with weak immune systems. The infection was found among AIDS patients who are poor, without homes and exposed to body lice. The germs are a risk to anyone, assert the researchers, but the risk is higher, and the ailment more serious, to those with weak immune systems. Infection can lead to complications including: anemia, weight loss, the growth of nonmalignant tumors and damaged heart valves. The disease is curable with common antibiotics, but it often goes undiagnosed. (Chicago Tribune, 1997)

With the high incidence of biohazard materials encountered by law enforcement officers, special precautions must be taken in the handling, collection, and storage of evidence that may possibly be contaminated with disease-causing organisms. Since humans may be infected with pathogenic (disease-causing) microorganisms and may not show symptoms of the disease, law enforcement officers handling evidence are at risk.

Property Control Officers must take precautions to prevent self-infection or the contamination of other evidence by infected evidence. All necessary precautions should be considered when dealing with any potential disease-causing organism that may be found in body fluids.

Protection Against Exposure

Property control personnel should take all necessary steps to reduce their exposure to pathogenic microorganisms.

As a means of preventing exposure to contaminated property, a disease control kit should be assembled and maintained in the Property Control Room and any other area where evidence is handled.

Infectious disease control kits. The contents of this kit should include:

- two pairs of disposal latex gloves
- two pairs of goggles
- two disposal masks
- a bottle of alcohol based cleaning fluid
- 1 large, orange, biohazard plastic bag
- several small plastic bags
- a quantity of biohazard labels sufficient to mark each plastic bag in the kit

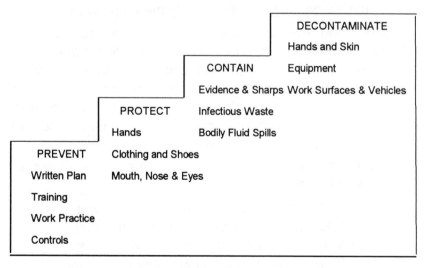

Figure 6.12
Steps To Exposure Control

Disposable gloves. The first step to protect the hands and keep them clean and away from the eyes, mouth and nose. Property control personnel having cuts, abrasions, or any other break of the skin on the hands should never handle blood or other bodily fluids without protection. When handling evidence of questionable origin; that may be infected with microorganisms, the best protection is to wear *two pairs* of disposable gloves.

Latex medical examination (surgical) gloves, in various sizes, should be purchased and kept in the Property Control Room for use by personnel when handling suspected items. These gloves should be disposed of in a clearly marked plastic bag. This bag is used for no other purpose than to collect the gloves until they can be disposed of properly. After finishing with any suspected contaminated materials or evidence, personnel should wash their hands thoroughly with soap and water.

Shoe covers. Property control personnel should also be aware that their shoes may be contaminated with blood or other liquids after an accidental spill or breakage of containers. Protective shoe coverings made of disposable plastic or paper must be considered for inclusion as a standard Property Control Room supply item. Without shoe covers there is a possibility that contaminates will be spread throughout the Property Control Room, the police facility, and possibly the employees home.

Protective eyewear. Caution must be exercised when handling bloody clothing that must be hung to air dry before being packaged. Flecks of dried blood may fly off the clothing when it is handled and infect the person handling it. Because of this, surgical masks and protective eye wear should be considered when handling dried blood particles, or liquid blood that may splash into the face or eyes.

To make sure all bases are covered, the following precautions should be taken:

- Employees should wash with soap and water immediately after removing gloves or other protective equipment, and flush mucous membranes following contact with any potentially infectious materials.

- Eating, drinking, smoking, applying cosmetics or lip balm, and handling contact lenses should be prohibited in work areas.
- Food and drinks should not be kept in refrigerators, freezers shelves, cabinets or on countertops or work benches where potentially infectious materials are present.
- Mouth pipetting/suctioning of blood or other potentially infectious materials should be prohibited.
- Broken and contaminated glassware should not be retrieved by hand but by other mechanical means. Likewise, contaminated reusable sharp instruments should not be stored or processed in a manner that requires employees to retrieve them manually.
- Contaminated laundry should be handled as little as possible, and bagged or "containerized" at the location where it is used, but not sorted or rinsed there.
- Containers should be properly labeled or color coded, and contained to prevent leaking. Employees handling laundry should wear gloves and other appropriate protective equipment.
- Training should be ongoing and documented. To prevent prejudicial treatment, officers should be taught to look at the disease and how it is transmitted, not who has it. Instead of focusing on highrisk groups, one expert emphasizes, focus on highrisk behavior.

The risk of contracting an infectious disease may be low, but it does exist. Officers should be trained to treat everyone with whom they have contact as if they have an infectious disease, and every piece of evidence as if it were contaminated. Personal protective equipment is important, but common sense is the best defense.

Sharp Objects

Property room personnel should be particularly alert for sharp objects that are contained in evidence packages. These objects include hypodermic needles and syringes, knives, razors, broken glass, nails, or any other sharp objects bearing blood. Even seemingly safe articles, such as the common metal paper staple, present a potential hazard. Staples harbor bacteria and viruses when used in the Property Control Room. Skin punctures can occur when removing staples from paper and potentially inject the bacteria or virus into the body. For this reason it is suggested paper or plastic tape be used whenever possible when packaging evidence.

Cases of accidental injection of police personnel with AIDS and hepatitis by needles and other sharp instruments have occurred, although rare. Narcotics case evidence should be handled with considerable care. Investigating officers and Property Control personnel should place hypodermic needles in puncture proof containers before wrapping and placing the evidence into the property control system. These "sharps" must be handled, and inserted into the protective container, using a "one-handed" method. In practice this means that the syringe must be inserted into the sharps container while the container is resting on a surface; not in the person's free hand. Plastic syringe, "sharps", containers made specifically for law enforcement use are available commercially and must be considered a standard supply item.

Many crime laboratories have adopted the policy of not accepting hypodermic syringes with the needle, or any portion of the needle, affixed to the syringe. Such policies are adopted to protect lab personnel against accidental inoculation. These policies should be considered for adoption in jurisdictions were it is legally feasible to do so and there are proper facilities to dispose of the needles.

Cleanup of Contaminated Items

The Property Control Officer is responsible for the proper periodic cleanup of the temporary storage lockers, minor spills that may contaminate the Property Control Room, and the disposal of contaminated items. Due to the health hazards posed by AIDS, Hepatitis B, and Tuberculosis, police agencies must develop policies and procedures for property control personnel to follow in situations involving the cleanup and disposal of contaminated evidence.

It is essential that law enforcement agencies contact their respective state health authorities to determine the proper procedures to be followed in disposing of hypodermic syringes, vials of blood, or other items stained with blood or body fluids. The disposal of such items into a garbage dumpster is not only irresponsible, but also a violation of state and federal laws.

Items that cannot be disposed of (evidence) and spills of bodily fluids should be cleaned thoroughly with a solution consisting of one cup of sodium hypochlorite (common household liquid bleach) dissolved in a gallon of water (a one to ten solution). The AIDS virus can be killed almost immediately with either the bleach solution or ordinary rubbing alcohol.

Disposal of Contaminated Items

Disposable items, such as gloves, masks and paper towels should be disposed of in a safe manner. Gloves should be turned inside out as they are removed and placed into a small plastic bag. Masks and other small items may also be placed into the bag and sealed. If an approved biohazard disposal container is not available all biohazard material should be place in a bag labeled with the internationally recognized biohazard symbol and then placed inside a second bag also labeled with the biohazard symbol. This procedure is intended to protect anyone handling the bag in the future.

Cloth wipe-ups or rags suspected of being contaminated with pathogenic microorganisms should be disposed of by incineration. If this is not possible, arrangements should be made with a local pathologist or hospital to sterilize the items by autoclaving and then disposing of them properly.

Large disposable items, such as bloody clothes that are not required to be maintained as evidence, and cleanup rags should be placed in a large, orange biohazard bag and the bag sealed. All disposable items should be placed in receptacle designated only for "Contaminated Waste."

Biohazard Warnings

All suspected items should be marked with appropriate warnings. This is accomplished through the use of adhesive-backed labels bearing the international biohazard symbol with space for writing the appropriate disease on the label. If such labels are not available, the package should be marked as a warning to others that may come into contact with it. This might include: "Caution! Contains Potential Hepatitis Case." This label will alert all persons subsequently handling the evidence; laboratory personnel, prosecutors, defense lawyers, and police officers of the potential medical hazards in the package.

To prevent the necessity of removing and handling evidence contaminated with infectious biological fluids, these items should be placed in transparent packaging only after they have been properly dried. The package should be marked clearly for identification and a warning label affixed stating the package contains suspected pathogenic material.

Notifications

Officers in the field have an obligation to inform support personnel (firefighters, paramedics, jailors, detox personnel) including the Property Control Officer, whenever blood or other body fluids are present, or if an individual made a statement that he or she has a contagious disease. Officers also have an obligation to clearly mark all containers containing biohazard evidence with the appropriate biohazard warning label.

Restricted Activities

Additional protection against pathogenic microorganisms is possible if personnel are instructed that no one at any time should be allowed to smoke, eat, drink, apply makeup or lip balm in the Property Control Room. Engaging in these activities brings ones hands to the mouth. This may inadvertently cause the ingestion of the microorganisms. Applying eye makeup brings the hand or makeup utensil close to the eye and the mucous membrane within the eye. Any microorganisms on the hand or makeup utensil may then be introduced into the body through the mucous membrane.

Mailing Biohazard Materials

Any evidence containing bodily fluids contaminated with AIDS, Hepatitis B, or other human pathogens to be shipped through the U.S. Mail must be in compliance with Part 72 of the *Code of Federal Regulations*. This regulation specifies that appropriate warning labels must be placed on the package and any liquid substances must be triple wrapped and sealed.

Additional information on these procedures may be obtained from the Center for Disease Control, Office of Bio-Safety, 1600 Clifton Road NE, Atlanta, Georgia 30333. Telephone instructions can be received by calling the Center at (404)329-3883.

Toxic Chemicals

Care must be taken to avoid storing hazardous substance evidence recovered from clandestine laboratories. Evidence seized from clandestine drug laboratories has a very high potential of containing hazardous toxic chemicals. Exposure to these chemicals can often be life-threatening.

With the rapid increase in clandestine drug laboratories throughout the United States, law enforcement agencies should develop policies and procedures pertaining to the handling, storage, and disposal of hazardous chemicals. The storage area or facility for these materials should be away from the regular evidence storage area and must meet EPA and OSHA standards. The best policy for preventing exposure to toxic chemicals is to prohibit their collection and storage by agency personnel. (DEA, 1991)

A relatively new method of manufacturing methamphetamine, the "Nazi Method", employs a sodium-ammonia method. This process uses chemicals readily available in hardware and chemical supply stores, pharmacies and super markets. While the method is particular to Missouri, Arkansas and the Pacific Northwest, the simplicity of the process and the rapid manufacturing time may cause it to spread to other geographic areas.

Several of the ingredients used are highly flammable, caustic, toxic and explosive. Ordinary kitchen utensils and glassware, buckets, mason jars, and drip style coffee pots have been found to be used in these labs for the manufacturing process. Disguised propane tanks; actually containing anhydrous ammonia, have been recovered from these labs. Anhydrous ammonia is corrosive and can cause cracking of the tank valve and corrosive cracking of the inner lining of the propane tank. This causes these tanks to be extremely fragile, and extremely dangerous.

The Drug Enforcement Administration (DEA) has provided information regarding telltale signs of a meth lab's existence. These include: thousands of white tablets in plastic containers, chunks of sodium metal in bottles of kerosene, and an extremely strong odor of ammonia emanating from a white powder. The common articles listed above should not be entered into the evidence storage system, or into bulk storage if it is suspected that they are associated with a clandestine laboratory. Common solvents and chemicals found in clandestine laboratories, and their hazardous properties, are identified in Figure 6.13

DEA procedures regulating the handling and storage of hazardous substances recommend treating all drug lab chemicals, glassware, and equipment as if they are hazardous waste. (IACP, 1991) Since fire department HAZMAT personnel generally have received comprehensive training in hazardous materials, law enforcement personnel should seek fire department assistance in developing training of Property Control Officers as well as the storage and disposal procedures for hazardous substances and materials.

Exposure Hazard

Exposure to toxic materials may be the result of inhaling vapors, getting chemicals in the eyes, absorbing chemicals through the skin, acids burning the skin, accidental ingestion of chemicals and other forms of contact. Some of the chemicals found in clandestine laboratories are also highly flammable and may explode with slight contact or heat. Ether, for example, is a common solvent used in clandestine drug laboratories. Vapors leaking from a container may travel to a source of ignition, and then flash back to the container. Vapor explosion hazards associated with many of these chemicals exist both indoors and outdoors. Toxic vapors from these chemicals may also permeate building structures, including the Property Control Room.

Law enforcement involvement with clandestine drug laboratories is a hazardous substance response operation that falls under the regulations of the Occupational Safety and Health Administration (OSHA).

OSHA regulations require the following actions by employers to protect employees that handle hazardous substances:

1. Employers must communicate clear and unambiguous warnings on the hazards and dangers of chemical substances

These warnings must be reinforced with training programs, as well as through agency directives.

2. Training of all employees regarding the exposure to hazardous substances

Property control personnel can be reasonably anticipated to come into contact with hazardous substances and must be trained in recognizing and dealing with safety and health hazards present in evidence seized from clandestine laboratories. They must also be trained in the use of protective equipment and safe work practices.

Evidence Disposal

Unsolved Crimes

Evidence associated with unsolved crimes can be purged from the property control system after the applicable Statute of Limitations has expired. The Statute of Limitations is the time period in which a prosecution must be commenced after the commission of a crime. These time limitations vary from state-to-state and are technical exceptions to these general rules.

The Property Control Officer should determine the time (statutory) limitations for various offenses in their own state and use them a guideline for the disposal of evidence associated with unsolved crimes. The prosecutor's office, or other legal authority, should be consulted before any final disposal action is taken.

Offense Type	Time Limitation
• Capital Crime	Generally held indefinitely
• Felony	Generally 2 to 3 years
• Misdemeanor	Generally 18 months to 2 years

	Explosive	Flammable	Toxic	Corrosive	Irritant	Degree of Hzrd.
Ammonia Gas		x	x	x	x	extra high
Benzene		x	x			high
Carbon Tetrachloride			x			high
Chloroform			x		x	medium
Coleman Fuel		x			x	high
Ethanol		x				medium
Ethylene Dichloride		x	x		x	high
Ethyl Ether		x	x			extra high
Gasoline		x	x		x	high
Hydrobromic Acid			x	x		high *
Hydrochloric Acid		x	x			extra high *
Hydrogen Chloride Gas			x	x		high
Hydrogen Gas	x	x				extra high
Hydrogen Iodide			x	x		medium
Isopropanol		x				medium
Lithium Aluminum Hydride	Explosive	Do Not Handle				extra extra high *
Methanol		x	x			medium
Methylene Dichloride		x	x	x		high
Nitrogen Gas			x			high
Petroleum Ether		x			x	high
Potassium Hydroxide			x	x		high
Sulfuric Acid			x	x		extra high *
Tetrahydrofuran	x				x	high

* These chemical should not come into contact with water since they may ignite in the presence of moisture or produce a flammable gas.

Figure 6.13
Common Solvents and Chemicals Found in Clandestine Laboratories

- City/county ordinance   Generally 6 months
- Extended time limitations may apply to certain classes of thefts, official misconduct, sexual conduct offenses, child pornography, and other specified offenses.

Appeals Evidence

Appeals from criminal cases, post-conviction cases, and juveniles court proceedings may require that evidence be maintained in custody after court judgement. The time to perfect an appeal requires that physical evidence be maintained for the time limitation for the filing of notice to appeal. The caveats mentioned for statute of limitations apply also to appeals evidence.

- Death Sentence

  Generally an appeal is automatically perfected. Evidence will generally be retained until all appeals are exhausted.

- Appeal From Judgement on Guilty Plea
  Generally thirty days after date of sentence

- Other Appeals

  Generally thirty days after final judgement appealed from

Department policy should be adopted to establish the responsibility of the officer submitting the property to notify the Evidence Section of the status of the evidence and the necessity, if any, to maintain custody the evidence beyond the date of the final court judgement in a case.

Chapter Notes

Cervenka, Valerie, *Entomology and Death: Solving Mysteries With Maggots*, St. Paul, MN, 1998.

Chicago Tribune, December 12, 1997; page 15.

DEA, EPA, U.S. Coast Guard, *Guidelines for the Cleanup of Clandestine Laboratories,* (DEA Office of Forensic Sciences), 1991.

DEA, "Officer Safety - Clandestine Lab Recognition" (undated mimeo)

National Firearms Act, 27 *Code of Federal Regulations*, 179.104.

International Association of Chiefs of Police (IACP), *Crime Victims' Bill of Rights*, resolution adopted March 12, 1983.

International Association of Chiefs of Police (IACP), *1991 Police Yearbook*, 1991, pp. 86-87.

The President's Task Force on Victims of Crime; Final Report, (U.S. Printing Office), December, 1982.

Washington State Patrol, *Physical Evidence Handbook,* (Crime Laboratory Division, Olympia, WA.), 1993.

Chapter 7

Record and Information Systems

A well planned record system is essential to the effective functioning of the property control system. In designing or modifying such a record system, several objectives must be kept in mind. A record system designed to achieve the objectives and comply with the records principles outlined below will eliminate wasted time, duplication of effort and unnecessary expense.

The lack of a sound record system will have significant adverse affects on the property control system. As stated in a well known text on investigations: "In the absence of a workable records system supported by uncomplicated forms, the security of evidence is considerably weakened, the chain of custody is in danger of being severed, and the opportunity is created for mishandling, tampering, stealing, or accidental loss of physical evidence." (Swanson, et al, 1992)

The planned use and adoption of computers and bar codes in the property room has become a major issue. There are numerous vendors offering stand-alone and integrated software, barcoding programs and equipment, and bar code tags. These products should be evaluated carefully before making the final purchase decision. Once a decision is made and a system is purchased it may be too late to assess the benefits of any particular product.

Objectives of Property Control Records

The design and operation of the property control records system should address the seven broad objectives statements below.

- Record custodial responsibility for evidence and property entered into the property control system
- Establish and maintain a continuous chain of custody
- Prevent loss or unauthorized release of evidence

- Record the description and location of each piece of property being held in the Property Control Room
- Record unique or unusual circumstances associated with the release or transfer of evidence
- Record the date, purpose, and signature of the person to whom property is released
- Document fully the destruction, auction, or agency appropriation of property

Property Inventory Report

The Property Inventory Report is intended and necessary to record the complete descriptions and circumstances surrounding the initial decision by an officer to take custody of evidence or property. The Property Inventory Report should include provisions for recording the offense or incident associated with the decision to take custody, any attempts to notify the property owner by the reporting officer, a complete and accurate description of each item of property or evidence taken into custody, and complete chain of custody entries.

A sample Property Inventory Report is shown as Figure 7.1. The form is designed to address many of the common problems encountered in the initial custody, processing and final disposition of property and evidence. Nine information elements should be included on the Property Inventory Report form. This information is intended to assist the Property Control Officer in accounting for all the property inventoried, the routing of property submitted, owner notification, and the disposal of the property. These nine elements are:

- Type of offense or incident
- Related report numbers
- Property status
- Owners notificationsDescribe each
- Property routing
- Special instructions
- Chain of custody
- Supplementary report
- Certification of receipt

The Property Inventory Report is not intended to take the place of an Offense or Incident Report. It is intended to serve as supplemental, documented information regarding property taken into custody. The Property Inventory Report should be a multi-copy form set to comply with legal requirements and sound record practices. The form shown in Figure 7.1 is intended to be implemented as a four-part form.

The first, or original copy, remains with the property and serves as the primary official record of custody. This copy is maintained in the Property Control Room file until final property disposition. After final disposition this copy is forwarded to central records where it is filed with the original case file documents.

The second copy accompanies evidence that is sent to the crime laboratory. The third copy is forwarded to the central records unit by the reporting officer along with the offense or incident report. This copy remains in the case file until the final disposition of all property. At that time the original Property Inventory Report form is filed and the copy is disposed of.

The fourth copy serves as a receipt for the finder of lost property, the owner of safekeeping property, or the person from whom evidence is seized in the execution of a search warrant. In those cases where a search warrant is served, the second copy may be used also as the "return copy" to the court issuing the warrant.

Four copies, the original and three carbons, serve the majority of purposes one might typically encounter. Should additional copies be necessary, the faceside of the original can be reproduced.

Request For Disposal of Property

The Request For Disposal of Property (shown in Figure 7.2), directed to the chief of police, is used to request disposal of evidence no longer required for case purposes and other property which is to be disposed of. The property information entered onto this form initiates the process of inventorying all property to be disposed of, notifies the chief of police of the quantity and nature of property to be disposed of and, serves as the basis for the issuance of the Approval For Property Disposal.

Police Department   **Property Inventory Report**   Report No.   -

1 Type of Incident / Offense	2 Property Inventory No.	3 Date

4 Related Report No.(s)	5 Property Status

5 Property Status
- ❑ Evidence
- ❑ Seized   ❑ Recovered   ❑ Contraband
- ❑ Safekeeping   ❑ Found \ Abandoned

6 Location Property Discovered or Found

7 Property Received From	Address	Residence / Business Telephone

8 Property Owner	Address	Residence / Business Telephone

9 Owner Notified   Date / Time   By: Officer Name \ Badge
❑ Yes ❑ No

10 Item	11 Quantity	12 Description: Make, Model, Color, Marks, Damage	Serial Number	13 Routing

PROPERTY ROUTING CODE: EVD. = To Property Section   INV. = Held by Investigator   C.L. = To Crime Lab   O = Returned to Owner

14 SPECIAL INSTRUCTIONS TO PROPERTY OFFICER	COURT ORDERED DISPOSITION

Item

COURT ORDERED DISPOSITION

❑Police Dept. to dispose of according to law

❑ Property Forfeited: _____

❑ Release Property To: _____

❑ Other: _____

_____

Judges Name: _____ Date: _____

Court Location: _____

Reporting / Inventorying Officer   Badge No.

Officer's Name / Badge_____

Figure 7.1
Property Inventory Report

Item	Date	Relinquished By	Received By	Purpose of Change in Custody

SUPPLEMENTARY PROPERTY REPORT

To Be Completed By Property Custodian

Record pertinent information for: (1) the return of property requiring identification or proof of ownership (2) Return of firearms; personal identification (drivers license, or identification number) and permit (number and date of expiration) (3) Return of property under unusual circumstances (claim of damage, property not returned: contraband, forfeiture, etc (4) If property auctioned, destroyed, or otherwise disposed of, record authority for disposal.

CERTIFICATION OF RECEIPT OF PROPERTY

I certify that I received the property described on lines (items) _____ of this Inventory in good condition.

X

| Owner's Signature | Address | City | State | Date of Return |

Department Employee Releasing Property: Name   Badge

I certify that I received the property described on lines (items) _____ of this Inventory in good condition.

X

| Owner's Signature | Address | City | State | Date of Return |

Department Employee Releasing Property: Name   Badge

I certify that I received the property described on lines (items) _____ of this Inventory in good condition.

X

| Owner's Signature | Address | City | State | Date of Return |

Department Employee Releasing Property: Name   Badge

Figure 7.1
Property Inventory Report

Policy Development

Policy statements governing the use the Request For Disposal Of Property form should include several important issues. A request for the disposal of firearms and ammunition should be contained on a dedicated list. Firearms often must be destroyed in a specific manner, or relinquished to a county or state law enforcement agency. The identification of firearms intended for disposal, and those disposed of in the past, is expedited when the Request For Disposal contains only firearms. Requests for the destruction of narcotics, dangerous drugs and drug paraphernalia should be restricted to a narcotics and dangerous drugs destruction request. Other property, if it is not of a sensitive nature, or with little economic value, should be included on a Request For Disposal form that contains a listing of general types of property and evidence.

Approval For Property Disposal

The Approval For Property Disposal, shown at the bottom of Figure 7.2, is the formal written approval and order issued by the chief of police to the Property Control Officer. This order directs the disposal or destruction of the property contained on the Request for Property Disposal. The order includes the date of disposal and, if disposal is to be effected by destruction, the identity of the officer assigned to witness the destruction. A copy of the Request for Disposal of Property should be returned to the Property Control Officer when it is approved by the chief of police. The original of the Request for Disposal should be maintained in a secure file in the chief's office. Duplicate copies of Requests and Approvals for Disposal provides an aditional measure of security if the forms are needed sometime in the future for audit purposes.

The Approval For Property Disposal is intended to serve as the official agency directive to dispose of property after it has been retained in excess of statutory time limits, is no longer needed as evidence, or is contraband subject to forfeiture and destruction upon seizure. This form, when completed, serves also as one element of the chain of custody and the property audit trail.

To: Chief of Police

From: Property Control Officer

Date:

The undersigned, Property Control Officer of the _____ Police Department, hereby requests permission to dispose of the property listed herein now in the custody of the _____ Police Department.

Disposal is to be accomplished by:_____
                                        Destruction, Auction, Appropriation

All applicable legal requirements for the retention of the listed property have been complied with.

    Complaint Number   Item Description

Approval For Property Disposal

I hereby approve the disposal of property, as inventoried above and in the manner requested. This disposal shall be completed by ___Date___, or a report shall be filed with my office on that date showing cause why the disposal was not carried-out.

Disposal By Destruction: I order that _____, an officer of the _____ Police Department, is assigned to witness this destruction. The assigned officer shall co-sign the Report of Destruction and return that report to my office within twenty four hours of the property destruction.

_____

   Chief of Police

Figure 7.2
Request and Approval For Disposal of Property

Report on Disposal of Property

The Report Of Disposal of Property (Figure 6.3) completes the forms necessary to document property disposals. After the order of disposal has been carried out, the Property Control Officer completes the Report Of Disposal of Property and returns it to the office of the chief of police. After appropriate disposition entries are made in the chain of custody section of the Property Inventory Report, the audit trail of the disposed property is complete.

The procedures described above ensures two copies of the property disposal forms are maintained by the agency. One complete file on each property disposal should be maintained in the office of the chief of police. The second file is maintained in the Property Control Room. In addition, after the disposal of property, the Property Inventory Report, with complete chain of custody information, is routed to the central records section and filed in the case file.

Disposition entries must also be entered on the Property Inventory Log, whether manual or computerized, to indicate the final disposal of the property, the date of disposal and the Property Destruction Number, if used.

Property Destruction Number

The Property Destruction Number is an optional property control numbering system. When used, a sequential destruction number is assigned each and every occasion property is destroyed. The destruction number is most useful when multiple property destructions are made in a short time period; several in one day or four or five in a week.

The property destruction number may be used also to indicate the number of property destructions that have been affected within a calendar quarter or year. Since destructions should be scheduled at least once a quarter during each calendar year, the property destruction number will indicate the number of destructions that year. This will expedite staff inspections of the property control function as discussed in other sections of this text.

To: Chief of Police

From: Property Control Officer

Date:

I, ———(Property Control Officer's Name)———, Property Control Officer of the
_____ Police Department, this day carried out the order
of the Chief of Police and affected the disposal of all materials
and items specified therein, and in the manner so ordered.

Property Control Officer

Exceptions To Disposal

I, _____, an officer of the _____
Police Department, this date witnessed the destruction of all
items specified on the Request For Disposal Of Property.

_____
Officer's Signature

Figure 7.3
Report On Disposal of Property

Property File Designs

Suspense Files

A suspense file devoted to property administrative matters
should be established. This file should use either the subject
classification or chronological filing method.

When evidence is checked-out for court or laboratory
analysis purposes an entry is made in the appropriate chain of
custody area on the Property Inventory Report and the form is
filed in a chronological Suspense File. This suspense file is a
tool to maintain control over the location of and length of time
that evidence has been out of the Property Control Room.

If the Suspense File is maintained on a chronological basis, one file folder for each day of the month, the Property Control Officer will have an indication of when the evidence should be returned. Examples of the use of this file are provided below.

Out for court. When evidence is removed for court purposes the Property Inventory Report associated with the evidence is placed in the Suspense File "Out For Court." This provides immediate recognition that the evidence was removed for court and reduces the potential of Property Inventory Reports being misplaced, misfiled or lost when no longer attached to the property.

For example, if an item of evidence is removed for court on the 10th day of the month with an anticipated return on the 11th day, the original of the Property Inventory Report is filed in the Suspense File folder for the 11th day. Upon checking that folder on the 11th the Property Control Officer knows what evidence should be returned on that day. If the evidence has not been returned at the end of the day follow-up action is necessary. This action includes contacting the investigating officer to determine the status and location of the evidence.

Evidence on loan. An Evidence On Loan file may be necessary when evidence is loaned to another law enforcement agency. The purpose of this file, if needed, is to serve as a central location for the Property Inventory Report and the letter requesting the evidence to be loaned, proof of mailing of the evidence, a letter of transmittal sent with the evidence and other pertinent documents.

One file folder should be created for each loan of evidence. These file folders are then filed chronologically; most recent to the back. The file folders should be checked periodically to determine if evidence has been returned promptly. Upon return of the evidence a memo is inserted into the file folder noting its return. The file should be transferred at this time to central records and filed in the case file.

Property Disposal File

In order to maintain a permanent record of all evidence and property that is disposed of pursuant to a Property Disposal Order a copy of all paperwork associated with the property disposal should be maintained in a Property Disposal File. Structured chronologically, with the most recent disposal in front, the file should contain a list of the property disposed of; the Request For Disposal of Property, the Property Disposal Order and the Report On Disposal of Property. Appropriate notations should be made also in the Property Inventory Log after the disposal has been completed to record the date and method by which the property was disposed.

Property in Bulk Storage

The Property Inventory Reports associated with property stored in a bulk storage facility should be maintained in a bulk storage file. This file provides an immediate inventory of all such bulk property as well as a convenient location to store the Property Inventory Report.

If extensive use is made of bulk storage facilities it may be advantageous to break the file classification down further into subclassifications. These subclassification might include construction materials, equipment/tools, household goods and other similar subclassifications of large items of property.

Assigned / Appropriated Property

An assigned and appropriated property file should be maintained. This file includes a copy of the Property Inventory Report of all property assigned to the agency by administrative action or appropriated pursuant to state statute. This file creates an audit trail of appropriated property and is intended to be used in addition to the permanent record of the agency's property inventory. The file should be maintained on a chronological basis.

Property Auction File

This file is designed to maintain records of property that has been auctioned. If questions arise as to the location or status of the auctioned property this file provides a convenient reference and reduces the need to access central records files. This file should contain a copy of the Request For Disposal of Property, Property Disposal Order, "Proof of Publication" (newspaper notice of the auction) and any other paperwork associated with the auction. The file should be maintained on a chronological basis with one file folder for each auction.

Property Control Records

Information Confidentially

Issue: Is police disclosure of a citizen's HIV status a violation of the right to personal privacy and actionable under Section 1983 the Civil Rights Act.

Facts: Plaintiff filed a civil rights complaint against Officer Tibbetts for an alleged violation of plaintiffs right to privacy and against the employing town for its alleged failure to adequately train and supervise Officer Tibbetts in the protection of the privacy of individuals with AIDS.

Officer Tibbetts came into possession of a mislaid container of prescription medication identified as belonging to plaintiff and which is used to treat AIDS patients. Officer Tibbetts later contacted plaintiff to confirm that the medication belonged to her. When plaintiff refused to explicitly identify the medication, Tibbetts told plaintiff he knew what the medication was. Tibbetts then asked the plaintiff if she was "HIV positive." Plaintiff, believing she would not get her medication without answering tibbetts questions, said she was HIV positive.

It was alleged that Officer Tibbetts later told a neighbor plaintiff was a "sad case," had an illness, and that children should be kept away from plaintiff's home. Sometime after the incident the plaintiff moved from her apartment due to the stress resulting from people knowing she had AIDs.

Officer Tibbetts testified he had received some training in HIV disease and its transmission. He was not, however, aware of the privacy rights of those with HIV infection.

The court found that plaintiff has a constitutional right to privacy which includes nondisclosure of her HIV status. (*Doe v Town of Plymouth*, 1993)

Introduction as Evidence

Police property control records are generally admissible as evidence under the "business records exception" to the hearsay rule. In order to qualify under this exception the records must meet several tests.

One Federal Appeals Court ruling held that the police property receipt for a weapon was properly admitted into evidence under the businesses records exception where the prosecution established that it was the regular and customary practice of the police agency to complete a property receipt for *any* type of evidence. *(United States v. Brown*, 1993)

Discovery of Police Records

The *Federal Rules of Criminal Procedure* provides that, upon request by the defendant, the government shall permit the defendant to inspect and copy, or photograph photographs ....

- In the possession, custody, or control of the government, and which are material to the preparation of the defense,
- Are intended to be used by the government as evidence in chief at the trial, or
- Were obtained from, or belonged to the defendant.

Federal Rules of Criminal Procedures, Rule 16(a)(1)(C).

This Rule applies to evidence inventories and receipts and other property control records that meet one of the two tests above.

Property Control Computer Systems

A computerized evidence and property system can generate more accurate and timely management data. Examples of such data include the number of property submissions each month, the number property transfers for court or return to owner, the number of drug or weapons cases received and the number of property disposals. These periodic reports are useful for documenting workload on a monthly, calendar quarter and annual basis. Yearly summaries can be used to project long-range trends to justify personnel and equipment needs in the development of the annual budget request.

Procedures assessment. Before considering the automation of the property control system a thorough assessment of the existing manual records system and property control policies and procedures must be conducted. A computer system, introduced into an inefficient and chaotic property control system, will only further add to the chaos. An automated system must be viewed as a *tool by which to accomplish the job;* not the answer to years of inattention to the property control function.

A second important consideration is the need to computerize. Not all police property control systems require the use of a computer to track property and provide reports. If periodic reports are needed for decision-making and control purposes the first questions that should be addressed are what decisions will be made, how often, by whom and for what purposes. The follow-up question is: can this information be obtained easily through a manual records system properly planned, designed and implemented? In either instance, deciding to automate or identifying management information needs, the manual property records system will have to be first analyzed and evaluated.

Life-cycle costing. Another consideration is the "true cost" to computerize Studies that have been conducted on the purchase of personal computers found that the purchase price is just 15 percent of the cost of installing, operating and maintaining the machine. Other factors such as reliability, technical support and training play major roles in the provision of cost-effective information technology.

Consideration all the long-range costs associated with computerization is referred to as "life-cycle costing". When evaluating computer hardware; such as a PC, monitor, printer, bar code reader, other equipment, and a software program initial purchase price should be but one consideration. Reliability, measured as "mean time between failure" should be considered. Manufacturers determine mean time between failure during the design of their product based upon the components used to build the product. To gain reliability better components are required, and that costs money. A bar code printer designed with a mean time between failure of 5,000 copies will be more reliable than another with a rating of 1,000 copies. The ease of acquiring maintenance services, the time required for typical maintenance and the relative ease of repairing the equipment are measures of the true costs of the printer over it useful life.

Technical support is another element to be considered. If the hardware or software does not operate in the manner it is intended then it is of little practical use. High quality, practical, cost-effective technical support from the vendor is an absolute necessity. If technical problems can not be resolved promptly, a back log of evidence and property to be processed will be soon become evident.

The length of time and quality of training that will be provided to system users must be considered also. Training to use a system effectively consumes time. The faster personnel are trained to use the system the quicker the full benefits of the computer system will be realized. It must be considered that not all vendors of property control computer systems are prepared, or knowledgeable in training users in their systems.

Assessing Property Control Computer Systems

Assuming there is in fact a need to automate property control records there is also a need to assess the many applications programs available commercially.

In smaller departments a relatively inexpensive relational database program can be structured and used to log property into, through and out of the property control system. Numerous smaller police agencies are using this approach and find it satisfactory for their needs. Larger departments have a justifiable need for more sophisticated computer applications. Property control application programs designed for larger departments are typically priced at $10,000 to $80,000.

Various options available in property control computer programs include:

- The generation of owner notification letters
- Requests for property auctions
- Property disposal requests
- Property maintenance activities and costs
- Bar coding and optical scanning
- Tickler files

- Data queries
- Auction management
- Auto impounds
- Prisoner property in custody

One computer program on the market will generate a chain of custody certification letter that is purported to be useful for introduction in court when the chain of custody must be proven.

Management information reports available in some computer programs include: statistics on monthly property submissions, property transfers, property returns to owner, drug and weapon cases received and property disposals. These reports can, and should be generated on a monthly, quarterly and annual basis and reviewed for trends and patterns in property submissions.

Bar Coding

A recent adoption associated with the increased usage of computers in law enforcement is bar code tagging of property and evidence. Bar codes, best known as the bands of parallel bars found on most items in supermarkets, can provide several distinct advantages over traditional paper tagging systems. The initial and most immediate benefit is the marking of evidence for identification through the use of computer technology.

Upon receipt of a piece of property or evidence into the Property Control Room, a computer file entry is created. The information in this computer file is the same as that entered onto the Property Control Log with one exception. Upon completing the initial data entry sequence, the computer program generates a printed label containing the parallel bars which represents the coded Property Control Number. Adoption of this system eliminates the need for a manual property control log since all information is entered and stored in computer files. This also eliminates the need to hand write or type multiple copies of the inventory tag if property is stored in several locations. With the use of gummed back labels for the printing of the bar codes, labels can be attached to evidence containers, tags, envelopes and file cards.

Case tracking and reports. Bar coding systems has been adopted by numerous police and sheriff's departments and crime laboratories across the United States. Crime laboratories use the bar code system not only to inventory evidence received for analysis but also as a means of tracking the chain of custody of exhibits as they are transferred from one laboratory section to another.

Depending on the sophistication of an agencies computer system, property tracking may be through a single stand alone computer terminal (a personal computer for example) or a module of a much larger computer network. In either system an entry is made into the computerized case file using the information contained in the Property Inventory Report. The computer requests specific information regarding the property including: the case number, the identity of the submitting officer, the type of article inventoried, description, victim and owner's name, which evidence is related to each party and any special instructions recorded by the investigating officer.

The system recognizes bar coded property labels through the use of an optical scanner. The scanner, when moved over the bar code transmits electrical impulses to the central processing unit in the computer which recognizes the bars as numbers. With this recognition, the computer accesses the pertinent file and displays the file information on the computer screen. At this time the computer terminal may require a password, badge number or identifying code of the person receiving the property, the nature and purpose of the transfer and other pertinent information. The date and time of the property transfer is automatically generated by the computer program. Thus, the computer file is edited and updated case information or chain-of-custody entries is made automatically.

In addition to tracking property inventory, the bar code system, through the computer database file, has the ability to search also by case number, description of the item, name of the seizing officer, length of time in custody, or any other data associated with a particular case, or group of cases.

In assessing bar code labeling three factors should be considered; the printer, the bar code software and the label itself. Of these three factors the printer should be considered last.

Bar code labels. The label is what solves the property and evidence identification problem. The quality of the entire bar code system depends upon the quality of the label affixed to packages of evidence and the label should be the first consideration. This includes the environment that the label must endure; temperature, humidity, dirt, etc. Another issue is how long the must label last; considering the time property is in police custody and how often it will be scanned. The types of labels that are needed in a particular application will dictate the printing technology that will be used. Label color is a very important element of a successful bar code application. Scanners do not see color but do see high contrast differences. For this reason bar codes should be printed in black on a white background. This is the most effective means of ensuring the scanner will be able to read the bar code.

The quality of the paper stock that is used for labels and the quality of the label adhesive are critical to an effective bar code system. Paper stock that will not produce clear, undistorted, long lasting bar code images will only frustrate attempts to improve the processing and disposal of property. Faded or smeared bar code images can not be read accurately by a bar code reader. This lack of label quality may require manual data entry into the computer file which will defeat the purpose of bar coding and its efficiencies.

A poor quality label adhesive will also frustrate attempts to improve efficiency. An adhesive that will not adhere properly to paper products, poly bags, metal and other common packaging materials used for property and evidence may be worse than no bar code system at all. If the label fails to adhere properly and semi-permanently, the identification of the property package may be lost with the missing label. At best time, will be expended locating the label and reaffixing it to the package. If lost labels becomes a frequent occurrence the benefits of the bar code system will be lost.

Bar code software. The printer software is the second consideration since it actually produces the label. If backlogs of evidence and property are to be avoided the label-printing and -application process is critical to property control operations. Another factor to be considered is the potential for other application for bar coding. It has been found that the initial implementation of bar coding fails to anticipate the other applications of bar coding in the police agency.

A flexible software program allows the separation of labels into fixed and variable information. Fixed information is entered during the design process using a variety of tools provided by the bar code software. This may include the police agencies name, a logo, and other standard information. The variable information includes case number, property control number, date, type of property and other pertinent case, or property information.

The scanning software is designed to recognize bar codes and funnel them to an interpreter where they are matched with the appropriate file.

If software offers checksum characters this should be considered a plus. After a bar code is printed, the characters in the bar code are added by the program and a mathematical calculation is performed to determine the checksum. When the bar code is read back, the mathematical calculation is again performed and compared to the checksum. If the bar code has been damaged while in storage this operation will ensure that the proper file is accessed and modified. This provides an extra level of data security. Damaged bar codes can frequently be reconstructed using the checksum, thereby saving the time necessary to retype case information into the computer. (Sharp, 1998)

Label printers. The printer is the vehicle for producing the label and it runs through the bar code software. Thermal and thermal transfer printers dominate demand label applications; different information on each label, the information is not known until the label is needed, and labels are needed one at a time.

The resolution of the printer must be considered. The lower the printer's resolution, the less dense the bar code must be in order to be readable. For most bar code formats, 300 dots per inch (dpi) is the lowest resolution that can be read by scanners.

The resolution of most ink jet and laser printers is well above 300 dpi.

The printer is that element of an otherwise sound system that can be expected to breakdown over time. Without the printer, labels can not be produced and a work backlog will result while the printer is unavailable.

Scanners. A bar code scanner is a combination of optical, electrical, and computing devices built into a small package. The scanner's function is to read the image--bars--on the label. The scanner sees the bars and spaces of different widths and decodes these patterns as number and letter combinations. Once decoded, the data are transmitted to the PC and processed by the software program.

Handheld scanners must operate fast enough to read the code while they are being held. This required speed translates into additional cost of the scanner. This additional cost must, however, be considered in relationship to the benefits of a portable, hand held scanner. The portable scanner allows data entry to be accomplished in the storage areas, or other locations distant from the computer.

While most scanners can read a wide variety of linear bar codes, they also have limitations. Before selecting a scanner it is necessary to find out exactly which bar codes will be read. There are several bar code symbologies in use. These include U.P.C., Code 39, Code 128, and PDF417

Contact scanners. Contact scanners, or wands, resemble heavy pens. Bar codes are read by pressing the tip of the wand against the bar code and drawing it across the bars. Simply placing the wand on the first bar, or in the middle of a code will not result in an accurate reading. The benefits of a wand scanners their low cost and ability to read bar codes of almost any length. Since they have no moving parts they are the most rugged, compact, and lightweight of scanning technologies. Contact scanners also possess some drawbacks. These include slow speed since the operator must manually scan the code, they are capable of reading only one-dimensional bar codes, and the bar codes must be of good quality.

Non-contact scanners. These scanners look like a gun with a short, wide barrel. There are two types of non-contact scanners; laser and charged coupled device (CCD).

Handheld laser scanners are at the high price end of scanning devices. Laser scanners use a laser beam to "see" the bar code. Although they are more expensive, laser scanners are fast and have a high resolution. They are capable of scanning bar codes at a distance of up to thirty five feet.

The less expensive charged coupled device scanner uses a row of light emitting diodes to light up the entire bar code. A CCD optical chip camera then scans and reads the bar code. These scanners are slower than laser scanners and their range is only a few inches.

Computer System Security

When evidence and property files are maintained on a computer system, whether a personal computer or as an application on a larger network, a management plan of action is essential to safeguard the computer system and the data stored on it. Senior management bears the ultimate responsibility for the analysis of risks to the computer system and the development of procedures to prevent unauthorized access, data manipulation, or the destruction of data. Operating managers, supervisors and the Property Control Officer also share the responsibility for system security and data integrity. Because supervisors and the Property Control Officer are so closely involved in the day-to-day operations of the Property Control function they are frequently the first to detect irregularities in the computer processing of property and evidence files.

Step 1. Computer system security audits must be concerned with prevention. The first step in prevention is the identification of high risk applications. One recent text on computer crime (Moulton, 1992) identifies several computer applications that should be considered high risk applications. These applications, in the context of the property control function, are:

- Make disbursements of large amounts of money
- Receive or process large amounts of money

- Process highly marketable merchandise [property and evidence]
- Contain valuable information [amount, processing and location of stored evidence]
- Are accessible by computer terminals
- Are accessible over commercial communication lines

Step 2. These risk applications apply to computers used to store property case information to the extent the application is run on a personal computer, a dedicated mainframe, or a shared mainframe computer system. The computer system locations that should be considered high risk locations include:

- The data center
- The data library, both on-and off-site
- Locations containing copies of programs and program documentation
- The master terminal from which privileged instructions can be entered and executed
- The system software generation function

Step 3. After an identification of the applications and locations that relate to the maintenance of Property Control Records, the next step is an assessment of the threats to the computer system and the data it contains. These threats can be classified into several categories for ease of evaluating the probability of threats to the computer system.

- Erroneous or falsified data input
- Uncontrolled system access
- Personal computers, especially if networked
- Programming errors
- Operating system flaw
- Communication system failure
- Civil lawsuits due to improper policies, procedures and practices

Step 4. The final step is the development of policies, procedures, computer access security codes and physical security measures. Training of all personnel using or having access to the computer system is also essential. During this training it should be stressed that preventive measures are the responsibility of all system users in addition to supervisors and the computer system manager.

Because of the need to maintain a defensible chain of custody an important feature of a evidence computer program is a computer-generated log of those that have accessed the system, the date and time of access, and the tasks performed on the system. This will provide an additional audit trail and strengthen any computer output chain of custody.

Chapter Notes

Doe v Town of Plymouth, 825 F, Supp. 1102, D. Mass 1993.

Hubben, Ed, "Picking The Right Scanner, *ID Systems*, Helmers Pub., Peterbrough, NH, Vol. 18, No. 7, July, 1998.

Moulton, Rolf, T., *Combatting Computer Crime: Prevention, Detection, Investigation,* (McGraw-Hill, Inc., New York, 1992).

Navas, Deb, "PDF417 Solves Evidence-Handling Glitches", *ID Systems*, Helmers Pub., Peterbrough, NH, Vol. 17, No. 9, September, 1997.

Rapaport, Lowell, "How To Print and Read Bar Codes", *ID Systems*, Helmers Pub., Peterbrough, NH, Vol. 6, No. 10, October, 1997.

Sharp, Kevin, "Selecting Bar Code Label Software", *ID Systems*, Helmers Pub., Peterbrough, NH, Vol. 18., No. 4, April, 1998.

Swanson, Charles, R.; Chamelin, Neil, C.; Territo, Leonard, *Criminal Investigations,* (Random House, New York, 1992). p. 47.

United States v. Brown, 9 F3d 907, 7 FLW Fed Crt 1081, CA11, FLA, 1993.

Chapter 8

Staffing The Property Control Function

Police agencies use various titles by which to refer to the employee responsible for the property management function. One encounters titles such as; property technician, evidence management technician, property control officer, property officer, property custodian and evidence officer. Regardless of the position title, if the individual is responsible for the official inventorying, custody, security, storage and disposition of evidence and property, the individual is functioning as a Property Control Officer.

The positions descriptions that follow address the issues associated with the essential knowledge and skills areas, duties and requirements under the Americans With Disabilities Act (ADA).

Property Technician

The Property Section is responsible for the receipt, storage, safekeeping, release and disposal of all property or evidence that comes into the custody, or under the control of the Police Department.

The Property Technician is responsible for maintaining security and control of property and evidence and ensuring the objectives of the Property Section are attained. Work tasks are performed under the general supervision of an administrative supervisor.

Position Duties

The Property Technician's primary assignment is to log, classify, store, dispense, destroy and release property or evidence to its rightful owner, for court presentation and / or for destruction and auction. The following specific duties are assigned to the Property Technician.

- Maintain all evidence, found, abandoned and safekeeping property in such a manner that the individual items are secure from theft, loss, or contamination, and can be located in an efficient manner.

- Maintain Property Inventory reports with property notations of any and all actions associated with the property; the "chain of custody."
- Ensure the timely and legally correct notification of owners and the release/disposal of property recovered, found, or seized by the Department.
- Operate computer terminals during case disposition research and to enter and retrieve other related information involving the classification and disposition of property items.
- Coordinate the disposal of unclaimed property and special disposal of narcotics, explosives, biological specimens, biohazard materials and firearms.
- Maintain a current knowledge of local, state, and federal laws involving property/evidence handling, storage and disposal.
- Deliver, or cause to be delivered, evidence to State and federal labs for testing or analysis as appropriate.
- Compile lists of property to be submitted to appropriate authority for an Order of Disposal.
- Monitor the status of evidence and property in custody, transferred temporarily for laboratory testing or analysis, and court presentation.
- Participate in property auctions, approved destruction, appropriation for Department use, and other final dispositions.
- Monitor and replenish as necessary all property control supplies, packaging materials and biohazard personal protection equipment.
- Maintain all property storage facilities in a clean, orderly and efficient manner.
- Make all necessary and appropriate recommendations for changes to department policies and procedures related to the property and evidence control function.
- Other duties and responsibilities as assigned by competent authority.

Equipment, Aids, and Tools

Equipment, aids and tools include pencil, pen, paper, computer evidence programs, FAX technology, pagers, answering machines, computer printers, telephones and Department vehicles.

Working Conditions

Position may involve occasional overtime after regular duty hours and on weekends. Potential exposure to hazardous waste, chemicals, narcotics, dangerous drugs and bloodborne pathogens.

Individual is subject to inside and outside environmental weather changes, lifting and moving heavy or bulky items weighing in excess of fifty (50) pounds.

Physical Requirements

Ability to walk, stand, stoop, stretch, reach overhead and under confined spaces, carry equipment, supplies and packaged evidence, climb ladders, grasp pen and pencil and operate a computer keyboard.

Required Knowledge, Abilities and Skills

Position requires a working knowledge of the principles and practices of evidence processing and storage. Requires also a working knowledge of State and federal laws and case decisions related to the custody of evidence and recovered property and City ordinances. Also, routine knowledge of Department rules of conduct, policies and procedures. Basic knowledge of computer operations and word processing and data base programs.

Position requires the ability to work with a minimum of direct supervision. Ability to effectively organize work assignments and establish work priorities. Ability to organize and maintain records files related to the storage and disposal of property and evidence.

Ability to interact effectively and courteously with the public and other members of the Department. Requires the ability to analyze situations quickly and objectively and make decisions, and to perform basic mathematical calculations (percentages, ratios). Requires ability to exercise initiative, independent judgement and resourcefulness. Ability to read, write and communicate effectively in oral and written form.

Position requires skill to handle and manipulate firearms and other weapons and operate Department motor vehicles. Skill in manipulating camera and balance or electronic scale.

Required Training and Experience

Requires knowledge, skill and mental development equivalent to completion of four years of high school. Must possess a current, valid vehicle operator's license. Must complete successfully an approved training course on Evidence and Property Management within one year of assignment to the position.

In a larger police agency there may be a need for a supervisor, sworn or civilian, to coordinate activities over several shifts, or to supervise the activities of several Property Technicians.

Property and Evidence Supervisor

This is a supervisory position of a technical nature involving the direct supervision of one or more subordinate Evidence Technicians. Individual supervises the receipt, custody, processing, security and disposition of evidence, contraband and recovered property coming into the custody of the Police Department. Work is performed under the general supervision of an Administrative Commander.

Evidence Supervisor
Position Duties

An individual assigned to the position of Evidence Supervisor is responsible for the direct supervision and performance of all property control functions, activities and tasks by Property Technicians. Position duties include the assignment of tasks and the setting of task priorities on a daily, weekly and monthly basis. The following specific duties are assigned to the Property and Evidence Supervisor..

- The direct supervision of Property Technicians and performance of all property control functions and activities.
- Provide general supervision of the Property Section personnel and daily activities.
- Review subordinates' completed work products for adherence to standards of accuracy, timeliness, and completeness.
- Conduct period performance assessments of subordinates.
- Develop work and task schedules and establish task / project priorities.
- Delegate tasks, establish task priorities and assign tasks on a daily, weekly, and monthly basis.
- Instruct Property Technicians in the duties, tasks and responsibilities of that position.
- Prepare requests for, and drafts of, Orders of Disposal and forward property disposal documents to the Office of Chief of Police for approval.
- Prepare cash transmittal documents and forward documents to Treasurer's Office.
- Prepare cash refund requests to be drawn from the Evidence Fund / Account for monies to be returned to lawful owners.
- Review completed Property Inventory Reports for accuracy and completeness.
- Prepare and forward, in accordance with established procedures, Deficiency Notices for evidence packaging and completed Property Inventory Report forms that do not meet established standards.
- Maintain adequate inventory of evidence management supplies and equipment. Requisition supplies and equipment as necessary.
- Answer questions pertaining to property control policies, procedures and records files.
- Conduct period unannounced spot checks of subordinate personnel and inventories of evidence and recovered property.
- Ensure the maintenance of a clean and safe work environment

that meets applicable federal and State regulations.

- Develop and submit Evidence Section management reports on a periodic and exceptional basis.
- Periodically review the Property Control Operations Manual for required revisions.
- Recommend and develop draft policies and procedures for Evidence Section management and operations.
- Maintain cooperative relationships, and coordinate Evidence Section activities with other Department sections and outside agencies.
- Maintain current knowledge of evidence related equipment, supplies, legal opinions and statutes.
- Maintain, or cause to be maintained, the physical security of Evidence Section processing and storage areas, records files, and computer systems.
- Supervise all property auctions, approved destruction and Department appropriations of property.
- Process, store and retrieve property and evidence as workload requires.
- Appear in court, or other locations in response to subpoenas and provide testimony as necessary.
- Other duties as assigned by competent authority.

Equipment, Aids, and Tools

Equipment, aids and tools include pencil, pen, paper, computer evidence programs, FAX technology, pagers, answering machines, computer printers, telephones and Department vehicles.

Working Conditions

Position may involve occasional overtime after regular duty hours and on weekends. Potential exposure to hazardous waste, chemicals, narcotics and dangerous drugs and bloodborne pathogens.

Individual is subject to inside and outside environmental weather changes, lifting and moving heavy or bulky items weighing in excess of fifty (50) pounds.

Physical Requirements

Ability to walk, stand, stoop, stretch, carry equipment, supplies and packaged evidence, climb ladders, grasp pen and pencil, reach overhead and under confined spaces and operate a computer keyboard.

Required Knowledge, Skills, and Abilities

Requires a thorough working knowledge of the principles of evidence processing, storage and management. Substantial knowledge of statutory provisions applicable to evidence management and the City Code. Routine knowledge of Department Rules of Conduct, policy and procedures. Also, knowledge of the principles and practices of police supervision.

Position requires skill to handle and manipulate firearms and other weapons, conduct field drug test analyses and operate Department motor vehicles. Skill in manipulating camera and balance or electronic scales.

Ability to interact courteously and effectively with the public and other members of the Department. Ability to analyze situations quickly and objectively, use considerable independent judgement and to determine the proper course of action. Ability to apply supervisory principles and techniques on a daily basis.

Training and Experience

Requires knowledge, skill and mental development equivalent to completion of four years of high school and a minimum of four years supervisory experience.

Must possess a valid driver's license. Must complete successfully an approved training course in Evidence and Property Management within one year of assignment to the position.

Selection and Training

The Property Control Officer plays a vital role in the security and chain-of-custody of evidence. The efficiency of Property Control Room operations is dependent almost entirely upon knowledge of proper procedures and the initiative displayed by the Property Control Officer. However, specific selection criteria should be used when making assignments to this position. These criteria should be used in conjunction with, or in addition to, other job duties if the Property Control Officer position is a part time position; i.e. Identification Officer, Evidence Technician.

Selection Criteria

Very little, if any, research has been conducted to determine the knowledge, skills, traits and abilities of the effective Property Control Officer. An analysis of the duties and responsibilities of the position however, lends itself to the identification of selection criteria.

Integrity. The very nature of the position requires, above all, honesty. The policies, procedure and methods developed for system operation obviously are no better than the honesty and integrity of the individual assigned to carry-out these responsibilities.

Perseverance. Perseverance is an important trait. Considering the general lack of attention to the property and evidence control function in the past, most property control rooms are in serious need of reorganization and the disposal of unnecessary evidence and other property. The task of overcoming years of neglect requires an individual that will persevere at the task of identifying and tracking down the origin of property in custody; very often with very little documentation or background information.

Perseverance is a result of patience. The chain of custody required for an adequate audit trail is constructed through detailed information entered onto property forms and logs. The Property Control Officer must possess the patience to deal with the collection and documentation of this information. This requires several entries on property inventory forms, property control logs, tags and other property control files. The Property Control Officer must have the patience, as well as the analytical sense, of an investigator to determine the owner of lost, found and recovered property.

Periodic, special and scheduled dispositions of property and evidence that no longer need be retained must be made in order to maintain the free-flow of items through the Property Control Room. This also requires a high degree of perseverance; knowing the dispositions will have to be carried out periodically if control is to be maintained. An understanding of the nature and value of physical evidence to the criminal investigative and prosecutorial functions and policies is also essential. Without such and understanding an individual may be tempted to otherwise prematurely attempt to dispose of evidence, or maintain it in such a manner that it loses its evidential value.

Knowledge of forensic sciences. The Property Control Officer should possess a basic understanding of criminalistics and forensic medicine. Criminalistics is "...the body of knowledge about the recognition, collection, identification, individualization, and evaluation of physical evidence." (Rini, 1992) A fundamental understanding of criminalistics will better prepare the Property Control Officer to recognize the need for the careful handling, packaging and shipment of physical evidence to the laboratory.

Forensic medicine involves the probative value of medical fact and opinion pertaining to evidence affecting human life or property. Forensic medicine includes pathology (the cause and manner of death), toxicology (the study of poisons), odontology (the study of teeth and bitemarks), serology (the study of blood) and psychiatry (the study of the criminal mind). With this understanding the relationship between physical clues associated with an offense and the evidential value of these items will be more readily apparent.

An understanding of the investigative and probative value of physical evidence will also provide greater insights into the requirement for an unbroken chain of evidence.

Human relations skills .The Property Control Officer has significant contacts with the public. It is very important that individuals considered for selection and assignment to this position possess the interest, motivation and the general ability to communicate effectively.

The ability to work well with others: patrol officers, investigators, civilian personnel and citizens, is very important considering the nature of the tasks and the interpersonal relations associated with the position. The Property Control Officer will be communicating with citizens who have lost property, are recovering stolen property, attorneys representing clients from whom property was seized and numerous individuals outside the organization that have interest in the property.

If the Property Control Officer is to be considered the "resident expert" on the storage, handling, and disposition of property within the department it is essential the person selected have the ability to communicate and interact effectively with others.

Creativity. Since the evidentury value of property may differ slightly to significantly in different criminal investigations even though they may involve the same type of offense, the Property Control Officer should possess a sense of creativity.

Creativity is defined simply as the ability to identify or create new relationships between existing pieces of knowledge. Thus, the property control officer must be able to create solutions to problems that may arise in the handling, packaging, storing and analysis of property.

Training

Concurrent with the assignment of an individual as the Property Control Officer should be a minimum of training in several related areas. When and where available the Property Control Officer should attend formal training on the Property Control function. The basic elements of a course in Property Control Management should include: the laws of property and property rights, seizure and forfeiture of property, property storage methods, disposition procedures and OSHA and EPA regulations.

Training should also include instruction in the proper operation and maintenance of records filing associated with the property control function, storage and shelving systems, security systems, property control report forms and logs and the handling of special classes of evidence: weapons, narcotics and valuables.

Basic evidence-handling techniques as well as crime laboratory standards for the packaging, handling and analysis of evidence and basic training in evidence collection and preservation may be found to be very helpful. If the Property Control Officer understands the procedures and policies relating to the initial collection and preservation of evidence he or she may better realize the scope of the responsibilities and procedures associated with the property control function.

Because of the increasing number of civil law suits involving the storage and return of motor vehicles to owners, attention should be directed to the legal standards established for the return of any type of property to its owner and the conditions under which it is returned.

The Property Custodian encounters firearms of all types, makes, calibers and particularly weapons with operating and safety problems. The Property Custodian should acquire a basic knowledge of firearms to include: firearms types and operation, safety devices and safety precautions. The Property Custodian should acquire a basic familiarity with semiautomatic pistols, revolvers, single shot, semiautomatic and fully automatic rifles, assault guns and shotguns. BB and pellet pistols and rifles--including paint ball guns--are other weapons that frequently are entered into the property control system.

The first safety rule is all firearms must be unloaded prior to packaging and submission. The second safety rule is all firearms should be handled and processed as if they are loaded, unsafe and ready to fire.

Bomb making instructions have become commonplace on computer bulletin boards. Since there is a greater potential for homemade bombs to show up in property control room, the Property Custodian should become familiar with the identification of potentially explosive devices. While department procedures should prohibit the introduction of any actual, or suspected explosive into the property control system these devices have, never-the-less, been found in property control rooms. An excellent source of information for identifying explosives is the *Firearms and Explosives Tracing Handbook*, available from the ATF.

Chapter Notes

Bureau of Alcohol, Tobacco and Firearms (ATF), *Firearms and Explosives Tracing Handbook,* Publication ATF P 7520.1 (Washington, D.C.)

Rini, Gary, *Forensic Science Services and The Administration of Justice,* (mimeo, Naperville, IL Police Department, 1992) p. 31.

Chapter 9

Property Control Audits

Four methods are available for maintaining control over property and evidence: chain-of custody, evidence / property transfers, property purge schedules and periodic audits. (Doran, 1993) In earlier chapters the first three methods have been addressed comprehensively. The final method, or step, is an assessment of the components of the property control system. This is the periodic audit.

Periodic audits of the Property Control Room should be the subject of formal, written policy. This is necessary to ensure the integrity of the property control process, to ensure all applicable agency policies and procedures are uniformly and consistently applied and to maintain exacting controls over evidence and property contained in the system. Audits assist also in determining if new or modified property control policies and procedures are required to improve system security. Audits of the property control function focus on specific control procedures and include tests of compliance as well as substantive tests.

Compliance Tests

Compliance tests are intended to collect and evaluate information as to whether internal control procedures have been adopted, are actually in use and operating efficiently. These tests evaluate the likelihood (risk) of material errors in the handling, storage and disposition of evidence and property.

Compliance tests are conducted by sampling, inquiry and observation. They are intended to answer the question: to what extent do internal control procedures reduce the risk of material errors? Where errors, omissions, noncompliance or insufficient internal controls are found to exist the greater the need for substantive audit tests of property transactions.

Substantive Tests

Substantive tests are intended to detect material errors in the property inventory, if they exist. The degree of testing, and the number of property cases to be examined, is influenced significantly by an assessment of the likelihood that material errors exist as a result of noncompliance with property control policies and procedures.

Audit Evidence

Audit evidence is defined as any information that corroborates or refutes a premise. Several types of audit evidence are available: internal controls (policies and procedures, internal inspections, performance audits), physical evidence, and documentary evidence. All three types of audit evidence should be considered when developing a property control audit plan.

Internal Controls

The primary question to be addressed is: are internal controls being employed correctly and efficiently? If internal controls are adequate and adhered to, strong evidence is created as to the validity of the physical inventory records. The adequacy of internal controls is a major factor in determining the amount of audit evidence that will be required and the sources of that audit evidence.

Physical Evidence

Physical audit evidence is the best evidence of the physical presence of items in the property control inventory. This evidence is collected through observation or count. United State currency is verified through counting both the number of bills, by denomination, and the total cash value entered in the inventory. Other items are examined for physical condition and for serial numbers matching those recorded on inventory forms. The auditor should be aware of the potential for the introduction of fraudulent items into the property inventory to cover the theft of the original item. Examples of such fraudulent items is a worthless check created deliberately as a means of concealing the theft of a bona-fide check in the property inventory system or the substitution of a powder substance for heroin.

Documentary Evidence

Documentary evidence is one of the most important types of evidence to collect during the audit. The value of a document depends, in part, upon its origination. A document created or originated by the Property Control Officer, for example, would be given less value than a document created by someone else in the law enforcement agency. A document originating outside the law enforcement agency would be afforded more value than one originating within the agency.

External documentary evidence. External documentary evidence includes written court orders, letters and memos from prosecuting attorneys and property owners regarding property held by the law enforcement agency, its condition, or procedures to be followed in the handling or disposition of the property. These are the best types of documentary evidence to seek during the conduct of the audit. Since these documents are created outside the police agency there is less likelihood they are the creation of a fraudulent intent.

Internal documentary evidence. Internal documents include the offense or incident report, Property Inventory Report, Request For Order of Disposition, and data contained in manual or computerized files. Consideration should be given to the type and nature of the document —it is possible for a dishonest employee to forge or create a document in its entirety.

Bank checks should be compared to the description on the original evidence inventory for an exact match of descriptions. Property destruction documents should be witnessed by someone, preferably outside the law enforcement agency, or a sworn officer from another division within the agency to preclude the opportunity for the forgery or creation of fictitious property control documents.

Scheduling Audits

Evidence and property control audits should be scheduled and conducted under the following circumstances:

- Whenever there is a change in command in a law enforcement agency

This audit is to satisfy the chief executive that the system has been operating in a secure and efficient manner under the previous administration as well as to establish a specific date when the new chief executive assumes full responsibility for the evidence and property stored in the system.

- Upon the reassignment of a Property Control Officer

The purpose of this audit is similar in purpose to the audit above with the exception that it is intended to provide the new Property Control Officer with assurances that evidence and property, and associated records, are secure and accurate.

If policies and procedures have not been adhered to the audit serves to establish a firm date prior to which any property or evidence was mishandled or misappropriated. This policy of periodic audits should not be construed as one by which to fix blame, but rather to fix responsibility for the proper operation and management of the property control function.

- On a periodic, unannounced basis but not less than once each year

These unannounced audits, conducted by a supervisor not organizationally or routinely associated with the processing or storage of property are intended to maintain system security and integrity.

Periodic, unannounced audits and inspections of the property control function should be conducted by a staff officer assigned by the chief executive officer. The individual assigned should be from a command other than that to which the property control function is assigned. The purpose of the inspection is to insure that good housekeeping practices are followed, records are maintained according to established policies and procedures, evidence and other property is maintained in a secure manner and periodic property dispositions are being affected.

A random sample of all property within the Property Control Room should be inspected physically and visually to ensure there has been no pilferage, inadvertent destruction, loss, or contamination. The use of a stratified, random sample of property items will provide a thorough audit of the handling, processing, storage, disposal and paperwork procedures actually employed in the past.

The audit should, in addition, determine if all evidence and other property within the Property Control Room have been properly documented on inventory forms, the inventory log, property tags and package markings, and computer file entries are complete and accurate.

- Whenever circumstances suggest an audit may be necessary to refute or affirm allegations of impropriety in the management of the property control function

Under these conditions an investigative audit may be warranted. An investigative audit is concerned with gathering physical and testimonial evidence to determine the nature of and the extent to which property in custody has been tampered with, misappropriated, or improperly disposed of.

Audit Scope

Audits should include the entire evidence and property control function subsequent to the collection and preservation of property by field personnel. Thus, the audit commences with the methods by, and locations at which, field personnel temporarily store evidence and property awaiting transfer to the designated Property Control Room or storage area. (Doran, 1991)

The scope of an audit should include the following elements as a means of identifying any system deficiencies or fraudulent intent:

- The manner in which property is stored prior to its receipt into the Property Control Room
- The procedures used to record the receipt and custody of the property to the Property Control Room
- The recording of chain of custody entries by the Property Control Officer
- The storage methods and procedures for controlling the storage of property; both physical security and age of the property

- Temporary sign-out for court and investigative purposes
- Procedures used to record and affect the final disposition of property and evidence

Audit Strategies

Three alternative audit strategies are available for use. These strategies include: inventoried items, active case files and final disposition transactions.

Inventoried Property

This audit approach includes a random selection of property items currently in inventory and the paperwork associated with each item in the audit sample. It is intended to determine that the property item can be located in the Property Control Room, the property is in approximately the same condition as when it was originally taken into custody and the recorded property descriptions on documents are identical.

The item and information entries are inspected and the paper work trail is tracked backward in the system to the original offense or incident report. The property description on the original and the copy of the Property Inventory Report are then compared.

Active Case Files

A random sample of active investigative case files is selected and the paper work trail is followed to the item stored in the Property Control Room.

Final Disposition Transactions

Closed cases are identified and randomly selected. The complete property control process is tracked from receipt of a property item by the original investigating officer to the final disposal of the property.

Preparation for the Audit

Preparation for the actual conduct of the audit of property and evidence should be as follows:

Random Sample

A random sample of evidence and property should be identified using the Property Control Log or other master record of property that has been entered into the system. This sample may be developed, for example, by selecting every fifteenth article on the Property Control Log starting with the eighth entry. This technique provides assurance of randomness of the audit sample. An additional benefit is it precludes the possibility of someone predetermining the audit sample. This would undermine the reliability of the entire audit process and the final audit results. A separate audit may be conducted of property currently in the system as well as an audit of property disposed of in the past.

Upon completion of the audit sample list the list should be reviewed to ensure it contains a representative sample of the various types and classifications of evidence and property. The audit list should contain sufficient items of Evidence, Lost and Found property, and Safekeeping property classifications to ensure a comprehensive audit and check on the integrity of the entire property control system. In addition, the audit list should be checked to ensure that sufficient number of weapons, narcotic and dangerous drugs, United Stated currency and other items of value are contained on the audit sample list. If these specific types of property are not contained on the list it is then necessary to go back to the Property Control Log and identify, again through a random selection, a sufficient number of weapons, narcotics and dangerous drugs and money for inclusion in the audit sample.

Sample size. The size of the audit sample is dependent upon the total number of items of property and evidence in the property control system as well as the time and manpower available to conduct such an audit. The lack of available time or personnel, however, should not be a justification for not conducting a thorough, comprehensive audit.

A sample audit format is shown in Figure 9.1. The property items that serve as the basis for the audit sample are entered on the list in chronological order.

Conducting the Audit

The physical audit process should be conducted in the order that each case falls on the audit sample list. Each piece of property or evidence should be physically located and, if necessary, the packaging opened. This access to the property may require the breaking of evidence seals affixed by the seizing officer or crime laboratory. If a thorough audit is to be conducted the property must be visually inspected to determine that it has not been contaminated, deteriorated or lost.

Case No.	Property Inventory No. Remarks	Item Description	Location	Located /
96-115	96-045	Brown leather wallet no contents	Bin E	
96-543	96-095	.38 b/s S/W revolver S.N. K521550	Gun Lkr.	
97-008	97-01	1 bag cntng. 2 vials cocaine	Narc. Lkr.	

Figure 9.1
Sample Audit Format

After inspection to the satisfaction of the audit officer the property should be repackaged and sealed. Any evidence seals broken should be reapplied and the initials of the audit officer and the Property Control Officer applied.

Narcotics

In some cases it may be desirable to conduct a substance inspection of narcotics and dangerous drugs. This can be accomplished through the use of a narcotics field testing kit or, where allegations of improprieties have been made, the substances may be submitted to a crime laboratory for analysis. In addition, the weight of narcotics and dangerous drugs and the count of tablets or capsules containing narcotics should be verified. Any discrepancies between the weight at the time of audit and the weight at the time of seizure, less the estimated necessity for these actions will be dictated by the circumstances surrounding the audit and any indicators of internal corruption through manipulation of evidence or allegations of misconduct.

Property Dispositions

The audit should, by policy, concern itself also with property disposals by the Property Control Officer. This will include property returned to owners, appropriated for agency use with proper authorizations, and property auctioned or destroyed. The purpose of this effort is to ensure policies and procedures pertaining to the final disposition of property are uniformly adhered to.

Specific procedures to be checked include the recording of signatures for the final disposition of property. This should include the signature of the property owner upon its return, the signature of the officer returning the property, date of return and any notations necessary when property is returned under unique or unusual circumstances. This would include, for example: very valuable property, damaged property and property requiring a license or permit for possession such as firearms and ammunition.

Property disposition audits should also review dispositions in relationship to: the statute of limitations on criminal offenses, time limits for appeals after sentencing, statutory requirements for the disposition of lost property, asset forfeiture cases and any state reporting requirements for forfeiture cases, federal disposition guidelines for "shared" or "adopted" seizures and statutory requirements for public auctions.

Destroyed Property

The audit of destroyed property is concerned with the receipt of proper court orders for destruction, an Order For Disposal by the agency chief executive and the certification of a witnessed destruction. The methods and procedures of destruction should also be reviewed. These include: the destruction of narcotics and dangerous drugs, biohazard materials, explosives and flammables, toxic and caustic chemicals and other materials regulated by state or federal law.

Appropriated Property

The audit should include property appropriated for agency use under statutory or administrative authority. This includes the recording of specific identifying information on the agencies permanent property inventory. If inventory stickers or other identifying marks are affixed to agency property, the inventory serial number as well as the unit or location to which the property was transferred should have been entered on the permanent property inventory. With the assurance the property was recorded in the agency's permanent property inventory, audit staff will be reasonably assured the property will be periodically inventoried with other agency property.

Audit Reports

The audit information collected through the processes above should be analyzed and be presented in a written Audit Report directed to the chief executive officer. The Audit Report should contain the original completed copy of the audit inventory list, a description of the facts and circumstances surrounding the audit, all audit findings and conclusions and any audit exceptions.

Audit Exceptions

Any property not actually located in the shelf, bin or storage area as indicated by the property records is recorded as an audit exception. Audit exceptions indicate that policies, procedures, shelving methods or data recording are not being adhered-to strictly.

Any weight or count discrepancy or property not located in its recorded location should be considered an audit exception. In addition, any evidence or property that is missing, shows signs of damage, contamination, deterioration or tampering in any manner should also be classified as an audit exception.

All audit exceptions should be noted in the "Remarks" section in the audit report and reported to the chief executive officer immediately, or upon conclusion of the audit report, depending upon the nature and seriousness of the audit exception. While there may be, and generally are, valid reasons for many audit exceptions they must be treated as compromises of the integrity and security of the property control system. These audit exceptions should be handled under established agency procedures for internal investigations.

Audit Briefing

Prior to concluding the actual audit work an oral briefing session should be held with the chief executive officer or his designated representative. The purpose of this briefing is to communicate preliminary audit findings and the initiation of the appropriate organizational response to the audit findings.

Chapter Notes

Doran, Robert, "Evidence and Property Management: Training Update For Chiefs and Command Officers." (paper presented at regional training conference on the police property control function, Elmhurst, IL., Oct, 1993), p. 5.

Doran, Robert, *Operations Audit of Evidence and Property Control; Decatur, IL, Police Department,* Report to the Director, Public Safety Services Department, Decatur, IL., Feb., 1991, p. 1.